# A Year with the Dubs

# A Year with the Dubs

*Daire Whelan*

Gill & Macmillan

Gill & Macmillan Ltd
Hume Avenue, Park West, Dublin 12
with associated companies throughout the world
www.gillmacmillan.ie

© Daire Whelan 2008
978 07171 4266 8

Print origination by TypeIT, Dublin
Printed by ColourBooks Ltd, Dublin

This book is typeset in 12pt Optima on 16.

The paper used in this book comes from the wood pulp of managed forests.
For every tree felled, at least one tree is planted, thereby renewing natural
resources.

A CIP catalogue record for this book is available from the British Library.

5 4 3 2 1

All photographs inside this book are © Inpho.

*To Trina.*
*No sporting passion can compare.*

'There is no past. All is future and hope.'

LOU BOUDREAU

# CONTENTS

# ACKNOWLEDGMENTS

First off, my thanks to Fergal Tobin of Gill & Macmillan who was taken with the idea of me writing a book about the Dubs and in so doing allowed me to combine two passions: writing and sport. (If I can ever get to combine writing, fishing and sport, then I really *will* have died and gone to heaven.)

Writing fan diaries is not as easy as one might think and there were many times (especially after the Tyrone game!) when I questioned my writing of the book. But first and foremost, this was most definitely a labour of love.

Thanks also to Claire Egan in publicity for all her assistance, and to Deirdre Rennison Kunz for her unfailing help and expertise with the proofs.

My love and thanks as always to my wife, Trina, who has never stopped supporting me in my writing. My love and thanks also to my family for allowing me to develop my love of sport through Gaelic games as a player and a supporter when I was younger; and to the Reas — Joe especially — for introducing me to the passion and beauty of Tipperary hurling.

I want to thank the different friends and Dubs fans I've gone with to Dublin matches over the years. A special word to John the Dubious Dub, never one afraid to stick his neck out, and to Dermot, as much a Waterford hurling fan as a Dublin football one — it's a tough combination in these times. We've all drunk, laughed and cried together and shared memories, good times and heart-break that will stand the test of time.

Finally, to the Dublin fans who are there come hail, rain or shine: from O'Byrne Cup matches in January to League games in April and the Championship in the summer, you make the Hill what it is and bring a colour and atmosphere that will never be replaced. I count some of my days on the Hill as the best I've ever had. What more could a fan ask for?

# INTRODUCTION

'The Hill? I wouldn't go there. Is it as bad as you hear? What's it really like?' Tell someone that you follow the Dubs from Hill 16 and you're invariably greeted with these lines. It's as if the famous terrace has its own aura separate from the rest of Croke Park and has its own rules and laws of which only Dublin fans know the secrets.

People watch on TV and see the massed hordes of Dublin fans; the camera zooms in and you might see a skinhead or someone with tattoos; then you might see a bottle being thrown at the netting behind the goal, and this becomes the pervading image of the Hill. To the outsider it seems to be a terrace that has embraced the culture of English soccer — from the violence to the chanting.

The Hill? Why would you want to go there, people ask. And these are not just questions from culchies. Most Dubs too wonder at what goes on and why anyone in their right mind would want to stand there for 70 minutes on a summer Sunday afternoon.

But it's not like that, you protest. It's somewhere with a great atmosphere and where, if the Dubs are in full flight on the pitch, it can be as good as any sporting terrace in the world. The Hill, like any identifiable terrace such as the Kop or the Stretford End, transcends its sport. It becomes an arena unique to the fans and its team.

In many ways it's exactly what the GAA doesn't want in twenty-first-century Ireland. It's coarse, uncouth, harsh and unforgiving. It has little regard for culchies and couldn't care less about farming quotas or crop prices. It likes sticking up two fingers at opponents and at the establishment. The odd burning of the Kerry flag doesn't go amiss either.

But on the other hand not all admire this version of being a Dub. Some don't look upon the 'Dublin-ese' swagger and attitude as something to be admired. I know many northsiders who look with disdain on what they see as a lot of 'put on rubbish' — from the blokes affecting Dublin accents, to those who think that if they sing Wolfe Tone songs and drink Bulmers they're living up to their cultural heritage.

There is confusion about what it means to be a Dub: where the line begins and ends is never clear. Dubs themselves often have no definition, but see the Liffey as a convenient symbol. Talk to country people and they just don't get it: why, they wonder, are Dublin people obsessed with which side of the Liffey they live on, and how much of a Dublin accent they have.

For one friend from Kilbarrack on the northside of the city, Dublin games amount to the worst examples of fake Dublin culture being brought together and hammed up on match-days. As we chatted in a pub one Saturday afternoon before a hurling match, we got to talking about the Dubs and what it meant to be one, and more particularly to be one that goes to the Hill.

Fifteen minutes later and I'd barely got a word in as this particular friend went on a rant, fulminating at the falseness and pretence of many he saw on the Hill at Dubs games.

'All right,' I said, 'if you feel that strongly about it, write it down and I'll put it in my book about the Dubs.'

'Fair enough,' he said, 'once you don't go printing my name or anything like that.'

So, let's call him 'John the Dubious Dub', and to show that this book isn't written through blue-tinted glasses, and that there are some Dubs (and northside ones at that) who think it's all bullshit, here then for the sake of balance is the other side's tuppence worth, courtesy of John the Dubious Dub. (These views do not necessarily equate with the author's, I hasten to add!)

*For all the misty-eyed eulogies it receives, the Hill on a match day can leave a lot to be desired: combine the usual (and unsafe) lack of stewarding, the often obnoxious anti-culchie routines (which, funnily enough, the 'hard chaws' often refrain from when there are fans from an Ulster team involved), the drunks and the inevitable stream of pig-ignorant, red-faced, middle-aged men who will never cease complaining, and you don't automatically have the makings of a wonderful day out.*

*There is far too much smug navel-gazing around Dublin matches. Oisin McConville was right to describe the circus of hype as a 'pain in the arse', and his Armagh team's reply to it was to deny Dublin their allegedly god-given right to get to an All-Ireland final in 2002.*

*Equally, there is an unspoken assumption that there is no atmosphere in Gaelic games other than that generated by the Hill during a Dublin match, which is nonsense. For non-stop noise look at a Munster hurling final, amongst many others, and many League of Ireland teams generate a far better repertoire of chants and songs than 'Come on ye boys in blue', 'Hill 16 is Dublin only', and 'Get off the Hill'.*

*Despite the scramble for Championship tickets on the part of Dublin fans, many of whom would not be found dead at a League match, far too many still come in late having found time to shoot down an extra pint at their leisure. In fairness there is nothing wrong with being a casual fan, but the type of Dubs fan who will claim beyond all reason, logic and truth to bleed blue whilst being unable to figure out why Parnell Park exists, let alone where it is, is a disheartening phenomenon.*

*For too many Dubs on the Hill on a summer day, image is all: the reason why they are there seems to fall into second place, unless Dublin wins. Or as one disgruntled Dub was heard to say: 'Some of those chancers wouldn't know the difference if there were two lads in the middle of that pitch playing fucking ping-pong.'*

So there you have it — the other side of the 'to be a Dub' debate. It should stir the pot at least and give some food for thought — either that or you'll be ready to chuck a stick, a bottle or whatever comes to hand at him.

But whichever way you look at it, the Hill does have a swagger and a cockiness, much of it stemming from its own history and meaning. The legend that it was built from the rubble of that seminal moment in Irish history — the 1916 Rising — gives it a status unlike any other sports terrace in the world. However, just as importantly the Hill has its own footballing history as well and boasts a lineage stretching back generations.

Fathers and grandfathers were there when the Dubs ended their longest ever All-Ireland famine in 1958, beating Derry and winning Sam after a 16-year absence — not forgetting of course the very sore defeat to Kerry in the 1955 final. At least that Dublin period saw only a 13-year gap between All-Ireland final appearances. (It was 16 years in total between All-Ireland victories.) It's worth noting that this current barren spell means we're now 14 years and counting without a title or even a final to talk about, and we're facing the serious possibility that the famine years from 1942 to 1958 could yet be surpassed.

Then there was the 1963 team that beat Galway, and with two All-Irelands in five years it was nothing short of a dynasty — in Dublin terms anyway. It was to be another 11 years before there would be another Sam Maguire in the capital. But what a time to be a Dub! Six All-Ireland finals in a row, three Sam Maguires and a rivalry and a golden age of the GAA that will never be equalled.

'Heffo's Heroes' captured the imagination of the city as Gaelic football had never done before, and suddenly everyone wanted to be associated with the Dubs.

Hughie Maguire was one of those who caught the bug in 1974 and has never looked back. He hasn't missed a match in the 34 years since — home or away, League, O'Byrne, Leinster or All-Ireland — and he has always been on the Hill to witness the Dubs in action.

'Sure there's nothing else like it,' he says, trying to explain the magic of the place. 'It's the only place to be. The buzz, the camaraderie . . . you won't get it anywhere else.'

He's seen changes on the Hill since the 1970s, of course, and reckons that at least now it's a lot safer than before.

'It could be dangerous back then, I tell you. Your feet wouldn't be on the ground most of the time. You could start the match at the back of the Hill and be at the front, stuck on the fence by the end.

'The place to be was on the roof of the old toilet at the back of the Hill. If you could get up there, you'd have a great view and wouldn't be tossed and thrown around.'

It's part of his life now and he wouldn't have it any other way, despite the disappointment and heartache. The regular match day routine sees him and around 20 others from the Dublin Supporters Club heading down the Handball Alley behind the Hill before the game and then on to Briody's on Marlborough Street to drown their sorrows or to celebrate afterwards. Away matches are Saturday mornings spent on the train or bus, book into a B&B, match and pints, then head back to the capital on a Monday morning.

Hard for him to believe, then, after the heyday of six finals in a row in the 1970s, that Sam Maguires would be only sporadic, rarely seen or experienced; hard to believe that there would only be two in the last quarter of a century. But for Hughie and many like him, it's not just about All-Ireland titles. There's Leinsters, Leagues and even O'Byrne Cups to celebrate and enjoy. A victory over

Meath is relished with extra vigour: 'Beating them is like winning an All-Ireland in itself,' he says, only half jokingly.

He has to put up with a lot more fairweather fans these days and is bemused by the fact that so many women can be seen at games nowadays. As for the Hill's bad reputation, he concedes there are a 'few bogeys there all right, but only a few' and says the vast majority are fine and just good GAA fans. It's all about the craic and the banter for him and other Dubs like him, and he can't quite understand the negative bias towards the Dubs: 'I mean, other counties have their bad few as well, you know.'

Hughie Maguire is an interesting antidote to John the Dubious Dub. Yet in many ways they are two sides of the same coin and sum up perfectly the paradox of who or what it means to be a Dub. In setting out to record a season spent following the Dubs from the Hill, I did not seek insights into the team or its affairs — most fans have no knowledge of that anyway. It was not intended either as a sweeping book covering the Hill and its many characters; instead I wrote this as a Dubs fan myself, as someone who has been following (and who once played) GAA all my life.

I was first brought to the Hill as a boy by my father in the 1980s and I can still remember the bleak, dreary scene as I stood on that half empty terrace while some 'fans' near us decided to put on balaclavas and sing IRA songs. But that was a different time.

Like many a good teenager before me, by the time the 1990s and secondary school came along, I was rebelling and finding fault with those things that had previously lit up my world as a kid. Gaelic games gave way to soccer; going to matches gave way to parties and hanging out.

It was only in college that I rediscovered and reconnected with many of my childhood loves: GAA and writing, first and foremost. Since then it's been agony and ecstasy each and every summer on the Hill. As I've got older I've started to question my place on the Hill and also, as I've seen the city and the country change so much in the last decade, I've begun to question my Dublin, Irish and GAA identity more and more.

In this book then I set out to record, in diary entry form for the season January to September 2008, my thoughts and observations from a Dublin fan's perspective. From the O'Byrne Cup to the National League and into the long-awaited summer months of the Leinster and All-Ireland Championships, this account takes it all in. You'll also hear from some characters like John the Dubious Dub and some of the fans I encountered on the Hill. Like anywhere and like any sport, those supporting it are never easily categorised or tagged. We're a mixed bunch.

Life went on for me in the interim and, like any other fan, there was work, relationships and the other myriad issues that adult life throws up at us all to deal with. I am a passionate Dubs fan but I don't separate my passion from the rest of my life. It is part and parcel of who I am. Work, relationships, sport, they all become one, become part of who you are. The problem is that the older you get the more you question your place in the world, and as you look around the Hill on a Sunday afternoon your place becomes more focused and seems to have more question-marks than ever before. The certainty you had as a kid is never rediscovered.

Like any year in one's life, this one has been a learning curve, with ups and downs. The season may have ended in disappointment but, as I write this, off the pitch the global economic crisis shows no sign of abating, house prices are still falling while unemployment is still rising. We face into the coming years with an uncertain future ahead of us. While the same may be said of us fans who have unsure expectations for our teams each year, at least we do have the reassurance of knowing that they'll be there, and that the season will come round once more.

# PROLOGUE
## THERE'S ALWAYS NEXT YEAR

**SEPTEMBER 26 2007**

*All-Ireland semi-final, Kerry 1-15, Dublin 0-16, Croke Park*

'We've found you a ticket. Face value. From a Kerry fan. But you have to be quick; he won't wait that long. Where are you?'

My mates had finally found me a ticket to the game — Dublin against Kerry in the most eagerly anticipated All-Ireland semi-final in years. But I was still a good ten minutes from the stadium. Shit! Having tried all week to get my hands on a ticket, here I was minutes from the throw-in and a ticket nearly in my grasp. I started into a run but struggled against the crowds who were streaming in their thousands to the game. Croker was to my right as I raced through Ballybough and the great stadium was already filling up. I couldn't miss this last chance of a ticket and let the Kerry fan walk away. My phone rang again and I answered, still racing along the streets and panting heavily now.

'How far are you? We're trying to stall him but you have to come quick.'

'Coming, fuckin coming! Just give me a minute,' I shouted breathlessly. The curry chips at 4 am after last night weren't a good idea.

Sweating from fear, beer and heat, I sprinted the last few hundred yards and made it to Gill's on the corner of the North Circular Road. The crowds were spilling out from the pubs. It was match time. Had I made it? Was I too late? And then I saw them on the far side of the street waiting impatiently, two Dubs and a lone Kerry fan trying hard to get away from these very curious city folk.

'And you have how many cows? That's amazing. Johnny, isn't that amazing?'

'Yea, amazing,' said Johnny. 'But tell me again about how many All-Irelands Kerry have won.'

My mates were working miracles stalling the Kerry fan and were on their last legs when I made it over to them

'Made it, lads!' I announced coming up behind them.

'About fuckin time!' muttered Gerry. 'I was even asking about his fuckin cows.'

'Now Seánie,' said Johnny, 'didn't we tell you he'd be here eventually? You know what Dubs are like for getting to things on time, eh? Sure we won't be late for the game. The Hill still have at least another round of drinks to get into them before they decide to wander down to the match. Loads of time still.'

'Seánie, is it?' I asked my saviour. 'Listen, thanks a million for this. You've made my week.'

'No bother,' said Seánie, my new best friend. 'Sure, better to give it to a fan than to a tout. Thirty-five euros it is then.'

Money handed over and I may as well have held Willy Wonka's golden ticket in my hands. My luck would start to run out sometime, I figured, but today at least, I was going to the game. It was Dublin's third All-Ireland semi-final in six years and the team had failed on both previous occasions. In fact it was twelve years since Dublin had last been into a final — the year the team won the Sam. All that stood between us and the final was Kerry, just the defending All-Ireland champions, the green and gold of The Kingdom that ever since the 1977 semi-final had always seemed to hold sway over us Dubs. Would today be any different, I wondered. At least I would be there in the stadium to find out.

I climbed the steps high up to the upper reaches of the Hogan Stand and was soon out of breath from the climb and from my dash through Ballybough. The short walk up to the Hill had its benefits at least, I thought, as another bead of sweat ran down my face. I was woken out of my self-pity as I turned the corner and entered the stand. 'Kerry! Kerry! Kerry!' A wall of high-pitched, screaming Kerry voices hit me. Christ! I had entered The Kingdom come to Croke Park. This little patch of Dublin was all Kerry for the next 70 minutes. Well, almost all. My Dublin jersey stood out in the sea of green and gold and there were good-humoured smart remarks as I made my way to my seat, edging past Kerry fans who were not interested in moving an inch to make things any easier for the Jackeen. It was going to be a long afternoon. But I had made it. I hadn't missed a Dublin game in years and didn't want to start with an All-Ireland semi against Kerry.

I took a deep breath and looked around from my lofty position. Yes, there was something different up here all right. Compared to the Hill, it was all a bit more . . . airy. There were no sweaty, drunken, heaving bodies pushing against you. The smell of dope wasn't in the air and there wasn't the danger of anyone getting sick beside you. Yes, the Hogan Stand was different right enough. It wasn't the Hill.

From up here you could look out over the Hill and see the buildings on Griffith Avenue stretching into Fairview and all the way out to Howth Head. These were all my old haunts as a kid growing up in Dublin, and sitting here waiting for the game to begin reminded me of just what the Dublin team and fans represented.

The game kicked off and, in fairness, for a land of John B. Keanes and Con Houlihans, the best they could come up with all afternoon was 'Kerry! Kerry! Kerry!' to slow rhythmical clapping. It was as if they were going into a trance-like state that was slowly building to a crescendo as they reached the last fever-pitched Kerry! Kerry! My banging hangover from the night before was getting a lot worse with each passing minute.

In contrast, from the Hill I could hear the first bars of 'In the Rare Ould Times' and 'Molly Malone' followed by 'Come on You Boys in Blue' and 'Get Off the Hill, Get Off the Hill' to finally the most poignant 'Sheep-shaggers nah-nah-nah, sheep-shaggers nah-nah-nah'. Imaginative, eclectic and thought provoking, no one could accuse the denizens of the Hill of being anything but colourful.

What the Kerry fans lacked in lyrics though, they made up for in their knowledge of the game. Discussing the strengths and weaknesses of every player, knowing the genealogy and footballing pedigree of even the referee, they were as religious in their preparations for this game as the Kerry players. Meanwhile, over on the Hill, cries of 'Hit him, fuckin hit him', followed by 'Culchie wanker' wafted over to intrude on the Kerry fans' intellectual ruminations of the hand pass versus the kicking game.

'You see, we don't have a problem with ye Dubs,'

explained the man sitting to my right who had flown in that morning from Glasgow for the game (and was flying home immediately afterwards). 'At least ye try and play football. Now those fuckers from Tyrone will do anything to beat you — eye gouging and the rest. But at least Dublin try and play the right way.'

Trying to play though wasn't working out as Kerry raced into an early lead. Their footballers played with a panache and a style that could only come from Kerry. They made it look so easy — pass, catch, kick — a simple game really. It's hard being a Dublin fan on these occasions. We lord it over the Meaths and the Laoises; we like to think we're one of the big boys. But then when we get there, we find out we're actually just pretenders to the crown. For Kerry, on the other hand, Dublin are just another team in the way. The lads in blue are a lot cockier all right and with a bit more swagger, but it is all the more enjoyable taking them down in the process. Hell, they even let us lead at half-time by a point — 0-08 to 0-07 — just to suck us in even more. Let them believe their own bullshit, they seem to be saying. All the more satisfying to kick it from under them.

And if one moment summed it up for the Dubs, it came with just thirteen minutes to go. Kerry's lead had been cut to one point and Dublin were hauling them back. The momentum was with the Dubs and for the first time the coolness of Kerry seemed to be ebbing ever so slightly away. One score in it and Dublin were in possession again. Stephen Cluxton, the enigmatic Dublin keeper gathered the ball and looked up to deliver it. The Dublin players were struggling to shake off their Kerry markers but were just about making space, while out on the right the Dublin midfielder Ciaran Whelan, who was having one of his best seasons in blue, was on his own, screaming for the ball — not even screaming, but yelling, waving his arms, doing everything but picking up a flag to alert Cluxton. But Cluxton looked only to his left. He hopped the ball, looked again, and with the Kerry forwards holding off like hunters waiting for their moment to jump on their prey, Cluxton decided he himself — the keeper! — would venture forth in search of space and territory. He reached the 45 (how far would he have got, one wonders, in some perverse alternative GAA universe) before he was found out.

The Kerry hunters had waited and waited, not believing what they were seeing, and were testing his foolhardiness. And then they pounced. The 45 was far enough for them, and as they closed in on Cluxton, a flurry of green and gold descending upon the stranded and isolated Dublin goalie, the soft underbelly of the Dubs was revealed. Cluxton panicked. The cool, decisive calmness of the Kerry pack was not what you encountered anywhere else in the country. Cluxton kicked the ball straight to Kerry's towering forward, Kieran Donaghy. The lights finally came on for Cluxton as he raced back to his goal — a full 45 metres away — to be joined by Whelan and the other Dublin players who had been screaming for the ball. But Donaghy and Kerry didn't join in the rush. They didn't panic or lose the head. They kept possession, working the ball down the wing, then moved it into the centre before going down the left channel where Seán O'Sullivan fisted an easy point. Kerry were ahead by two points now. There was daylight between them and their opponents. There was only a minute left and the slightly creaking ship had been steadied.

As for the Dubs? Well, they dusted themselves down and tried to come back at Kerry. But the damage was done. The momentum was lost. And when the final whistle blew, Kerry had won and were into their fourth All-Ireland final in a row. Another missed opportunity for Dublin. It was twelve years and counting now since their last final appearance. We would be heading into a thirteenth season next year wondering when it would ever be our year. The hunger worsened with each passing season. Maybe we would never see the good times again.

'Trying to play football,' I said shaking hands with the Kerry fan beside me. 'Will we never get past ye?'

'Aye, sometime. Not today though,' replied the Kerry man with a broadening smile. 'But there's always next year.'

Another year over. Another season of dashed hopes and disappointments. Pained and disconsolate, I turned my back on Croke Park for another season and headed down the stadium steps. But there was nowhere else I'd rather have been. They were still my county and my team. And sure the Kerry fan was right. There was always next year.

# DECEMBER–JANUARY
## WINTER HIBERNATION

### The Blue Stars

I hate October and November if only because you're left wandering aimlessly around the house on a Sunday afternoon. The normal routine of going for pints and to a match has been interrupted and there's not even team selections or match scores to liven up the conversation. Even the Premier League and Champions League seasons are only just beginning and not worth glancing at.

The clocks going back is the final nail in the coffin. It will be dark by four o'clock in the afternoon and after that I don't feel much like venturing outside the house. Better to be in by the fire and contenting yourself with *All-Ireland Gold*. At least I might get to see glimpses of Dublin when they used to win All-Ireland titles. Flashbacks to the 70s when Moran was in full flight; cut to the 80s when Mullins was decking all around him; and even picture the 90s when Sherlock was in his pomp. Linger too long, however, and I might get unlucky. TG4 might be showing (yet) another Kerry victory, with Spillane running like a fairy down the wing or Páidí lifting the cup as if it alone was giving him the elixir of youth. And then there was always Micko prowling the sidelines, watching it all like a chess grandmaster — more Kasparov than Fischer, it has to be said. (Who would be the Bobby Fischer of the GAA is an interesting conundrum for those brave enough to ponder.)

Time passes quickly and before too long I've become familiar with the endless Christmas ads and jingles. All that's left to worry about are the multiple get-togethers that are colliding the week before Christmas. The luncheons and meetings are held with boozy accompaniments. They run late into the night, and before I know it I'm waking up the next morning wondering where it all went wrong and what time I've to meet another bunch of friends I haven't seen since last year. Some want to talk about poor old Bertie 'only' getting a €33,000 pay rise and having to make do without a Versailles or Chequers to live in; others bring up the Cork players going on strike. Me? I like to leave politics, religion and Cork out of the conversation and stick to the year that's been (feckin Kerry!) and the year to come.

The liver and stomach might not be able to hold up for Christmas, but at least my sanity will, for this time of year means that the season is just around the corner. The Blue Stars clash is held soon after Christmas Day, and then it's January with the O'Byrne Cup followed soon after by the football and hurling leagues. After that, the Championship is only a short hop of the ball away.

Christmas and Stephen's Day have passed off without incident. I'm glad it's all over for another year and now, like a madman, I'm standing on the sideline in the freezing rain watching a Dublin team play another Dublin team!

Yes, it can only be the annual Christmas fest known as the Blue Stars matches when the hurlers and footballers play against a selection of other Dublin hurlers and footballers. They are the traditional matches to blow off the cobwebs that signal the season has come around again. After its brief hibernation the season is ready and willing to serve up another year of highs and lows, victories and defeats.

A large crowd of men, women and children stand around in north County Dublin in the freezing cold. Despite the red noses and frost-bitten fingers, we all carry a look of smug satisfaction as if Santa has come again. The Blue Stars have come down the chimney once more and the fans (fanatics/lunatics/madmen) are lapping it up.

Even Dublin Bus has obliged us by laying on courtesy buses from the DART stations to Naomh Mearnog's ground. Next year all we need is for the game to be played in our own back gardens while we watch from the comfort of our living rooms with a drink in one hand and nachos in the other.

Glancing away from the match and casting my eye on those standing on the sidelines, I wonder just what it is that compels all these people to come out here on this December day each year. The free bus rides and the *Evening Herald* sponsorship show how popular this event has become. Who needs New Year's Eve celebrations or hogmanay when you have the Blue Stars clash? Can the Dubs really mean this much to all these people, I wonder. What do they do in their months off and what did they do before they ever discovered their love of the Dubs?

Ten years ago while I was living it up in college, if someone had told me I'd be wrapped up in Dublin GAA gear standing here watching a challenge match at the end of December, I would have pointed them towards the nearest madhouse. Now, though, I'm 30 years of age, I have a mortgage and credit union loans and am about to get married later in the year. (August actually; if the Dubs make it to the semis, the honeymoon may have to be postponed!) Life, in other words, is starting to get serious and is stretching out before me in a haze of work and bills.

You know the old saying, that youth is wasted on the young, but at 20 years of age living the high life in college with five hours of lectures a week, it doesn't get much better than that. We don't really spend four years of our lives studying to get degrees. It's four years of indulgence so we can get it out of our systems and then hopefully be ready in our mid-twenties to get serious about a career and all that.

Some college habits are harder to shake off than others, however. And sometimes you find that life's lessons don't come until a good deal later. I'm 30 for heaven's sake and I'm standing here like a child in the freezing cold, feeding a joyful habit that really should have been consigned to the shoe box under my old bed with my *Match* and *Shoot* magazines.

It's funny though. The older I get, the more I hanker after my youthful habits and pastimes — football, sports, fishing, dogs, writing, mountain climbing and whatever you're having yourself. You may give them up as you hit your teens, but they never really leave you. The worst mistake you can make is to ignore them entirely as you get older, and the sooner you take them back out of their boxes the better. And all the better if you have done so before you meet your future wife/life partner. At least then she has been given sufficient warning and if she still wants to go ahead and marry you, then she knows that certain things, like you disappearing every other Sunday for Dubs games, comes with the territory.

So, I stand here and freeze. It's the madness of it that has to be appealing. The giving in to it and not caring. The way as a kid you could roll yourself down a hill and not worry about bumps or bruises or anyone watching you. So I stand here, hands deep in my pockets, looking to hide them from the cold air. It's only a Blue Stars match, but it's part of who I am and want to be now. The Dublin GAA badge of identity is not about the team or the county, but about me, about who I want to be and the passions I choose to follow — not some middle-aged hankering for the likes of golf or cigar smoking. I must make do by pulling the collar of my jacket tighter around my neck and wondering when I'll ever hear the final whistle.

The games go to penalties (penalties in the GAA!), but I lose interest by the time the final whistle blows. The cold has penetrated my bones now and I need something hot to soothe me. Like Christmas Mass and the Leopardstown Races, another Christmas rite has been accomplished. Our appetites have been whetted.

 *O'Byrne Cup first round, Dublin 2-12, Wicklow 0-09, Parnell Park*

I've survived New Year (another year celebrating it at home with friends, family and Jools Holland) and like everyone else am having to get used to writing

2008 now. In the days after, I always like to sit down and go through my plans, my 'must dos' and 'want tos' for the coming year. Between building our house, getting married and concentrating on work commitments, I'll be surprised if there's much time left for anything else. But Sundays will be left free when the Dubs are playing and I'm hoping that this year I might finally be able to get on the Parnell Park ticket scheme (I'm not holding my breath though) and save myself the hassle of the scramble for tickets during the Championship.

That's all a while away, but for now I've no problems getting into Parnell Park for the first game of the new year against Wicklow in the O'Byrne Cup. Mick O'Dwyer is managing Wicklow still. It's amazing to see the man as hungry as ever for the game. You'd want to have some hunger all right to be seeing Wicklow through a few seasons, but he does seem to have lifted things in the county. It's a far cry from his Kerry heydays of the 70s and 80s, but Dublin fans have always had respect for O'Dwyer, for what he's done for the game and for his rivalry with Kevin Heffernan.

It's a bitterly cold January night in Parnell Park tonight, but Dublin, despite being just back from their break and with only one training session under their belts, manage a comfortable nine-point win over Wicklow. Some new names are being blooded in these early months. Eamonn Fennell gets a place in midfield while Ciaran Whelan is rested; Barry Kennedy continues in the forwards after doing well in the Blue Stars last week. Only six regulars are in the line-up. Still up front, plugging away in the middle of winter, is Jason Sherlock. It's hard to believe that Sherlock is still tipping around and his running and eagerness for the game, even in an O'Byrne Cup in January, is remarkable. Is he a future O'Dwyer in the making, I wonder.

Next up is the visit of Westmeath, but Monday means a return to work after the New Year. The Sunday blues are kicking in already. I just need some of that O'Dwyer/Sherlock enthusiasm to get me through it.

**JANUARY 10 Thursday**

I hear that song, 'There may be trouble ahead', playing in my head. For the first time in GAA history a county was unable to field a team due to strike action when Cork's Waterford Crystal Cup tie against Limerick IT couldn't go ahead. The strike action the players called back in December has been allowed to drag on and the fact that the footballers are in South America and not due back until next week hasn't helped matters. It must be suddenly dawning on all concerned that this could potentially escalate into something more serious. If it's Cork, you're guaranteed some sort of ruckus. Watch this space.

**JANUARY 11 FRIDAY**

I read that Alan Brogan has been named Dublin captain for the coming season. He's a class act, but captain and leadership material? He's been a great servant and forward for Dublin football these past five years, but surely you want someone with more experience and presence on the pitch. I would have gone for Sherlock. He's someone you would look up to and listen intently to anything he had to say to you. Plus, if this is his year, it would be some way to finish off his career by lifting Sam in Croker in September.

**JANUARY 12 SATURDAY**

## *O'Byrne Cup quarter-final, Dublin 1-16, Westmeath 1-06, Parnell Park*

Another Saturday in the freezing January weather and where else would you be but Parnell Park to see the Dubs in the O'Byrne Cup? I honestly think I'm going batty since I've made the first two O'Byrne Cup games and haven't had anything better to be doing with my Saturday nights, especially as the games are on Setanta anyway. I just need a hobby that doesn't involve standing out in the bitter cold, wind and rain. Scuba diving in the Pacific would be more like it.

All I can say is I must have been a very bad person in a previous life to put myself through this. I'm just hoping the Dublin GAA gods have spotted me and will look benignly on me when I'm chasing through the streets and pubs around Ballybough in August and September looking for tickets.

It's a facile ten-point win for Dublin this evening and I don't know if the Dublin management team will have learned much from such an easy victory. I've learned one thing though: I must be losing my marbles. I spend the rest of the night drying and thawing out while the missus looks at me with that 'Why? Will-someone-just tell-me-why-he-does-it' look.

**JANUARY 16 Wednesday**

The only thing that knocks the players' strike from the conversation in Cork is the release of Wayne O'Donoghue from prison this morning. Give it a day or two and they'll forget about O'Donoghue and go back to the only thing that really gets them going down there: Cork GAA.

**JANUARY 19 Saturday**

*Postponed O'Byrne Cup semi-final, Dublin v Carlow, Parnell Park*

First postponement of the year. It's expected at this time of the year really, but I hope it won't be a portent of things to come. Getting the GAA to reschedule games in an orderly fashion is like trying to accommodate 32 different warring factions. It's been lashing down for the last few days and while the game has been rescheduled for next Tuesday, if it keeps raining like this the games will again have to be called off and the O'Byrne Cup will be running into the League.

I stay in to watch highlights of Leinster and Munster in the Heineken Cup. Munster win heroically to qualify for the quarters, while Leinster lose pathetically to go out. Same as it ever was. Hope the Dubs don't catch some of those Leinster rugby failings. Maybe it's in our east coast DNA.

**JANUARY 22 Tuesday**

*Rescheduled O'Byrne Cup semi-final, Dublin 1-15, Carlow 2-12 (aet), Parnell Park*

I much prefer these midweek fixtures and am looking forward to the game against Carlow tonight, although you do have to feel sorry for the Carlow set-up having to make it across Dublin city for a 7.30 pm throw-in. But even Dublin selector Dave Billings is having a go and says it's awkward for some of the Dublin lads to make it!

'Even from our point of view,' he said, 'we have players

coming from all over the city, and getting there for a 7.30 start is difficult. A later start would have been preferable. It is an amateur game and people have to work.'

I reckon if the fans can make it on time, then the players should be able to.

Traffic issues didn't affect the players' appetites this evening. What a game, although not one you'd be expecting Dublin to be drawing or losing. A bit of extra time probably didn't do their legs or fitness any harm.

Dublin managed to get a late equalising point to take it into extra time. They then took control going three points up before Carlow got a controversial penalty to level things again. It was back and forth all the way before Carlow got an equaliser deep into injury time.

Not great from the Dubs' point of view, but great entertainment. If word gets out about how good these games are in January, they'll be switching the O'Byrne Cup to Croker soon. What with the warnings about the Irish economy and housing prices dropping, the GAA might just be our only feel-good distraction this year.

**JANUARY 26 Saturday** The GAA finally wake up to the fact that the Cork situation is no longer just a Cork problem, especially now that League games could be affected. (Are they worried about the sponsors' reaction or the fans, I wonder.) Kieran Mulvey, chief executive of the Labour Relations Commission, has bravely taken on the job of trying to find a way through the problem. It's pressure time now as the League games are coming up and there's no sign of any side backing down.

Talks break down this evening after 18 hours. The

A YEAR WITH THE DUBS

clock is ticking on Cork GAA's year. Will it be too late to save it, and why was it left until the last minute before the GAA got the finger out and intervened? Still though, just when you thought the New Year would be quiet, leave it to Cork to provide us with plenty of talking points.

Seán Óg Ó hAilpín gives an insight into the players' thinking and attitudes in an excellent piece with Tom Humphries in *The Irish Times* today. He traces the current dispute back to the last strike in 2002 when the players had the upper hand and reckons that county board officials are now looking to row back on those improvements and re-exert their own power by appointing yes men into the management roles.

His point on extracting every last ounce and percentage to win All-Irelands is well put, but when you read about the politicking and manoeuvring that goes on in the background, it makes Machiavelli seem like a Green Party TD in coalition by comparison. The interview is a fascinating glimpse into the players' minds. Calling on Frank Murphy to resign won't have helped matters either. This row has a long road ahead of it. Will be glad to get to see the Dubs tomorrow and get back to matters on the pitch.

**JANUARY 27 Sunday**

*O'Byrne Cup semi-final replay, Carlow 1-07, Dublin 1-15, Dr Cullen Park*

I don't know what's more remarkable: it's still only January and already the Dublin footballers have played four games; or the fact that I stand here in Dr Cullen Park in Carlow for an O'Byrne Cup semi-final replay surrounded by nearly 5,000 Dubs supporters. I have to double check the programme once more to make sure I haven't got the O'Byrne Cup mixed up with the Leinster Championship. No, there it is in black and white, confirming that this is indeed a low-key, warm-up competition — in Carlow, in January, with 5,000 Dubs in attendance.

The first game in Parnell Park the week before was a humdinger of a battle. Sendings-off, goals, penalties, mêlées, blown leads and extra time were all the ingredients that couldn't separate the teams in a pulsating game. And so it was that Dublin were forced to leave the capital and travel down to Carlow for the replay.

I leave in the morning, expecting an easy and relaxing drive to Dr Cullen Park. But driving past the Red Cow roundabout and on to the N7, there was a phalanx of other Dublin cars, some with their flags from last year flying from their side windows, all with the same idea in mind. A replay against Carlow in the O'Byrne Cup was, on this Sunday, an attractive fixture for the Dublin fans. Arriving into Carlow two hours later, and the traffic is bumper to bumper as if it is the height of the Championship. Cars are parked in industrial parks, church car parks and the perennial favourite — grass verges on the side of the road.

Dumping the car on a pavement, I head down to the ground still marvelling at the crowds of Dubs doing the same. And then it hits me. Most of these cars haven't come from Dublin at all. They've all probably driven in from the outskirts of County Carlow itself. We may be two hours from the capital, but we are most definitely in the commuter belt. The Dubs are now like the Irish Wild Geese, forced to flee their own land and find refuge in the locales of Kildare, Meath, Carlow and Wicklow. With so many tossed around the province, the notion of away games in Leinster might soon be a thing of the past for the Dublin team.

On all sides of the ground could be seen blue jerseys and blue flags. What other county, I wondered, could drum up such support for an O'Byrne Cup replay in January. Wasn't this the closest thing the GAA had to a hard-core fan base? In the same way that Munster fans (and Leinster fans somewhat) as well as soccer fans in Ireland and England identify closely with their teams, so too this Dublin team was being closely wrapped up as 'theirs' by Dublin people. And, it appeared, this Dublin fan base was growing year on year. With their city changing in physical and cultural terms, what it meant to be 'Dublin' was being latched on to, preserved and celebrated through the county team. And more and more want to be part of it.

'Fucks sake, Kennedy! Yeah, go on. Get off the pitch. Ye're fuckin useless anyway.'

'The referee's a crack addict. Go on, ya prick ya, Bannon!'

The Dad, in his forties, wearing his Dublin jersey and with his Dublin flag wrapped around his shoulders, turned to his companions laughing to see if they were joining in the fun too. His three companions — his 8-year-old son, 6-year-old daughter and a 4-year-old girl, looked up laughing, wanting to join in and understand what was going on. You can take the fan out of the Hill, but you cannot take the Hill out of the fan. It was Hill 16 on tour for the day in County Carlow.

On my other side another group of fans sipped from their Budweiser bottles and passed the spliffs around. Bedecked in their Dublin jerseys, they had flags wrapped around themselves in mock uniform. In front of me stood three blokes in their twenties, no jerseys or blue on them. They weren't drinking or smoking and spoke quietly among themselves about Dublin's chances for the year. Beside them stood two oul' fellas in their fifties, small, stocky and with pot bellies earned through years of hard work in the pubs. Both identical in their Dublin jackets and jeans, they barely said a word to each other during the match apart occasionally from shouting, 'Ya bollix ya, Bannon!' to the ref, before retreating back into their silent concentration on the game.

The Dublin crowd is a complex mix all right, and here in Carlow you would get no better place to see their different hues. From the headbangers to the early morning drinkers to the quiet and sedate fans, Dubs fans embrace all types. 'Bogey buzz dat, ya mad ting!' 'Ger ourra dat, ya cunt ya!' The worst excesses of Ross O'Carroll's stereotypes weren't, it seemed, entirely based on fiction.

There is definitely something unique about Dublin people and Dublin fans. Whether that is a good thing or not is for each to decide for themselves, but 70 minutes of such verbal abuse began to give me a splitting headache.

Dublin suffers from an identity crisis and class divide, not knowing who or what it is. Divided by the river, people on the southside generally want nothing to do with a Dublin accent which they associate with the northside. Instead, they shun the accent and its associated trappings and embrace a mid-Atlantic tone which is neither Dublin nor culchie but is instead neutral enough to appeal to British people whilst at the same time not appearing west Brit to the Irish. More and more though, it seems that American affectations such as, 'That is like so oh my God fabulous!' are being taken on by those for whom mid-Atlantic is the norm. They are in fact going further west all the time.

And then on the other side of the divide are those who like to class themselves as Dubs. They are proud of being Dublin and like to highlight their Dublin accent and use Dublin sayings like 'bleedin' and 'deadly' in an unconscious parody of themselves. Southsiders to them are 'poshies' and 'faggots', while they are the ones that 'keep it real', smoking Johnny Blues and drinking cider or Bud.

And then somewhere in between are the Dubliners who don't want to be either. Much as IRA violence gave Irish nationalism a bad name, so too the self-parodying northside and southside Dublin cultures that are exaggerated are the ones that many people don't want to be associated with and choose instead to turn down the volume on their own accents. Following the Dublin team though seems to mean an identity with the worst excesses of the northside culture — from the accent to the sayings to the drinking habits. Being on the Hill on Championship days, this culture is magnified a thousand-fold.

But is there an acceptable middle ground? If rugby fans are the typical southsiders and Dublin GAA fans the northsiders, where then for the Dublin neutrals? Or maybe we just have to put up with both sides of the divide. Going to Ireland or Leinster rugby games, you just have to expect a certain behaviour by the fans, and with the Dublin games likewise. At a Celtic League game in Donnybrook once, when Leinster were hammering their opponents, the crowd began a chant of 'Let's run riot! Let's run riot!' Down in Thurles in 2001 for the replayed Dublin-Kerry All-Ireland quarter-final, it was the time of the foot and mouth outbreak when farmers (and culchies by extension in Dublin fans' thinking) were most badly affected. Before the game, outside the pubs in Thurles where the Dublin fans congregated, chants of 'La, la, la, your sheep are dead! La, la, la, your sheep are dead!' were sung at horrified Kerry fans walking past.

Geographically, culturally and mentally we are a city divided. And in the middle you have to fit the Dublin people who just want to get on with supporting their respective teams. One thing is certain though. In the brave new world of Celtic Tiger Ireland, Dublin fans now know how to get to the likes of Carlow and Kildare. They've become practically cosmopolitan in their outlook and lifestyle ('Pass the Americano there, Anto'), but when following the Dubs, they'll revert back to type. 'Cider and spliffs, anyone?'

Dublin outclassed and easily beat Paul Bealin's Carlow by eight points this day in January and the 5,000 Dubs headed home happy with the win. For some, they didn't have far to travel. Carlow was now the county they called home. But Dublin was still the place they clung to.

**JANUARY 30 Wednesday** The Cork saga drags on and is now affecting other counties. GAA HQ has acceded to Cork's request and a postponement of the Meath v Cork game has now been passed. I'd say Dublin fans are nervously keeping an eye on things. Hundreds of them will be planning a lost few days in Cork in February when the Dubs are set to play down there.

But it looks like dragging on as lines in the sand are being dug deeper. Last night the Cork County Board met and fully supported Teddy Holland and Frank Murphy. They're sticking it up to the players. It's hard to see how any normal relations can be restored when it's all finally done and dusted.

You have to pity Kieran Mulvey in all this. The chairman of the Labour Relations Committee has the county board and the players in separate ears. Some are saying not even Kofi Anan or George Mitchell could solve this impasse. If Mulvey does manage to find a solution, he should be nominated for the Nobel Peace Prize and taken around the world to Israel, Iraq and Chechnya. He'd find those places a piece of cake compared to Cork's internal strife.

**JANUARY 31 Thursday** Thankfully we can forget about Cork for a bit and think about the Dubs who start their League campaign in Parnell Park on Saturday against Westmeath. It will be closer than the ten-point drubbing we handed out to them a few weeks back and should be a good game — once we get the weather.

It's strange to still have the O'Byrne Cup on our minds with the League starting, but next Friday is the final against Longford. We're getting into the busy period now for the Dublin fans — football and hurling league matches to get to over the coming months. Then it will be long, bright evenings and the start of the Championship. I can nearly smell the Croke Park grass. The cobwebs have been dusted off and the Dublin jersey taken out of the closet (miraculously it still fits). The winter hibernation is finally at an end.

# FEBRUARY–APRIL
## LEAGUE MATTERS

### *National Football League, Dublin 1-07, Westmeath 1-05, Parnell Park*

It's a strange first outing in the League to look forward to. The O'Byrne Cup final has still to be played next Friday and, well, a final is a final, even if it is only the O'Byrne Cup. Tonight is just the first round of the League, but every game counts this year as promotion has to be the one and only objective for Dublin. Whether the Cork game goes ahead is another matter, but there will still be games against Meath, Armagh, Roscommon, Cavan and Monaghan to deal with, and Pillar's men will need to improve on previous League outings.

The Dubs appear to have sprung out of the traps this year and aren't looking to ease themselves into the Championship. The Dublin lads have looked as fit and physically superior as I've ever seen them. Hopefully Pillar can use the League games to try out a few new faces and work out what his full back line should be and whether a few new faces emerge among the forwards. This is the time for tweaking and improving before the summer arrives. Proving themselves over the coming weeks and months will be foremost in Dublin fans' minds.

Playing Westmeath again so soon after beating them by ten points in the O'Byrne Cup has a feeling of *déjà vu* about the place. The game was anything but similar though. Dublin were five points up early on, but then Dessie Dolan came to life and hauled Westmeath back into it. It was a bit of a free-kick and wide fest from there on in, and somehow Dublin managed to scramble over the line with just two points to spare. It's not impressive and it's not pretty, but it is a win.

Is it too early to start worrying about form and the way the team wins? Probably, but that won't stop the Dubs fans discussing tonight's win as if Sam Maguire depended on it.

Not a good omen for the season either. Went down to the Church end of Parnell Park and met a load of Dublin 'fans' drinking and smoking hash. Looks like the fuckin eejit brigade has jumped on the Dublin bandwagon early this year. Pity. At least the Hill is bigger and you can't smell them as bad.

Maybe I'm just getting old. I'll want to be sitting down at games next.

**FEBRUARY**
**3**
**Sunday**

It's the Super Bowl tonight. Most of my friends think I'm nuts, but I'll always take the Monday after a Super Bowl off. I stock up on the beer and popcorn and get ready for the advertising-cum-sporting fest which will run from 11 pm until 4 am. I've always loved American sports — from baseball to basketball to American football — and can explain the rules better than most Americans themselves. Is it just part of my sports obsession? Probably, but I can still remember being given a present of an American football and a New York Mets cap from an uncle returning from holiday in the States when I was about 6. I've been hooked ever since.

American sports do entertainment, marketing, merchandising, glitz and glamour better than anyone else in the world. Even if living a couple of thousand miles away on the other side of the Atlantic, I still follow the goings on in the NBA, MLB and NFL.

This year has been special as well. The most dominant team in recent years with three Super Bowl wins in six years, the New England Patriots, are chasing a perfect season. They have already gone 17-0 in the regular season and are through to another Super Bowl against the New York Giants. It's all about the Patriots and their perfect season, but somebody should tell the media and the fans that the Giants are there to play as well. It's not quite the Dubs, but I remember their All-Ireland in 1992 against Donegal when Dublin just had to turn up to win the Sam Maguire.

Food, beers and frosted mug beside me, I settle in for the long run. Everybody else goes to bed shaking their heads at the thought that I'll be still up for another five hours watching a game that takes ad breaks every two minutes. But hey, this is the life of a sports fan. You don't choose; it just happens and you go along for the hugely enjoyable ride. Tonight I could be watching sports history in the making. How often do you get to say that?

**FEBRUARY**

**4**

**Monday**

Wake up at 11 am very bleary eyed and with a heavy head. Got to bed at 4.30 am. I think back to the game and groan. With less than two minutes on the clock and 14-10 up, it looked like the Patriots had things sewn up. The perfect season would be complete and history would be made as probably the greatest American football team of all time headed for glory — a bit like Kerry going for their five in a row against Offaly in 1982.

And then. With 1:15 on the clock, the Giants had the ball on their own 44 yard line. Quarterback Eli Manning receives the ball and is looking to throw the pass, but two Patriots linemen close in on him and are about to sack him. One of the Patriots actually has a hold of Manning's sleeve, but somehow Manning wriggles away and launches a 32 yard pass which is caught in mid-air by a falling David Tyree. Four plays later and with 35 seconds left, the Giants get their game-winning touchdown and record the greatest upset in Super Bowl history. By the width of a sleeve is how close the Patriots came to winning and I am gutted for them. I have been following them for the last number of years. But it serves as a reminder of just how small the margin between winning and losing can be, no matter how much of a favourite you are. Just ask the Kerry team of 1982, the Dubs in 92 or 94, or Tyrone, Armagh and Mayo. Any team can point to heroic defeats or glorious victories, and the gap between the two is oh so small.

Why the hell then do Kerry footballers make it look so easy picking up so many All-Irelands year in, year out? And why do Dublin footballers make it look so hard? If there are only inches and tiny percentages in it, how come we always seem to come out on the wrong side of the line and Kerry on the right side?

Anyway, this is too much thinking after so little sleep and with such a heavy head. I think I'll get out the *Dubs in the Rare Ould Times* DVD and remember the good old days. I curl up on the couch, feel sorry for myself and wallow in some Colm Meaney-induced nostalgia.

**FEBRUARY**

**6**

**Wednesday**

Busy week this week sportswise. I finally recover from my Super Bowl hangover and get my tickets for Friday's O'Byrne Cup final. Friday night makes a nice change for the Dubs and should add to the atmosphere. Find it hard to believe we're still only talking about the O'Byrne Cup and there's already such interest in it.

First things first though, and this evening Brazil are in town for a friendly against Ireland. It's not often you get to see the Samba Boys in the flesh and watch their skill close up. Ronaldinho and Kaka might be missing, but it's still Brazil and even their third team I'm sure would beat us.

The Ireland team is still managerless since the sacking of Steve Staunton. There've been rumours of Giovanni Trapattoni being in the running, but I'll believe it when I see it. Anyone but Terry Venables, please. After the disaster of Steve Staunton you wonder just how many fuck-ups the FAI can make. If they keep up at this rate they may just disenfranchise the entire Irish soccer population and send them into the GAA's hands. Maybe GAA HQ is praying for Venables to be given the job after all.

Brazil win 1-0 and the match is crap. With Dunga in charge, it just shows how far Brazil have sold their footballing soul to match European physicality and organisation. It's a bit like Kerry trying to mimic Armagh or the Dubs. Well, you know what I mean.

The FAI had better appoint someone good and someone fast, otherwise the Irish team will be playing in front of a half empty Croke Park come the autumn. Play the Dubs against Italy and you'd be guaranteed a full house. I'd like to see Ciaran Whelan taking on Gattuso with Sherlock up front and Cluxton in goal. The more I think of it, this could be the answer to everyone's problems. The Dubs get to play all year round; the FAI get away without paying the players; and we get to qualify for World Cups and European Championships.

**FEBRUARY 7 Thursday**

The Cork saga rumbles on and it looks like the Cork County Board are looking to completely end affairs with the players. They have attempted to divide the players and public by revealing some of the negotiating positions that were taken by the players' representatives including, the board claim, the fact that the players were willing to accept Teddy Holland as manager.

This is surely going to explode. Dubs fans, you can forget about the Cork game now.

**FEBRUARY 8 Friday**

*O'Byrne Cup final, Dublin 2-12, Longford 1-14, Parnell Park*

Sure enough, the Cork players hit the roof with yesterday's county board statement. 'We are furious at the spin and misinformation put out by the board,' say the players, 'culminating in yesterday's board statement which said that we would accept Teddy Holland as football manager, which is totally and utterly untrue.'

Time is running out and they only have until the middle of next week before they get kicked out of the leagues.

Friday night and I'm heading down to Donnycarney for the O'Byrne Cup final. The taste of live action is something Cork people won't be having for a while, it seems, although I wonder if Dublin players would be as willing to stand up for such principles if they were backed into a corner.

I can't remember such interest in the O'Byrne Cup before. The Friday night fixture has a lot to do with it and the fact that Dublin are now becoming a year-round attraction. I'd say there will be more here tonight than were at last week's Westmeath game.

And what a game we were treated to. Dublin were chasing their tails for most of the game, dominated by Longford, and were four points down with only minutes to go. What is it they say about form being temporary and class being permament? On 70 minutes Jason Sherlock pounces on a rebound from a Bernard Brogan shot and buries it in the back of the net.

It's still not enough however, as Longford go back upfield and get an insurance point for themselves to leave them two points up deep into injury time. But this Dublin team just doesn't know when to stop or give in. They still had time for one more attack and had to go for goal to win it. Dublin's new find in midfield, Eamonn Fennell, launched one into Sherlock again, who caught it, swivelled and buried it in the net. Goal! And that was it. The final whistle went and Dublin had won by a point with two Sherlock goals in the dying minutes. Unbelievable stuff.

It wasn't quite the Camp Nou in 1999 but Jesus, it was close. Pitch invasions and everything else followed as the Dublin supporters celebrated as if this was Sam itself being won.

Nothing for it but a few celebratory pints this evening as we looked back on a remarkable match. What would it be like if we actually did win an All-Ireland, we wondered.

Any excuse though, and it was nice to be celebrating something so early in the year. The hard road lies ahead though. Longford in the O'Byrne Cup in February is nothing compared to Kerry in an All-Ireland in September. My stomach jumps even thinking about what can still happen this year. But it's been a good and enjoyable start and I get another round in. Cork, you don't know what you're missing.

It's quite the busy, hectic weekend. We drive down to Tipp in the morning to visit the in-laws. Reading the paper at lunchtime and I notice that the Tipp footballers are playing against Clare this afternoon just down the road in a place called Ardfinnan. This would be something new for me, I figure, and decide to head down with the dogs to have a look. It's Division 4 of the League and I'm intrigued to see what standard the football is and just who would be at a football match between these two hurling strongholds.

My first surprise was seeing the rows of cars parked along the side of the road — it reminded me of Donnycarney. I was expecting just myself, the dogs and a few loons standing on the side of a field. Surprise No. 2 was the lovely little ground and stand that Ardfinnan GAA have. An even greater surprise was the €10 I had to pay to get in! At least the dogs were let in for free. The game had just started and I walked to the far side in the sun and sat on the grassy hill near a few of the Tipp fans.

There were a fair few hundred at the game and even Clare had some vocal support with them. Meanwhile the kids behind the goals were knocking a sliothar back and forth with their hurleys — I knew some sort of hurling couldn't be too far away around here. The football was of club standard in Dublin but was one of the most enjoyable games I have seen in a long time. It was such a novel experience to be sitting there on the grass (a tenner for that!) looking across at the Knockmealdown and Comeragh Mountains while the blue and yellow of Tipp and Clare fought it out with a football. For someone as sports-hardened as myself it's rare you get to see something new in sport, but today was it. I have yet to meet anyone from Tipp who has seen their footballers in action. It took a Dub to inform them how good it was.

Tipperary ran out winners in the end. The result was a footnote in the papers the next day, but I learned that you ignore the smaller counties at your peril. These guys are busting a gut training all week to run out for their counties at the weekend. There's no glamour or glory in Division 4 football between Tipperary and Clare, but their spot in the papers is not a fair reflection of the games being served up. I reckon the Dubs will do well to match today's game between now and September. This afternoon at least, my romantic notions about sport have been rekindled once more.

**February 10 Sunday**

*National Hurling League, Dublin 0-22, Antrim 0-15, Parnell Park*

Back and forth, back and forth. It's the return leg in Dublin today and somehow I'm also able to catch the Dublin hurlers in Parnell Park in the afternoon. It's the hurlers' first outing in the League and a chance to get some hurling back into my system. What a strange weekend this is turning out to be. I travel to Tipperary and watch a football match, then come to Dublin to see hurling. But of course all talk is still centred on the 'Cork situation' as we like to euphemistically call it. They always seem to be having 'situations' in Cork, but this one is proving even messier than the previous ones. Last night the Cork players held a meeting where they rejected a proposed 'memorandum of understanding' and have confirmed their commitment to pursue their strike action.

Heading into Parnell Park it's good to get away from the talking, the allegations, claims and counter-claims and remind ourselves of what the GAA does well. A fine seven-point win in Parnell Park for Dublin over Antrim and all is well in the GAA world this side of the country. The hurlers face Kilkenny next week which will be a real test, but in the meantime it will all be about Cork.

Get home to watch the highlights of the Manchester derby on the fiftieth anniversary of the Munich air disaster and you're aptly reminded that sport is just a game. It's a business game as well though for commercial entities such as Man Utd (and increasingly the GAA). The crass commercialism of the anniversary strikes home. The team wore a special 1950s style strip for the game (how much in the club shop, I wonder) while a beautiful mural commemorating Munich which was unveiled earlier in the week was spoiled when the club inserted their main sponsor's logo into it. Despite the fans' protests, they refused to take it down and for anyone that visits Old Trafford they can remember that tragic day fifty years ago brought to you by AIG. I hope we will never see that sort of commercial intrusion into the GAA, but I'm doubting it more and more. Will we soon see a Croke Park Bloody Sunday memorial on Jones's Road sponsored by Vodafone?

United seem overwhelmed by the occasion and play poorly, losing 2-1 to City. I read up some more on the internet about the remarkable talent that was Dublin's own Liam Whelan who died in Munich, a Dub whom Bobby Charlton described as the most talented and skilful player he had seen, no less.

A busy day all round. It's a Six Nations weekend and, no surprise there, Ireland lose 26-21 to France, but already I'm losing interest in the Irish rugby team. They have gone stale and tired under O'Sullivan and today's game doesn't look like they've shaken the disaster of last year's World Cup off their backs. It could be a testing Six Nations campaign for them. But the Gah is back so I'm not really worried.

Between the hurlers, the rugby and Man Utd, I get away with murder in watching all three. I don't know for how long this state of grace will last, but I give my thanks to Sky+. I work in the media and try to say all this sport is for 'research purposes'. Not sure for how long that one will work. And there's still the Champions League to come. At least the Championship is on in the summer when there are few other sports playing. I'm sure I'm walking a tight line as it is. Valentine's Day is next week, so maybe I can earn some extra brownie points then.

**FEBRUARY**
**12**
**Tuesday**

Some chink of light finally in the Cork saga. The county board have agreed to binding arbitration with the LRC's Kieran Mulvey. The ball is now firmly in the players' court. You have to wonder why the county board were so quick and agreeable to the binding arbitration. Do they know something the players don't?

**FEBRUARY**
**13**
**Wednesday**

Still no word as to whether the Cork players will take part in the binding arbitration. You have to be fearful for the players in this. If they don't do it, they will start to lose public support and look like they are digging their heels in too much. But why did the county board agree so readily to the arbitration? If the players jump in and then are told they have to accept Holland, they will be stuck in no man's land.

And in the midst of all this GAA fighting, the FAI announce Giovanni Trapattoni as the new Ireland manager! The one organisation that could never get its shop in order is the only one at the moment acting responsibly. Wonders will never cease. Who would have thought it, former Juventus and Italy supremo Trapattoni managing Ireland after the calamity of Steve Staunton's reign. The FAI are nearly making the GAA and IRFU look like incompetent schoolkids. I'm sure it won't be long before Merrion Square makes some sort of gaffe, but until then I'll be digging out my old Italia 90 jersey. Dublin for the Sam and Ireland to win a few games? The good times could be coming back.

Valentine's Day and there ain't much love in the air in Cork. But maybe Cupid's arrow has hit someone down there. The players have agreed to the binding arbitration. They had little choice really. The ball is now firmly in Kieran Mulvey's court. His decision will be final (one hopes). I don't have a good feeling for the players on this. Why were the county board the first ones to jump in on the arbitration option? They must feel that Mulvey will stick with Holland and leave the players and board to sort it out in the summer. It's going to be a tense 24 hours for all concerned. Up here all anyone really cares about is if the Cork v Dublin game is still going ahead.

Going online to read the Dubs fans' thoughts on things, I can understand their frustration not knowing what is happening about Saturday's game, especially those who have booked transport and accommodation. (Luckily I'll be in Tipp where the missus is from, and I intend to drive the hour or so down to the game.)

But I can't understand their griping at the Cork players taking a stance over such a vital issue. Would Dublin fans like it and accept it if John Costello *et al* started picking Pillar's selectors? Or if the Dublin County Board treated the players and management with disdain and barely concealed contempt? If it's not all right for us then it shouldn't be for anyone else.

It's a curious difference in mentality between Dubs and Corkonians and it's coming more to the fore this week as I follow the Dubs fans' discussion online and in the pub. They all pretty much see the Cork players as holding the country, the GAA and the other counties to ransom as if this were a Cork-only problem or that the issue isn't of sufficient importance to be of interest to the rest of the country.

You can't argue with Seán Óg Ó hAilpín when he said in an *Irish Times* interview nearly three weeks ago that all they wanted was the best way to prepare for and win All-Irelands. Be it preparations, standards, equipment, food or management practices, these are players looking to win. In this GAA age that and only that can win titles. You don't see Kilkenny players left wanting for anything or lacking in preparation or facilities.

Ó hAilpín was right in characterising it as a battle between county board officials who don't like being told what they ought to be doing and players who are trying to get the best conditions. What has been remarkable has been the players' steadfastness and belief in all of this. They know the consequences and not one of the sixty has broken ranks. If they give in now, where would that leave them in future years? At the behest of county board officials looking to cut corners and control things for a bit more power?

You have to admire the Cork players for standing up for their principles, for what is right and for seeing it through, no matter what. It's the main difference between them and the rest of the country. I doubt if the Dublin players (or any other county's players) would have the balls or the stomach to fight for such principles or be willing to stick it out for so long and in the face of such opposition.

I hate to bring up the 'S' word, but with Saipan and Roy Keane it was the Cork people who backed their man and believed in principles, while it was noticeable that large numbers of Dublin people saw Keane as a traitor. Don't rock the boat seems to be a Dublin mantra. Maybe all that time being the Pale and the centre for British rule in Ireland has had some effect on us. It was after all the Dublin people who spat in the faces of those involved in the Rising when they were arrested and taken away. It was only when the country started to have sympathy for the Insurgents after being shot in Kilmainham that supprt for the Rising swung in their favour. It is noticeable now, four and five years after Saipan, that the *I, Keano* audiences in the Olympia in Dublin chant and cheer Keano's name at the end.

We are great, it seems, at revisionism. But until then don't rock the boat and cause hassle for the establishment. It's a kind of unsettling picture of Dublin people, isn't it? But it's one that comes to mind as I read the criticism of the Cork players by Dubs fans.

**FEBRUARY 15 Friday** I keep an ear cocked all day for word on Kieran Mulvey's recommendations, but by lunchtime there's still no word. It's a bit like waiting for exam results. You just don't know how you've done and are half expecting the worst. The GAA confirm that the Cork-Dublin and Waterford-Cork games this weekend are off (I can hear the Dublin fans' wails from here already). It looks like they're expecting a resolution today and can then get back to organising the games. I'm not going out tonight and while watching the telly have the laptop on my knee and am constantly scanning for any news.

Finally, late in the evening Mulvey has come to his conclusions. Surprisingly, he appears to have sided with the players and recommended that Teddy Holland step aside. Not only that, but any new managerial appointments should be done by a committee of seven, of whom two members will be players. Finally, he says the players must agree to never strike again, although this seems a bit far reaching. Still though, getting the removal of Holland was basically an endorsement of the players' view and the players should also be entitled to a say in team affairs.

The county board are to hold an emergency meeting tomorrow — with their tails between their legs hopefully. Fair play to the players who stuck their necks out for what they deemed best in helping them and the county win All-Irelands. Meanwhile, away from the spotlight they resume their daily gym and training schedule and the Dublin fans go on bitching and moaning about their lost weekend in Cork. On this one though I'm firmly in the players' camp and they've been proven right. If the Cork County Board hadn't tried to brush the issue aside back in December, the League games would never have had to be postponed/cancelled in the first place.

Teddy Holland fires one last spiteful arrow across the players' bows. Releasing a statement tonight he lambasts them saying:

*The notion that the players somehow monopolise a desire to win is a myth. Last year's All-Ireland final was the most chaotic, abject capitulation in the history of Cork football. It lacked all the qualities which I stand for and which I hope the players can learn in time. In their more honest moments, the players might reflect on their performances that day and use them as a motivation to drive them forward.*

It smacks of bitterness and petulance, and the bilious manner of his going only adds to the overall ugly effect of the whole affair.

Maybe we should remember the words of Kieran Mulvey who at the end reflected, 'I do not see the events in the Cork GAA as an exercise in "player power". Rather it is a local dispute relating to specific circumstances and their own unique chain of events.'

They're different down there all right.

**● ● ●**
**FEBRUARY**
**16**
**Saturday**

## Postponed NFL, Dublin v Cork, Pairc Uí Chaoimh

Today was supposed to be the day when the Dubs played Cork. Hundreds of pissed-off Dubs venting their anger online and on the street. Even selector Dave Billings has a go: 'There's been a lack of respect from Cork towards Dublin — a lack of respect from both Cork County Board and players. They've let a local squabble run out of control and I would welcome an acknowledgment of that.'

A lot of the fans' anger is because they had planned a weekend's piss-up in Cork and now that's been taken away from them, and it's understandable the Dublin set-up is annoyed at having their plans and arrangements cancelled at the last minute. Still though, sometimes you wish the bigger picture could be seen in all of this and that everyone wasn't just fighting their own corner.

Hopefully it can be put to bed now, Cork can move on and the League can continue. But you just have a nagging suspicion that it won't be laid to rest completely and some other county will have some problem or other somewhere down the line. Only time will tell.

## NHL, Kilkenny 1-21, Dublin 2-10, Nowlan Park

**FEBRUARY 17 Sunday**

A win against Antrim is a win against Antrim, but a game against Kilkenny down in Nowlan Park is a different kettle of fish altogether. Manage to catch snippets of radio reports in the afternoon, but by the sounds of it the Dubs were never in the game. It ends up being an eight-point defeat. Let's hope the hurlers can take it on the chin and push on again. Sure it's only Cork next and after their match today against Waterford was cancelled, they'll be itching to start off with a bang against us.

**FEBRUARY 18 Monday**

St Vincent's heroics in the All-Ireland club championship has really got my interest. It's great to see a Dublin club doing so well, but the fact that it's the old sleeping giant, Vincent's, who gave so much to Dublin GAA, only adds to it all. This is a club that's got a history and a pedigree and God only knows what an All-Ireland title will do for the club, the area and the kids playing the game.

I'm not a Vincent's man but am appreciating more and more the club championships. The GAA is about the local and while the county scene gets more cynical and professional, you start to glory in what the clubs can offer. I love nothing better than travelling across the country to an unknown village and seeing the effect the club can have on a community. Wasn't it Caltra in Galway that

43

won an All-Ireland club football title in 2004 with a population of just a few hundred?

Next Sunday Vincent's face Crossmaglen in Navan in the All-Ireland club semi-final and I start to make plans for the journey. If the Marino men can overcome those bejaysus scary south Armagh boys who have numerous All-Ireland club titles to their name, then you know Vincent's can beat just about anybody.

There's another Cork County Board meeting tonight to vote on removing Holland and his selectors.

**FEBRUARY**
**19**
**Tuesday**

Catch the result from last night's Cork board meeting on the radio this morning. It is 89-18 in favour of removing Holland and his cohorts, but why it had to be dragged on so unseemingly smacks of petulance on Holland's part. It seems like I've been following Cork GAA affairs more than Dublin ones these last few weeks. If I start saying 'boy' at the end of my sentences, just smack me in the mouth.

**FEBRUARY**
**20**
**Wednesday**

Never a dull moment for the GAA. Between strikes, postponements and actually organising competitions, I'm surprised they have any time to raise money at all. But have no fear. If there are millions to be made, they'll make sure it happens.

The GAA's TV rights are announced, and surprise, surprise, RTÉ get 40 of the 50 games on offer to go with the TV3 deal (God help us all!) announced back in December. It's set to bring €25 m into the GAA coffers over the next three years and should go some way to paying for the player grants.

Nickey Brennan scoffed at notions that the GAA were out to extract every last penny (he would though, wouldn't he):

*There was an awful lot spoken out there that the GAA would sell their soul. I can tell you quite clearly, while I'm not going to answer any questions about how much money the GAA is getting from any of the service providers, I would say that it is significantly improved on the last contract.*

*But I would like to make one thing absolutely clear. The GAA did not take this for money. If this was a money deal we might not have had the outcome we had today. We went for a combination of finance, quality of coverage, experience and obviously the new dimension brought to it by TV3.*

*We feel we have met the requirements of the broader spectrum of GAA people across the country and that the end result will be very positive.*

But if the rumours are true that RTÉ is to be one of the hurling sponsors, then the GAA-RTÉ marriage makes quite a bit of sense and puts into proper perspective Brennan's comments. I can't believe however that a winning broadcaster could also have the rights to sponsor the same competition. We'll have to wait until the sponsors are announced, but I can see another unholy row brewing if the rumours are true.

As for the RTÉ-GAA marriage of convenience, does this mean Montrose will become like Sky Sports in being merely a cheer-leader for a product in which they have such a vested interest? Will we see the end of Brolly, Spillane and O'Rourke? Or will they just bring in the *Après Match* character Mickey Kelly from the GAA Assimilation Committee? In the immortal words of Mickey, 'If you can turn a fella G-A-Y, you can turn a fella G-A-A. Are you with me, Pat?'

**FEBRUARY**
**24**
**Sunday**

*All-Ireland Club Football Championship semi-final, St Vincent's 2-09, Crossmaglen 0-11, Navan*

Surprisingly, it's only a short spin up to Navan from north Dublin. We head up the M1 and cut off just past Drogheda passing through Slane. There's little or no traffic this way and we hit Navan in only forty-five minutes — thank God for Google maps. We pull into the town wondering where to park when a sign appears out of nowhere for €2 parking in the school grounds. We're only five minutes' walk from Pairc Tailteann and get a great spot in the stand. That and knowing Dustin the Turkey won Ireland's Eurovision spot last night means I'm in good form today.

Vincent's burst out of the blocks scoring two early goals and Crossmaglen can't cope with their speed, movement and quick ball. Even the introduction of Francie Bellew in the second half can't inspire the Armagh club and

Vincent's hang on. They're into an All-Ireland club final for the first time since 1985.

It feels like I've been in one of those Heineken ads and can hear Van Morrison singing 'Days like this' in my head. Maybe I should do the Lotto tonight.

## MARCH 1 Saturday — NFL, Cavan 0-07, Dublin 1-09, Breffni Park

I'm sorry but I just can't bring myself to do it. Tonight it's Dublin against Cavan up there. But in all honesty could I really be bothered? The Dubs will win for sure, the match will be crap, I'll have driven for four hours there and back, be cold, miserable and knackered, and I'll have to stay in for the rest of the night bitching and moaning. I know, I shouldn't be saying this, let alone admit it. And yes, being a fan means thick and thin, hot and cold, Laurel and Hardy and whatever else you're having. But some days you just want to stay in, sit by the fire, put the telly on, keep warm and snug and enjoy a few hours' entertainment.

Am I being mad? Besides, watching Ireland lose to Wales in the Six Nations in Croker has put me in bad form. Losing in Croker, again! The egg chasers should be ashamed of themselves.

The game is on Setanta and I settle in for a few hours' restful Dubs watching. It's absolutely pissing down at the ground and I turn the fire up and get another beer knowing I've made the right decision tonight. Fair play to the supporters who did go, however. (Especially as afterwards fans told of paying to get into the stand and being told it was full and having to stand on the terraces getting drenched all evening.)

It's too much of a wet and dirty night for a decent game of football and all you want to do is get the win and get the hell out of there. It's not pretty but the Dubs grind it out and win by five points in the end. A job well done from the comfort of my couch.

Two hours later I haven't moved as I channel flick in blissful comfort. I glance at my watch and think of the poor bastards still on the road back from Cavan. The joys of being a fickle fan.

**MARCH**
**2**
**Sunday**

Cork footballers make their long-awaited return to action. It's against Roscommon away and despite the rustiness Cork should be strong enough for them. Good to see the players back where they belong, on the pitch and doing their stuff. They come through in the end, winning by two points. The footballers and hurlers need good seasons now to put the backstabbers and snipers back in their place.

**MARCH**
**4**
**Tuesday**

Reading more post-mortems on the Cavan-Dublin game, came across this great story from a Dubs fan on reservoirdubs.com, telling his tale of woe up in Cavan.

*Got off a bus one evening in Cavan with splitting headache. Bought a packet of well known pain killers and repaired to nearby hostelry where I ordered a pint and took two tablets. A minute later the pint was removed and I was requested to leave as they didn't want — quote — 'Dublin druggies' around the place. Cue shamefaced retreat Embarrassed So wherever you stay don't engage in any exotic behaviour like eating paninis or letting your missus talk back to you.*

**MARCH**
**9**
**Sunday**

## NHL, Dublin 2-16, Cork 3-18, Parnell Park

Dublin finally get to play Cork, but unfortunately it's the hurlers instead of the footballers. Cork just to spite everyone will probably go on and win everything before them this year. That would be real Cork all right. The Dubs end up losing 2-16 to 3-18, and if anything it flattered Cork. How much of it was Cork rustiness or Dublin improvement only time will tell.

But Dublin being nine points up in the first half was quite a shock. Cork's return from exile was looking like a lost cause and there was a lot of huffing and puffing going on. But typical Cork. Second half comes, they get the finger out, lift the performance level and soon come back into it. Fair play to Tommy Naughton's men however. Years before they might have capitulated, but not this new breed of Dublin hurler. They kept scrapping and went back into the lead before Cork again pegged them back and ran out five-point winners.

There was a fair-sized crowd in Parnell today — most of them drawn by the lure of Cork you'd have to say. And I was one. It's always good to get a chance to see some of the best hurlers in the country in the flesh in Dublin (no offence to the Dublin lads).

It says a lot about Dublin hurling when a five-point loss to Cork is disappointing. But in fairness the story today was all about the return of the Cork hurlers. One game in and they've well and truly put the last few months' upheavals behind them.

**MARCH 12 Wednesday**

Busy getting tickets for Saturday's League game against Monaghan, but it's the club finals on Paddy's Day that I'm really looking forward to. Decide to go through Ticketmaster to get the tickets so I can make sure we're in a good spot that is covered in the Hogan Stand. You know Paddy's Day — always pissing rain. Get through to some UK office talking to an English bird who does quite well trying to pronounce Portumna, Nemo and Birr. Tickets being posted out to me. And if I don't get them on Friday since it's a bank holiday on Monday, I ask. 'Oh you can collect them from the box office on the day at Croak Park,' she says.

**MARCH 14 Friday**

Denman wins the Cheltenham Gold Cup and no sign of club final tickets from Ticketmaster. Bad day all round as I had money on Kauto Star to win and then was given a 'good each-way tip' for Neptune Collonges which was about 12-1. I forgot to put the money on, and of course Collonges comes in third. €240 could have been mine this evening. Instead I'm down about €150 for the week from Cheltenham. Never again, I say, ripping up the Kauto Star slip. Of course I'll be at it again next year. The bookies must be licking their lips in anticipation.

## Postponed NFL, Dublin v Monaghan, Parnell Park

**MARCH 15 Saturday**

It's been pissing rain for the last few days. Wonder if it will let up in time for tonight's match. I always look forward to the visit of a Nordie team. You're always guaranteed a bit of extra spice, especially in these conditions when anything can happen.

Luckily, I decided to check hill16.ie one last time before heading down to Parnell Park. There it is in black and white: game called off. Nothing to be done about it, I suppose, as it has been raining solidly for the last few days. Still though, would hate it if I was stuck on the M50 and found out, or even worse, was at the ground. Monaghan fans must be cursing us. I'm starting to get cabin fever however, stuck inside watching an abysmal and depressing Irish defeat by England in the Six Nations. O'Sullivan must surely be on his way out after this and the World Cup campaign.

Postponements and water-logged pitches. That's football in March for you.

## NHL, Wexford 2-09, Dublin 0-15, Wexford Park

**MARCH 16 Sunday**

The hurlers get a draw down in Wexford today. I wonder what that says about Wexford hurling and what it says for the Dubs that we can now be seen as genuine county contenders in Leinster. It says a lot about the steady developments and improvement in Dublin hurling when it's a disappointment to only come away with a draw against Wexford. They need to start building even more on what they've achieved and start winning games against the Wexfords on a consistent basis. If they can do that, then there are a few thousand fans just waiting to climb on to that particular bandwagon.

Looking forward to seeing Joe Canning and the club hurling final tomorrow.

**MARCH**
**17**
**Monday**

*All-Ireland Club Finals Day,*
*St Vincent's 1-11, Nemo Rangers 0-13*
*& Portumna 3-19, Birr 3-09,*
*Croke Park*

Sure enough, my tickets hadn't come by Friday. I ring Ticketmaster in the UK to confirm I can pick them up and now am told there actually isn't a ticket pick-up facility at Croke Park. Feck's sake! I have to get them to cancel the payment on my card and arrange to get down a bit earlier to get new tickets. That was a wasted hour talking to Ticketmaster. The world would be such a great place if it wasn't full of people.

I'm travelling up from Tipperary today for the club finals (long story; don't ask) and feel like a proper GAA fan. Not many would be travelling from Tipp to watch club finals that don't even have clubs involved from the Premier county.

But surprisingly, I'm not the only one standing on the Thurles railway platform heading to the games today. As I await the Cork train, I overhear snatches of conversation from three old farmers beside me. They are Tipp men and they are hurling men.

I'd say they've been to all of Tipp's games over the last fifty years, but here they are on St Patrick's morning travelling up to Dublin to see a hurling match between an Offaly team and a Galway team. These are the real fans and real GAA people, travelling the two hours from their farms to Dublin to watch the best that club hurling has to offer in Ireland. They were not doing it because of any GAA renaissance but because they had always done it. Hurling was in their blood and who they were, though they probably didn't see it in those terms.

Their talk rarely wavered from hurling, the state of the counties and the talents of Tipp players. Occasionally it would veer to the weather and farming, but always it would return to hurling. Theirs were faces that were deep set and well worn. Lines engraved spoke of a thousand tales and you knew you would just love to spend a couple of hours listening to them. It's a pity there aren't more of them around. And you'd worry for the future of the GAA with some of the morons that go to games nowadays.

I get to the ground and have to queue down in Ballybough for tickets while I curse Ticketmaster under my breath. There was a good crowd out today and it wasn't raining, so it promised to be an entertaining afternoon.

We sat in the Cusack among a mixture of Portumna and Birr fans and there was even a smattering of tourists sitting around. They were right as well. Never mind the shabby parade. The real Ireland was here in Croke Park today. Was it Micheál Ó Muircheartaigh who said that the All-Ireland hurling final should be a national holiday as we knew how to hurl long before we knew about Christianity?

My money is on Portumna and I'm taking particular interest in seeing Joe Canning in the flesh today. I have been following his exploits since he burst on to the Portumna team three years ago. 'Watch Canning. Just watch what he does,' I tell my father beside me.

Canning doesn't disappoint. Sidelines, hitting points from either side, frees from his team's own half, he can and does do anything he wants with a sliothar and a hurl. It's an easy ten-point victory for Portumna in the end, but the real entertainment comes from being among these hurling folk from Galway and Offaly. Some have obviously been on the sauce all weekend and have had a few tipples this morning to ease them into the day and in honour of St Patrick himself.

'Chunky! Chunky! You're playing like a fuckin donkey!' comes one cry. Then when Canning scores another sublime point, I can hear one of the Portumna lads say to an English visitor beside him, 'And he's only 12, don't you know. He'll be fuckin mighty when he's 13.'

'He is something else,' agrees my Dad after the match as he rips up his betting slip that had a Birr-Nemo double. 'Why didn't you tell me about him before I made the bet?'

It's amazing to see, but many of the fans now head for the exits. The hurling is over; they've seen all they want to see. For many of these hurling people, Gaelic football isn't even a proper game at all. It's either hurling or nothing.

I've never been a sports sectarian. I've always embraced all games involving a ball and some form of competition. You want to know about baseball, hockey, badminton, basketball? I'm your man. I've never played hurling. ('That game is too dangerous,' said my mother all those years ago.) But I have fallen more and more in love with it and will gladly travel the country to catch a top-class hurling match. How could I ever forget my first Munster hurling final in Pairc Uí Chaoimh between Cork and Tipp?

Gaelic football has always been my game. Kevin Moran posters were the first that went up on my bedroom wall and playing in Croke Park was a childhood dream. Because Moran was at Man United, they too became my team and so my other dream was scoring the winner at Wembley for them in the FA Cup final. All day and night I would be out on the street kicking a ball around — against the wall, against the kerb, or on the pitch if there were enough lads around for a game. I was still only 7, but my mum thought I might as well be with a club and so marched me down to the local soccer and GAA clubs. I was too young for soccer, but the GAA club was starting a Saturday morning coaching and training session and I was welcomed into the fold.

That's the beauty of GAA clubs. They become like a second family. Soon a gang of us would meet up and head down each Saturday morning with our boots, shorts, gloves, socks and T-shirt. We might as well have been the Dubs playing in an All-Ireland, for that's how we saw ourselves. Then afterwards into the bar at 12 pm (we started early) where a pint of Ribena set us back 10p. With that and a packet of crisps, we set ourselves up in front of the telly to watch *Football Focus* on the BBC where we would hear about Man Utd and see how Kevin Moran was getting on.

They start them young in the GAA all right and we were

treated as little men. We were the future of the club and to this day those Saturday mornings are some of my favourite memories of growing up. One of my biggest regrets, which I still ruefully look back on, was when I was 15 and decided I would try my hand at soccer and leave the club after eight years. The soccer petered out as many things do when you're a teenager, but I never returned to the GAA fold, thinking it was too late. It was like a family member leaving me and never returning but one I always thought fondly of and wondered how they were getting along.

Now I'll never get that member back, but my way of keeping in touch is by going to games and not just Dublin games. That's why I'm here on club finals day and will (fingers crossed and ticket permitting) be at the Munster final in the summer.

The St Vincent's fans start to stream in behind us and have brought great support with them for the day. They only had a short walk down Griffith Avenue to get here, and it's been over thirty years since they won their one and only All-Ireland club title. But the Vincent's renaissance is well and truly under way under Mickey Whelan and the Marino club is setting itself up to be one of the greats of the national club scene once again.

They're up against a giant in Nemo Rangers, but in a tight and cagey affair Vincent's come through by a point and are All-Ireland club champions once more. Fans stream on to the pitch and the Vincent's faithful are going mad. And fair play to them. You can't help wonder if they would take this instead of Dublin winning an All-Ireland title later in the year. It's the beauty of the GAA. Local takes pride of place every time.

I head home and catch highlights of the Patrick's Day parades from Dublin and around the country and am all the happier to have been in Croke Park today.

**MARCH 18 Tuesday**

Every year is the same for me once the Championship comes, scrambling around for tickets, ringing and texting people I barely know, trying to tap them up. If I had any respect for myself it would probably be shameful, but when you have to, just have to get tickets to the match, you'll do absolutely anything. And I mean anything. You know what I mean, don't you?

This year I decide I will sign up for the Parnell Park ticket scheme. It's a worthy idea whereby you pay an annual fee of €175 and for that you get in free to League games at Parnell Park and are guaranteed a ticket for Dublin games in the Championship. Yesterday was being coined the St Patrick's Day Massacre when €3.5 billion was wiped off the Irish Stock Exchange, but I'm feeling like an Irish stock price right now as the hopes I had with the ticket scheme are plummeting fast.

The problem is that every other Dublin supporter not attached to a club has cottoned on to it as well. I arrive at Donnycarney to pick up the application form and the bloke behind the counter wishes me luck with it. 'Sure you never know,' he says unenthusiastically. I think of slipping a twenty into the envelope with the application. After all, if it's good enough for Bertie . . .

I'll find out at the end of April, they tell me, but I'm not hopeful and can see another heart-breaking summer of chasing around and selling myself and my dignity for tickets. I won't though go to the lengths of one Dubs fan I know, who similarly sick of desperately trying to get tickets the week of a game, decided to join the local GAA club down in Ballybough. Of course that meant actually having to train and play, and when he got a call one Friday night in the pub telling him to be on the pitch by 10 am the next morning, he knew he had bitten off more than he could chew.

He had probably last seen exercise when he was playing for the under 10s. He was told he would be a sub that morning, but when they handed him the No. 3 jersey he nearly had a heart attack. 'You're having me fuckin on,' he gasped. 'I haven't played in about 15 years.'

'You'll be grand,' the manager told him. 'You're big and lanky. Just catch the ball and kick it away.'

Luckily for him, the full forward he was marking was about 20 years older and about 20 stone heavier. Paddy was slow, but the full forward he was marking made the tortoise look like Ben Johnson. When after 20 minutes he had to go over to the sideline to puke up last night's cider and curry, Paddy knew he would get through that day's game, but only just. He bitched and moaned about his aches and pains for the next four weeks but produced the Dubs tickets when it counted.

It all soon faded out, however. The training and playing ('I didn't know I'd actually have to do it') got in the way of too many other things, and soon he was back to scrounging around a few hours before the throw-in for tickets.

As I say, we'd do anything for a Dubs ticket. Well, nearly anything.

**MARCH**
**19**
**Wednesday**

Out of the blue — well, kind of — Eddie O'Sullivan announces his resignation. A disastrous World Cup campaign followed by a tepid Six Nations and it was obvious that O'Sullivan had plateaued with this group of players. Why the IRFU handed him a contract extension *before* the World Cup is anyone's guess, but that's blazers for you. O'Sullivan will get his pay-out, but going from the highs of last year and being spoken about for the Lions job, how quickly things turn if you outstay your welcome. It's getting a bit like that for Bertie down at Dublin Castle as well. But the last thing he needs is another pay-out from his bosses to have to explain to the Tribunal.

Later this evening I read about the GAA's new multi-million euro sponsorship deals. Much like the Champions League model, GAA HQ has embraced the multi-sponsor model and are set to cash in on more millions in sponsors' money. The football championship is being sponsored by Toyota, Ulser Bank and Vodafone, while hurling is being financed by Guinness, RTÉ and that well-known Irish airline, Etihad Airways. I can't get over RTÉ being allowed to be one of the title sponsors for hurling while also being awarded the broadcast rights. Surely this is a first in broadcasting and sponsorship terms?

It all seems very Irish and very cosy. But when the GAA starts talking about its brand, its corporate identity, and employs UK advisers who work with the Premier League, you know the euro is king now in Jones's Road. It makes a mockery of the fact that the government is the one having to pay the €3.5 m annually for the player grants. Next they'll be talking about the 'Gaelic games family' the way FIFA's Sepp Blatter does. Isn't there such a thing as being too commercial and taking too much money? I fear for the day, as has happened at the Olympics and World Cups, when kids wearing T-shirts with rival sponsors' logos are refused entry to Croke Park.

## MARCH 23 Sunday — *NFL, Dublin 1-10, Monaghan 0-13, Parnell Park*

Second time of asking and Dublin finally get to meet Monaghan. A win today and we'll be well on our way back to Division 1. But it's the Dubs and the course of things never runs smooth.

Monaghan have been doing well themselves and are pushing for promotion. There's a good contingent down for the match and it's another packed house in Parnell Park. Evenings like these and I often wonder if Dublin could do with a 20,000 seater stadium.

From five points down the Dubs clawed their way back into it to be ahead by five points, but Monaghan — greatly aided by referee Syl Doyle — didn't give in either and got the equalising point in injury time.

Again though, it's the off-pitch incidents that people end up talking about afterwards. The Dubs' disciplinary record is being questioned with Mark Vaughan sent off early in the second half for a second yellow. Something was going to blow in fairness and we could see it coming. Vaughan was on a yellow and a tick and had been missing frees. On top of that he had some Nordie mouthing off to contend with and it doesn't do much for your state of mind listening to their crap.

Sure enough, just a few minutes into the second half Vaughan lands a late dig on Monaghan's Damien

Freeman. Dublin are down to 14 men, but Vaughan gets a handshake from Caffrey as he goes off. (Should he not be getting a bollocking for reducing the team to one man less?)

Referee Syl Doyle had to be given a garda escort off the pitch at the end as the Dubs fans hurled abuse and bile in his direction. It was one of those games — 55 frees, 8 bookings and Dublin reduced to 13 men (Bryan Cullen was sent off for a second yellow with a minute to go). Monaghan were also complaining of their players being 'accosted' by Dubs fans after the whistle. County board chairman John Connolly didn't do himself and Monaghan any favours by having a go at the stewarding and claiming there would have been a riot if they had retaliated and then shot himself in the foot moaning about kids being allowed on to the pitch at half-time.

There was a tense atmosphere at the game all right, but it wasn't helped by Doyle's refereeing. Monaghan's whinging just showed them up for the moaners they were on the night. The Dubs fans were glad to see the back of them tonight, although we may be seeing more of them next year again if we both get promoted. That would make for an interesting return trip to Clones.

With all the excitement in Parnell Park this evening it was easy to forget that the Dublin hurlers were also playing today. (What jokers scheduled the hurlers on the same day as the footballers?) It was their last outing in the League this year and the hurlers have been taking small steps of late. I catch word on the radio on the way home however that it was a six-point loss down in Waterford. Still though, six points can become three and then one and then none in due course. Hurling however is still the minority sport in Dublin fans' terms.

What the hurlers need is a win against one of the big boys to ignite interest in them. We're a fickle bunch and used to performing on the big stage with the footballers, so as soon as the hurlers can start to mix it with the Waterfords and Corks, you'll see a guaranteed upsurge in support. At least they retained their Division 1A status and can look to being the second team in Leinster now.

I get home and watch the highlights of Sky Sports *Super Sunday* from this afternoon between Man Utd and Liverpool, and Chelsea and Arsenal. Pity the Sky cameras weren't down in Donnycarney today. That was a real Super Sunday. Head to bed exhausted. All that shouting, abuse and nail biting is nerve-wracking stuff.

**MARCH**
**24**
**Monday**

Shit is starting to hit the fan in the press today. Never mind the Dublin fans' abuse and jostling of the ref and Monaghan players. It turns out a Dublin official was up to much worse. Word is coming through that one of the Dublin management headbutted Monaghan's Tommy Freeman. Will be watching this one carefully. Who is the mystery headbutter, we all wonder. And people thought it was our fans who were the ones behaving badly.

Come across a little light relief on reservoirdubs.com in the midst of all these recriminations and allegations. One Dublin fan describes his attempts to follow the first Dublin-Monaghan game from India:

*Didn't see the match yet as I'm away in Goa, in a*

*steamy hot internet cafe at the moment. For the last week I was under the impression that we'd played Monaghan the first time and that Jayo had banged in 2 late goals to save us again — my sister was instructed to check the match in progress on Setanta and text me the scores as they happen. Of course, she knows nada about sport in general and assumed that the Longford/Dublin O'Byrne Cup final which was shown in place of the cancelled Monaghan match, was the match she was to report 'live' on. So, basically I spent most of last week, sprawled on a beach, sipping pina coladas fetched by local sepoys, with the sun blazing above, my eyes watering at the thought of how Jayo 'once again' saved the day with late goals and how we should really rename Dublin airport after him.*

*Then I finally log on and find the bleed'n match hadn't even happened. Jesus!*

**MARCH**
**28**
**Friday**

The *Irish Independent* names the Parnell Park headbutter as Ray Boyne, the Dublin team statistician. He was down near the sideline where Tommy Freeman was and, it seems, decided to give Freeman a bit of a Harold's Cross hello while down that way.

You have to wonder what state of mind these guys are in. And these are supposed to be the responsible officials? Is it any wonder the Hill is the way it is and Dublin have a reputation for thuggery wherever they go? We won't be living this one down for a long time.

And I thought the League was going to be dull this year.

**MARCH**
**30**
**Sunday**

## Postponed NFL, Armagh v Dublin, Crossmaglen

Mulled it over about taking a spin up to Crossmaglen for the Dubs clash against Armagh. Being on the northside of the city, the drive up the M1 is handy enough. Would be back in time for dinner and keep in the good books. But look out this morning and it's pissing rain. Actually it's been lashing down for most of the month so it shouldn't be a surprise. But when you've been planning a trip somewhere and the Irish rain just doesn't piss off (pardon the pun), you can either resign yourself to it and get soaked or decide life is too short. If it was in Parnell Park I'd be thinking differently, but 'up there' is never a fun place to go, doubly so if you're getting soaking wet. Pneumonia would be one more thing I could blame the Nordies on.

I'm like the dog in the morning poking his nose out the door at the weather. A downpour and it's no thanks, I'd rather not lift the leg this morning if it's all right with you. 'You're not seriously going to the game today?' the better half asks incredulously. 'Of course not,' I say. 'Do you think I'm that daft? Don't answer that,' I respond before she has a chance to. Sometimes you have to listen to the voice of reason. And when even the dog won't venture out, then the fan should really stay put.

I'll see if I can bury myself 'in work' later on and get out of any DIYing that needs to be done. Not only are we getting married this year but I'm changing jobs and we're also building a house. Three stresses into one won't go and a weekend without a Dubs game is starting to feel like work. Soon I'll be an expert in doilies and home-made curtains.

Jesus Christ, thank God I never made it up to Cross. The game was called off just 40 minutes before the throw-in with most Dubs either already there or on the way and forced to turn back in disgust. Poor bastards! Going all that way and then being told it's off. I know it's been doing pretty much nothing but raining since the League began, but the Dubs fans have had to contend with three cancellations or postponements out of only six games already.

We hear about the millions being made by the GAA and how they are pumping it back into the counties and the grass roots, but you wonder how much of it is going to proper pitch drainage systems. Fans, players and officials are all losing out when games have to be called off — not because of excessive rain, but because of poor drainage.

What's worse, it's been announced there will be no refund for those who had paid for their tickets. They are talking about free admission on a rescheduled date on Wednesday week. No refunds and now a midweek rearrangement for the fans to contend with. As my father was wont to say about women drivers: if they had brains they'd be dangerous.

**APRIL 1 Tuesday**

No April fools, but the first resignation of the year with the announcement that Roscommon's John Maughan is stepping down after just 30 months in the job. It didn't help that Roscommon were hammered by 11 points against Westmeath and also suffered heavy defeats by Monaghan and Armagh, but the real reason appears to have been personal abuse being directed at Maughan by the Roscommon fans. Maughan cited a growing group of people who seemed determined to turn up at matches for the sole purpose of abusing both players and management. While getting hammered certainly didn't help the fans' view of their team's efforts, fan abuse does seem to be growing. Maughan himself acknowledged that each manager is now in the results business, but results at any and all costs? Only a handful of counties are capable of winning titles in any given year.

Just look at the abuse Kieran Donaghy received when playing in Mayo for Kerry in the League — coins, even a piece of wood being thrown at his head. Any wonder he gave these so called 'fans' the finger? In fairness to the man, he apologised publicly a day later, but it shouldn't have been him apologising.

Once it was Dublin fans who were accused of being the yobbish element in the GAA, of bringing soccer hooliganism into Gaelic games. That now seems to be spreading throughout the country. Where once jeering and abuse was the preserve of Dublin fans, now other counties' fans are taking on the same characteristics. As with Dublin and the rest it is always a minority, but it always seems to be the vocal minority that get noticed. The question now is what are county boards doing to eliminate such elements from their grounds? What are stewarding and policing arrangements like at all inter-county games and not just the big ones?

With the GAA becoming more popular and more important in people's lives there will inevitably be an increase in the number of gobshites going to games. But perhaps the increase in abuse is a growing phenomenon reflective of our changed psyche. People will point to the Dublin fans and their history of abusing opponents and even their own (Mickey Whelan and Tommy Lyons immediately spring to mind). But as the country has grown and developed and has become increasingly urbanised, the other counties are now importing the worst features, from drugs to arrogance and aggressiveness. These were all common traits in grounds in England in the 1970s and 80s, but it wasn't until the FA did something about seating and stewarding and the police got their act together in terms of policing these hooligan elements, that the game improved significantly and became more spectator friendly. Now look at it.

Are we at a crossroads in the future development of the GAA, I wonder. If county boards, the clubs and the Central Council let things slide any further, perhaps we will see a more violent form of GAA fan emerge. Hooliganism, violence and abuse are not soccer's problems alone.

A lot of fans are probably thinking that's rich coming from a Dublin fan who spends time on the Hill. And yes, there are a lot of fuckin idiots who come on to the Hill every summer, curse and scream abuse at anyone, give the finger and wanker sign to opponents' fans in the nearby Cusack Stand, and then throw plastic bottles and cans in the direction of the pitch. (The netting behind the goal isn't just to stop the ball going into the crowd.) And OK, it doesn't help when Dublin officials decide to headbutt opponents, and yes, that's another area that needs cleaning up by the GAA — keeping officials in designated areas. But let's deal with one headache at a time at least.

It was probably never seen as much of a problem, more a Dublin thing that had to be tolerated. But when it starts spreading to other counties, then surely the GAA needs to start acting. We've seen the Cantona kung fu kick at a fan in Crystal Palace and the NBA player going up ten flights of stadium stairs to start punching a fan. Will it be long before a player or an official in the GAA decides to do something similar?

It's only Tuesday but already my head is starting to hurt. I need a few feel-good GAA stories — and soon — to help calm my nerves. It can't be all bad, can it?

**APRIL 2 Wednesday**

The Roy Keane national holiday and media fest didn't get its annual outing today. It turns out that the bould Bertie wanted to upstage the blind labradors and announced he's stepping down on 6 May. I won't get into political chicanery here (I'm sure that will come later in the summer), but by day's end after wall to wall coverage I was nearly missing the Keane mouthfest.

You have to admire Keane's talent and determination and what he has achieved, but when stars hang around too long you kind of get sick and tired of hearing them mouth off, don't you? Maybe the media are worse in the way they fall over him any time he comes back to Ireland like some sort of uncrowned king. (Was Mick McCarthy his Kitty O'Shea?) If he farted it would probably make the news. But he's starting to sound like a broken record and one that's out of touch now (not fully appreciating the Cork players' situation, for one example).

This isn't a Dublin v Cork thing (but Jesus, they are

annoying people). Only Bertie the Dub doing his standing down trick could have knocked Keane off the front pages and media programmes. Maybe it was all a ruse and come 6 May he'll decide he actually wants to wait for his own Taoiseach's palace to be built before moving. (Although isn't that what the Bertie Bowl was supposed to be?) Pity he's going though. His fantasy reality at the Mahon Tribunal was actually keeping the GAA grants story off the front pages. Leave the politics to the main stories and the sports stories to the back pages, thank you very much. At least that way it will be discussed by sports people who know what they're talking about instead of news hacks pontificating about something they only discovered when they realised the mass of the great unwashed had an interest in it.

A bit like Roy Keane really, whom we find the Marian Finucanes of this world fawning over. Just as the population has moved on from Bertie's reign, the fans have moved on from Keane. He may be our Princess Di figure as Father Ted creator Arthur Mathews famously said of Keane, but we should start talking about his influence over here in past tense terms as well.

## *NFL, Dublin 3-20, Roscommon 0-07, Parnell Park*

**APRIL 5 Saturday**

I like these Saturday night games in Parnell Park. You have time to have a few quiet pints beforehand, head down to the match, enjoy a decent Saturday evening's entertainment before heading back out with something good to talk about in the pubs later on. Plus, if you've got kids (I don't), you can bring them along, earn your brownie points and head out for pints afterwards with a clear conscience.

Calling it entertainment tonight though is probably stretching it a bit too far. In the wake of John Maughan's resignation and the team's resultant disarray, the Dubs win by 22 points — 3-20 to 0-07. I doubt if a Dublin team ever had it so easy. Roscommon just didn't want to know and are in free fall, managerless and rudderless. You have to pity the players who put in the effort day in, day out, only to be slaughtered on the pitch by their opponents and off the pitch by their own people.

They must question themselves at times like this and wonder, why bother? I really admire athletes at times like these. There's nothing but heart-break and pain in it. Imagine training twice a week, going to the gym on other nights, breaking your balls to get fitter and stronger — and all for nothing. A bit like Scott getting to the South Pole, only to discover Amundsen got there first. I'd have given up long ago.

Actually I did. And this is why I'm here on the sidelines watching and having pints later on. Do I wish I had that same purpose in my life as the Roscommon footballers? Probably. But do I wish I was putting that purpose into Gaelic football? Definitely not. I don't know the feeling of absolute dedication and commitment that it takes to get to the top in sport and I don't think I could ever have envisaged myself expending that much effort in pursuit of a sport which I love so dearly. As Wayne Rooney once said, there were players better than him growing up, but he was the one who stuck it out day and night, determined not to let anything stop him becoming what he wanted to be.

If only the rest of us here on the sidelines tonight could discover that one thing that would lead us to obsessive dedication for the rest of our lives. Or maybe we found it and just couldn't be bothered. Maybe that's why we will be in the pubs later on tonight talking a good game instead of playing one. As for the Roscommon players, their dedication has been giving them nothing but heart-break and you wonder how much longer they can keep at it.

One thing of note from tonight: as the game got easy and boring, more attention turned to Bertie Ahern in attendance. Only three days after announcing he was stepping down you'd think he'd be on the lash or going out with a bang. No, the bould Bertie was in Parnell Park watching the Dubs in a walk-over against Roscommon. And he hasn't lost his power over the people just yet either. As he entered the stand two minutes into the game, the crowd all stood up as if they were in the presence of royalty — northside royalty, I suppose. With his uniform of anorak and tie and a diet of Bass and Gaelic games, that's the bould Bertie that only his mother and the Dubs could love.

**APRIL**

**12**

**Saturday**

Armagh giving free admission to tomorrow's game because of the last-minute cancellation two weeks ago is tempting, but I've never been a fan of away games up north. Although it's on a Sunday afternoon and will cost nothing but the petrol, I have a feeling it will be a wasted journey. I've never fancied Dublin teams going up north. It's as if we're going into the bullies' backyard and I don't expect us to have the stomach for the fight. Although at this stage of the season could you expect them to?

Armagh have suffered some surprising defeats already in the League and people are talking about them in the past tense and about the possibility of relegation. Nothing better to sting them into action, I reckon. Armagh's brand of football has caught up with them in recent times. Other counties are as fit and as physical as they are nowadays; it's just the likes of Kerry (and occasionally Dublin) that have been able to marry the physicality with skill thrown in. But any talk of Armagh being over the hill and we know what will happen. Footballers like Steven McDonnell and Ronan Clarke don't become bad players overnight. Here's hoping it doesn't decide to pour down an hour before the game starts. How many Dubs will risk another wasted trip?

No surprise this evening when the media report that GAA delegates have voted to accept the player grants issue. God bless technology and the internet. After years of using espn.com and si.com for web video and live streaming, RTÉ have already been carrying GAA matches online, but are now thankfully broadening their coverage into other sports areas.

The GAA Congress was broadcast online this afternoon and it's great knowing you can be sitting at your desk working and also be able to catch up on and watch events like these. Just the other day I was working on my laptop with Sky Sports, Setanta Sports and RTÉ.ie all on my desktop with live streams, while I was also on Google Talk with a friend and on my mobile phone. Just don't ask me to write a letter.

The Congress isn't exactly riveting, on-the-seat-of-your-pants viewing, but it's great to be able to watch the corridors of power at work. No surprise in the vote as well. After the DRA ruled that the grants didn't infringe the GAA's amateur status, it was only a matter of time before Congress voted to accept it.

There's been outspoken criticism of it by prominent GAA people such as Donal McAnallen and the Of One Belief group who have called it the start of professionalism and pay-for-play.

Opposing the grants, Derry's Seamus McCloy declared, 'accepting these payments will accept the introduction of sham amateurism', which is a bit rich considering that the only true amateurs in the GAA are the players themselves. What about the under-the-table payments made to county and even club managers? What about the professional administrators throughout the GAA? And what about the millions signed in sponsorship deals as the GAA gets into bed with multinationals?

Sham amateurism has been alive and well in the GAA for decades. It is a typical Irish attitude to turn a blind eye to it and pretend it doesn't exist (just like Church abuse and political corruption). Then when something official is passed through, the head-in-the-sand brigade cry foul while conveniently ignoring the unofficial professional activities that have gone on for years. Fair dues to GAA President Nickey Brennan for coming out and saying he will be looking to strictly codify the amateur status of the organisation.

But what I've always wondered is, can the rules be bent and can a major business effectively sponsor an entire county squad for a season and pay those players their training and living 'expenses'? What is to stop a J. P.

McManus or Seán Quinn character from sponsoring a county squad to train full time for the season? If such sponsorship and expenses means players can give up working and concentrate solely on training and playing, what can the GAA do about it? More sham amateurism perhaps, but is there really anything to stop this becoming a reality, as it surely will in due course?

## APRIL 13 Sunday — NFL, Armagh 3-13, Dublin 1-10, Crossmaglen

What was that about Armagh being a spent force? Catch snatches of the game on the radio as I drive out and about. Stuck traipsing around DIY stores with the missus. Tiles, floors, bathroom suites — who would have guessed there was so much in it? I'm on my mobile half the time anyway catching snippets of updates on the mobile internet. The sooner they introduce MobileTV streaming in Ireland the better. What could be better, if you're stuck DIYing, than watching the game on your mobile?

My bad feeling about the Armagh trip was right. Dublin get blown away 3-13 to 1-10. Massacre in Crossmaglen and all that will be in the papers tomorrow. Amazing how after one defeat for the Dubs and suddenly they're a bunch of wasters. Mustn't be much fun being a Dublin player picking up the papers the Monday morning after a defeat. In fairness to them it's the first one of the year and it was a make or break game for Armagh. Still, there's that nagging question mark about Dublin playing against the big boys, especially in their own backyard. Today Kerry went to Salthill and beat Galway easily by five points to ensure another League final appearance for the Kingdom. For Dublin though, sometimes it seems they're so busy proving they are tough that they forget about winning the match. Even DIY hunting was preferable to watching that mauling.

On a positive note, I make sure to get home for the *Sunday Game* later on to watch a resurgent Tipperary beat Kilkenny and prove that Brian Cody's men aren't quite invincible. Galway beat Cork and young star Joe Canning had a stunning senior debut for Galway. After seeing him in Croker on club finals day the neutral hurling fan could be in for one of those memorable summers if he and Ger Loughnane's Galway start to blossom.

**APRIL**
**14**
**Monday**

Predictably enough the demise of Dublin has been reported this Monday morning. Forget about Sam, Leinster and whatever else. Understandable maybe why Pillar Caffrey is so distant towards the media. One bad loss and it's hyped to spell the end of the team; one good win the next week and it's Championship glory all the way. It's the manager's job to keep the players focused and on an even keel, but at the same time Caffrey has to understand that that's the nature of the media and the fans. It was always that way and always will be. The only difference is that the media cycle is now 24/7 as opposed to once or twice a week years ago.

But sift through the debris and doom and gloom of the Monday papers and as usual Eugene McGee in the *Irish Independent* talks sense about the Dublin team deficiencies, although I still wouldn't agree with the total doomsday scenario being painted. He does point out the weaknesses in the Dublin defence and how McDonnell and Clarke for Armagh cut through them too easily.

To win All-Irelands you have to be able to shut down players of this calibre. It's only April, but where is the watertight Dublin defence to lock things down come the Championship? Heart-break could be around the corner again this year. If we don't have the quality among the backs, it seems the only way we can overcome top sides is by outscoring them. But to concede 3-13? It's rare that a Kerry or Armagh team would ever let that happen. I'm getting a headache thinking about all the problems and permutations and it's still only April. How must Caffrey be feeling!

From one hype to another and you'd swear Joe Canning was the next Christy Ring. The kid is only 19, but after winning an All-Ireland club title with Portumna and now finally making his senior debut for the Galway hurlers and helping to defeat Cork to reach the League final, Canning is hitting the big time.

He is that good. He can do anything on a hurling pitch. You just hope the county's hopes don't fall completely on his shoulders. But with his brother Ollie around and with Ger Loughnane in charge, they'll make sure this doesn't happen. You can't help but lick your lips at the prospects this coming summer — Kilkenny proving dominant, Cork coming good, Tipperary resurgent, and Galway with Canning leading their attack. The real dream will be when the Dublin hurlers are up there as good as the rest of them. Now what a summer that would be — Dublin footballers and Dublin hurlers taking on the best in the country. I make a mental note to get to some of Galway's hurling matches in the Championship this summer. This kid is that good that you would travel across the country just to see him in action.

**APRIL 18 Thursday**

Did I hear right? A 2 km parking exclusion zone around Croker on match days? I catch snippets of radio reports and only manage to read through the story properly this evening. Dublin City Council in their wisdom have decided to implement a 2 km no parking exclusion zone around Croke Park on match days. This one came out of left field and obviously without any forward thinking on it.

So, one wonders, where are the extensive parking facilities to cater for the exclusion zone? I'm presuming of course that they have thought this through and will have park and ride facilities, special transport and parking in place which will allow this scheme to be implemented properly. Because announcing such a decision without thinking of the consequences wouldn't be like councillors, would it? Joined-up thinking comes naturally to such esteemed citizens, I'm presuming.

**APRIL 19 Friday**

Dublin v Meath is looming. It's only the League, but it's Dublin v Meath. They could be playing tiddly-winks and there would still be an edge to it. The Division 2 title is up for grabs and the final placings will be worked out after this weekend. Meath are out of it, but they'd love nothing better than to stop the Dubs getting there, especially in our own backyard. As I say, it's only the League, but with Dublin and Meath there's no such thing as only.

I won't be in Dublin this weekend and can't make the game. You can forgive missing the Roscommons and Wicklows, but Meath? It just won't feel right not being there in person to throw some bile their way.

I check on the internet and discover that, of all things, the game isn't even on TV. Understandably the hurling league final is the live game on Sunday on TG4, but you'd think there could have been some back-up plan to show the game on RTÉ, Setanta or even online. There will be 12,000 packed into Parnell Park and thousands more locked outside who won't be able to watch it. The hurling final between Tipp and Galway will be a fantastic game, but Dublin v Meath is box office, isn't it?

I'm stuck down in Kerry of all places for a few days this weekend, about as far from the capital as I can get and in a county that would look down its nose at a Dublin-Meath clash. Sure doesn't the Kingdom have a Division 1 football league final against Derry to concern itself with next week. Kerry football has been proving itself awesome and invincible of late. They seamlessly go through different managers, seem to have an endless supply of new talent coming through and coupled with their experienced All Stars and All-Ireland winners, they can lift their game into fifth gear when needs be.

Under pressure in a game in Salthill last week, people wondered if Pat O'Shea's men wouldn't mind losing to Galway as it would give them some rest ahead of the Championship. And then they come out and blow Galway away by five points in their own backyard to qualify for another League final.

Do Dublin have that ability yet? I don't think so,

especially when you see how they were annihilated by Armagh in Crossmaglen. But it's only been one loss so far this year. Going up against Kerry though, and you would wonder. Do we have that mental toughness and cute hoorness to see the match through all the way?

We're a bit like the Irish rugby team under Eddie O'Sullivan. We might have won a few Triple Crowns along the way — Leinster Championships in GAA terms — but when it came to the final push and getting over the line for Six Nations Championships and World Cups, the team was found wanting. Take Munster by contrast, and you just know that when it comes down to vital games in Europe they will come through. They have that inner belief and steel that no matter what, they will be ahead come the final whistle. Where does this steel and belief come from? Maybe the Dublin players should take a leaf out of Vinny Murphy's book and spend a few years in Kerry hoping the X factor down there might seep in. They could always commute to their games in Parnell Park and Croke Park, and if we won Sam again, would we really mind if they were Kerry based anyway?

### NFL, Dublin 0-13, Meath 2-06, Parnell Park

**APRIL 21 Sunday**

I'm staying near Sneem in the Ring of Kerry for a few days. Looking out of my window I can see the Atlantic Ocean which is starting to whip up with the waves crashing against the rocks and the ocean spray climbing high before falling on to the shore (an omen for the game today perhaps). Behind and around me are barren mountains rising up from the shore; sheep and lambs dot the landscape as do a myriad of bungalows. The few bushes and trees continuously shake from the impact of the wind coming in off the sea. The dirt track trails off into the distance and for the first time in a long time I feel alone and truly isolated.

I have left the city far behind me. Cars and people are a rarity here and I feel like I am back in the Irish countryside with all it has to offer. I have come to realise that we are shaped by what's around us — by the mountains, vegetation, coastline. Our moods, outlook and view on life can be influenced by external influences. And here I am loving the isolation and peace it's bringing. If only I could fly to Parnell Park for the Dubs game — even the match on telly would do me now. But the best I'll get will be updates on the radio while trying to picture the action and the scores.

I'm thinking about what I said two days ago about Kerry and Munster folk having an inner strength and steel, and I honestly do think it has something to do with the landscape down here. I'm surrounded by mountains revealing only bleak barrenness and pock-marked with occasional bungalows. You learn to live with yourself down here. You don't have people, houses and cars crowding around you. There are only two channels on the telly and one on the radio.

A great silence envelops the house and the only sound is that of the wind blowing across the land and through the trees. I am forced to be still. I have no choice but to listen to myself and calm my racing thoughts. Work is a million miles away; people and money problems can do for another day. For the first time in a long time I have to be comfortable with myself as there is nobody else or nothing else around to distract me from that.

Growing up in such an environment, is it any wonder that Kerry footballers and Munster rugby players know the depths of how far they can go? Pressure only comes from within and if you're used to dealing with yourself and asking yourself questions on a daily basis, then game day pressure is just another series of questions to be answered. Answer them and you win. No sweat, no pressure. I start to day-dream and imagine if I had been born and raised on one of these Kerry peninsulas, would I have been playing in All-Irelands. Then I picture Colm Cooper or Dara Ó Sé and think, perhaps not.

Thanks to the Dubs fans' site, reservoirdubs.com (tag line: We came, we saw, we kicked it wide . . .), a link has been posted to get live commentary on the game from local Dublin station NearFM. It's slightly surreal as I sit by the kitchen window looking out at the Atlantic and the mountains whilst listening to the commentary from Parnell Park. I feel like those people who used to sit around the wireless listening in to the world heavyweight boxing fights from another world. I am worlds away from the game but can hear the Dublin crowd booing every time Graham Geraghty touches the ball. I'm hundreds of miles away and feel like doing the same myself. Even some of the choicest derogatory chants are being picked up by the radio mics. I can almost smell the Bulmer's and Johnny Blue cigarettes wafting in the air.

Incredibly, or maybe not, according to your view on Dublin-Meath clashes, there is a bit of a bust-up just a few minutes in and four players are sent off — two from each team. It seems a bit harsh and over the top from what I could hear. Unbelievably, just minutes later Ciaran Whelan gets sent off and it's 12 v 13. Memories of Dublin v Galway 1983 all over again!

Every few minutes the stream drops out and I have to reconnect. Invariably it's just as a Dublin forward is bearing down on goal. I find myself listening intently to the game. It's a novelty sitting here having to focus and force myself to concentrate. The noises and sounds help me picture the scenes as they are unfolding. Despite the numerical disadvantage, Dublin steam away from Meath in the second half and lead by seven points. A thrashing for the Royals. What a day to be in Parnell Park! But this is Dublin so you can't get over-confident.

And sure enough, with just ten minutes left Meath score a goal bringing the deficit down to four. Another minute and another Meath player waltzes through (I'm picturing) the Dublin defence that's now sleep-walking. Two goals in two minutes and Meath are back from the dead. I'm glad I'm not there in Donnycarney to be going through this agony. Instead I'm going through agony in Kerry and I don't know which is worse. Unbelievable stuff and I only have the sheep in front of the house to shout at. Mark Vaughan now has a free to try and stretch the Dublin lead. 'Vaughan steps up with the ball in his hands not far from the posts,' the NearFM commentator informs us, 'and he ...'

Silence. The stream has dropped again. 'Not now,' I scream, 'not now!' Double click about five times and iTunes tells me it is rebuffering. Oh so slowly. It reconnects just as I hear the score. Vaughan has missed the free and

Dublin are still leading by just the one point. But thank God the final whistle goes soon after. Dublin have clung on to their win despite their own best efforts and are now into the Division 2 final and are promoted to Division 1 for next season. Job done, but Christ, what a nerve-wracker. Typical Dubs. Just when they're strolling and seem to have things wrapped up, they let the other team back in. Today epitomises what it is to be a Dublin supporter, but thankfully on this day they've come through on the right side of the scoreline. I just hope we haven't used up too many of our nine lives today because we are going to need them during the summer.

**APRIL 20 Sunday**

### NHL final, Tipperary 3-18, Galway 3-16, Gaelic Grounds

I might not be able to watch the Dubs, but today's Hurling League final is on TG4 and has been one of the most anticipated in years. Tipperary are starting to come good under Liam Sheedy, Shane McGrath in midfield is being touted as one to dominate this year, and the bad vibes from the Babs Keating years are well and truly forgotten. And why shouldn't they be? Beating Kilkenny by five points in Nowlan Park is one confidence booster, that's for sure. Up to then Kilkenny were unstoppable and heading for their fourth League final appearance in a row and probably another All-Ireland double. Cork were the only team that could get close to them, but how their strike action will affect them only time will tell.

In truth it was all getting a bit predictable with Kilkenny and Cork leading the way year in, year out. Now suddenly we have two more teams that are promising to upset the hegemony. Despite only winning on average an All-Ireland once every decade, Tipp still see themselves in terms of royal pedigree when it comes to the Championship. For once they might not be flattering to deceive. Throw them, Waterford and Cork into the mix and aside from the All-Ireland the Munster Championship could be one of the best yet.

As for Ger Loughnane and Galway? Well, what hasn't already been said of Loughnane? He stated when he was taking over Galway that anything less than an All-Ireland was a failure. He may have struggled in his first year, but now into his second and with the introduction of Joe Canning on to the seniors, Galway folk are whispering about another coming. Can Loughnane do it again with them? With Canning anything can happen, and once Loughnane spreads the burden of expectation throughout the team, then who's to say we couldn't have five top quality teams — Kikenny, Cork, Waterford, Tipperary and Galway — all capable of scalping each other and winning the Liam McCarthy Cup. Tipp v Galway is only a League final, but is it a taste of things to come?

I tune in to TG4 and am grateful for the ability to see what's happening this time although I'm ashamed to admit that I can't understand most of what I'm hearing. 'Puc saor' and 'Joe Canning' are about all I can catch, but this League final is more than worth it. Tipp come through in the end, but only just. Galway are dragged back into the game with a superb goal from Canning, but Tipp hang on and win their first League title since 2001. Hurling fans across the country can't wait for the summer proper to start. Perhaps Denis Walsh should start penning a *Hurling: the Revolution Years* sequel.

Dubs fans meanwhile look forward to the summer with the usual beating heart, excited, nervous and fearful, for we never know what the summer will bring us. And with the Dubs around, things will never be quiet. I wonder how the Dublin-Meath fighting will play out. TV is showing the bust-up over and over again.

**APRIL 21 Monday**

Into Sneem for the morning papers, knowing there will be wall-to-wall coverage of yesterday's fracas. I don't relish the fact that the focus is on the fights, but one part of me loves the fact that there is so much coverage of the game. I can happily spend hours going through the pages and read all the minutiae of the events. Let the post-mortem begin . . . not just yet though.

It's a shock to realise that it's nearly 10 am and the papers still haven't arrived in this part of Kerry. I can be in London or Europe and get *The Irish Times* easier probably. Thank God for the interweb. Fifteen minutes later I'm back in the house and logging on with my cup of tea. But still I miss the feel of the paper in my hands and seeing the pictures and articles laid out on the pages. Online reading just isn't the same.

Predictably enough, hyperbole is the order of the day. 'Blue murder', 'Red card five' and 'Stormy affair' are just some of the headlines and it's the twenty-nine man brawl that gets most of the attention. Surprisingly (or should that be unsurprisingly?) the hot tea that was thrown at Ciaran Whelan after he was sent off gets little coverage. In light of what I'd been saying about fan abuse nowadays, it seems that off-pitch stuff barely warrants a mention, while player fisticuffs garner all the headlines. I can picture a Cantona-like incident happening down the line if something isn't done.

But for what it was really like I'll always check out the reservoirdubs.com forum. As usual the fans on it are spot on, not given to over-exaggerating things and usually give their observations with a good dose of humour thrown in as well. I particularly like the Dubs fans' refusal to write the word 'Meath'. It's normally M**th. My latest favourite is that used by one fan, calling them Mordor.

On the scuffles most of the Dublin fans accept Paddy Russell's decision to send off the players involved and most think Whelan was downright stupid in what he did. (Common sense from Dublin fans? Whatever next!) As for the tea-throwing incident and other fan issues:

'As for the M**th arsehole who threw his coffee at him when he was off, well, less said the better. He was very lucky not to have been lynched by the Dubs fans around him. Luckily, he was removed by the Gardai. Fair play to the M**th fans who pointed him out to the Gardai', says one fan.

Another hits the nail on the head when talking about idiots at all the games nowadays:

*It's a thing that gets me down that Dubs matches used to be great crack and good clean fun (god im sounding like an ould fella) but more and more it seems to be an excuse for arseholes to have a day out.*

*It just seems the Dubs and even the GAA as a*

*whole is more and more becoming an outlet for a yob mentality nowadays.*

*I dont think stewards or the gardai can sort this one alone, I've been at a few soccer matches in the UK where the Stand up Speak out effort see anyone stepping over the line gets a warning and then ejected as a result of being reported by other supporters. I think being a vigilante doesn't work but the great majority in Parnell park should show these ejits that their behaviour is not welcome.*

Unsurprisingly, it's the players' fisticuffs that is the talking point in the media this morning, but it should be the minority fans' behaviour that should be highlighted more. Now we're all waiting with bated breath to see what suspensions will be dished out to the Dublin players and will Whelan be missing now for much of the Leinster Championship. It might only be the League and April, but already the butterfly wings are flapping and starting to cause a tornado at the thought of the summer to come.

The GAA have been quick out of the blocks on this one. They seem determined to make an example of the players and teams involved in the Dublin-Meath fracas on Sunday. Nickey Brennan was on RTÉ Radio yesterday denouncing them and palpably frothing at the mouth.

Sure enough, today the media are reporting that sixteen players — eight from each side — will be hit with bans ranging from four to eight weeks. The media are having a field day discussing and denouncing the culture of violence among players and teams. But will heavy bans work in the long run, I wonder. Remember Semplegate between the Cork and Clare hurlers last year. The heavy bans handed down there didn't stop the mêlée on Sunday. Although, maybe, just maybe, this will serve notice for the Championship.

Brennan was right though, in criticising county board officials for their hypocrisy in attempting to fight any bans handed down. As Eugene McGee writes in today's *Indo*, there's never any apology, never anyone owning up. There is no culture of responsibility.

Doesn't this sound oddly familiar? Don't we live in a political culture where responsibility is a dirty word? No one is responsible for the shambles in the health service or transport. When dodgy bank payments are spotted in a Taoiseach's account, the first action is to prevaricate and take the accusers to court. Is it any wonder then that county boards follow similar routes?

The problem isn't with the mêlées in the first place; the problem exists within the game and what is and isn't allowed. Rugby Union is constantly reviewing and revising its laws of the game to improve it as a sport and a spectacle. For years now people who follow Gaelic football have been critical of the development of the game with the emphasis on possession and the increasing physicality of the players. New rules need to be introduced to reflect the changing nature of the game and take the sly digs and mass brawls out of the equation. Severe punishments for those involved in the scuffles at Parnell Park on Sunday will merely be a warning for the year but won't stop the long-term malaise of the game.

Until the GAA get its head out of its arse and looks at

deeper change and stops worrying about media and sponsors' reactions, then Gaelic football will continue to lurch from one crisis to the next.

P.S. They've announced the venues for the League finals next Sunday: Dublin against Westmeath in Navan next Saturday at 7 pm. Wonder if the Meath fans will be out with pitchforks to give the Dubs a warm welcome up there on Saturday night?

**APRIL**
**24**
**Thursday**

It's my last day down here in the beautiful and spectacular ring of Kerry. I'll be sad to leave it behind but glad to get back to the capital for more violence, muggings and assaults. Discover Dublin!

I feel as if I have been disconnected from the uproar following the Dublin-Meath fracas last Sunday. I have been following it in the newspapers and fans' forums online and quite incredibly it's still rumbling on. There are now even letters from concerned citizens in *The Irish Times* pages. It's unbelievable and maddening.

I just have to get this off my chest. The *Liveline* brigade has jumped on to 'the-Dubs-and-the-GAA-are-too-violent' bandwagon and are now getting an airing in any media outlet that will have them. When you get non-sports people up in arms about something they don't know anything about and are then being aided and abetted by non-sports sections of the media, it's a recipe for blathering and disaster.

I can't help feeling that Nickey Brennan is pandering to this middle Ireland *Liveline* brigade. His comments, especially about the 'presentation' of the games, show you where his thinking on this lies: in trying to appeal to as many 'customers' as possible i.e. non-GAA people who could be attracted to the games and therefore pay money to see them, watch them on telly or buy their merchandise. It's classic sports marketing tactics in not sullying the brand and fawning to non-sports people who don't have a clue about sports.

The whole issue hasn't been helped either by the sports hacks bewailing the fracas in terms of something more sinister and deep seated within Dublin GAA. There are three issues here at play for the GAA which need to be separated out: Dublin player indiscipline, Gaelic football development which has seen mêlées like this break out, and fan discipline and abuse at games.

Dublin player indiscipline has been in evidence throughout this year and does seem to be a case of players not being disciplined internally by management for their actions (Caffrey's handshake with Vaughan when he was sent off against Monaghan comes to mind). Is Caffrey trying to portray the Dubs publicly and privately as a team not to be walked on?

Gaelic football development. The GAA, unlike the rugby authorities, has not kept up with the physical and tactical developments of the game. Hand passing, keeping possession and swarm defence are all modern aspects of the game which have invariably resulted in closer, more hand-to-hand contact which will occasionally end up in this kind of brawl. What is the GAA doing to encourage a more flowing game and cutting out the cynical fouling in the game? Just look at how much Rugby Union has benefited from rule changes and adaptations in recent years.

On this point, secondly, the GAA's disciplinary rulings have not been consistent or stringent enough and there is little culture of respect for disciplinary bans being handed down (ironically enough it is Dublin who appear to be the exception). Rules on bans are seen in many counties as a means to get off scot-free, whereas true respect for games discipline should see bans sorted quickly and cleanly.

There must be clear rules introduced (a la Aussie Rules) on other players who join mêlées so that players know exactly where they stand. And when they break the rules the bans should be handed down harshly and quickly. Dublin and Meath are being made an example of this time around, and if it means that this is being used as a marker for future misconduct, so be it. Do we reckon there will be many mêlées later in the summer now knowing the consequences? I reckon players and teams will think twice about it. This culture must be consistently upheld from here on in, with the GAA letting counties know they will do it again in a flash.

Finally, fan culture and abuse must also be addressed. More customers coming to the games invariably means more idiots, but it's also reflective of an Irish society where people are generally more aggressive and belligerent. Again this is helped by the fact that they know they will get away with such conduct. Stewarding needs to be seriously stepped up for every inter-county game with rules and procedures in place for what a fan can be thrown out for.

Stewards need to be trained in such tactics and county boards need to work with the Gardai to have policies in place for what and how fans can be ejected and then banned from county grounds. What has happened for example to the person who threw hot tea at Ciaran Whelan? Was he ejected from the ground? Can he get into a GAA ground again whenever he likes? Why is the GAA not addressing this fundamental issue of conduct?

We are not yet at English soccer standards and thankfully the fans do not have to be segregated, but why not learn from the country which has the most experience and most knowledge in dealing with fans and stewarding.

Taking all of the above, there's a lot for the GAA to be dealing with. But the organisation is such an unwieldy behemoth and its wheels of power turn so sluggishly that it's hard to see any vision or lasting change being implemented.

End result? They will continue to have knee jerk reactions when an issue gets sufficient media attention, but in the meantime the problems will become worse and more deep seated and it will only be when something really serious happens that they will be stung into action. Will it be a player attacking a fan in the crowd? Will it be a fan hurting a player with something deadly? Will it be serious fan violence at a game? Or will it be a brawl that sees a player seriously and permanently injured?

Any of the above could eventually happen and are worst case scenarios, but unless the little things that are slowly worsening are kept in check, then it's a road the GAA could be going down.

And so to the media-society problem. It's not helped when you have other issues thrown into the mix such as the sports media cycle which is 24/7 nowadays and which means there are more media outlets and commentators voicing opinions and covering the story from every angle at some hour of the day. You also have the rise of the commentator in the media which means opinions, and shit-stirring opinions are prized most highly above reporting. Sound bites are the media currency of the day.

And if all that wasn't enough, you have the non-sporting sections of society and the media which feel they can throw their ignorant tuppence worth into the equation because a) the GAA wants to be attracting itself to these future/potential customers; b) politics has got so dull and apathetic that society and the media increasingly turn to sports now as a means to generate coverage, listeners and readers; and c) we live in a media-obsessed society now where every concerned Mary and Joe becomes a voice in the story and gets a soap-box to stand on.

The media coverage is not reflective of those with actual vested interests and understanding in the story. It is more reflective of the cranks and mouths who will always find something to whinge and moan about. They make the most noise of course and will be given an outlet in the media. And it is because of this, the GAA thinks they must appeal to them, thereby soothing the conscience of the nation.

In contrast, most right thinking people see the cranks for what they are and for the fools the hyped-up media and customer-obsessed sports organisations are as well. In all of this where has GAA leadership and backbone been? All we have seen is knee jerk reaction from every section concerned and this sort of 'situation' where people are 'concerned' and up in arms will keep on arising for different reasons and in different areas until somebody with vision, strength and leadership can stand up and say, 'Hold on, stop over-reacting. This is what's being done. Now let's move on.'

We have lived for too long in a political and organisational culture that seeks to plaster over little cracks and soothe every minor complaint, all in the name of consensus and not rocking the boat and keeping the masses happy.

Ignore those who don't understand Gaelic games and are up in arms. GAA people instead need to be asking themselves and their own organisation why necessary change isn't being taken (not because of anything the *Liveline* brigade might say but because of what football and hurling people can see what needs to be done), and why the GAA feels the need to pander to people who know nothing about the game instead of dealing with the real issues at stake.

Phew! I feel much better having got that off my chest and can breathe easily again. I can now read *The Irish Times* letters page in a calmer frame of mind.

### APRIL 26 Saturday — NFL Division 2 final, Dublin 0-10, Westmeath 0-15, Navan

It's the third meeting between these two teams since the new year and there's been a lot of water under the bridge since Dublin handed Westmeath a ten-point mauling in the O'Byrne Cup quarter-final back in January. It feels like a lifetime ago. Dublin have been taking a battering in the media and on the airwaves for their part in the scuffles against Meath last week — could it only have been a week? — so determining what kind of mind-set the Dubs will be in will be hard to judge.

We're down to the bare bones of a squad without the Parnell Park Eight — Ciaran Whelan, Eamonn Fennell, Ross McConnell, Paul Flynn, Tomás Quinn, Bernard Brogan, Diarmuid Connolly and Paddy Andrews. Brogan, Connolly, Quinn and Andrews were told this morning that their bans were being upheld, so that means the Dubs' Championship opener against Louth on 8 June will be missing Brogan, Connolly and Whelan.

At least Caffrey had the balls to come out in the run-up to this game and speak out about the over the top reaction to the Parnell Park punch-up, saying Dublin were being hung out to dry. It could work in our favour though. Caffrey needs to act like Alex Ferguson now and build up an Us v Them mentality around the team and county.

It's certainly emerging in the fan base as Dublin fans feel as if the whole country is out to get them one way or another. You'd worry it could spill over into something nasty if tempers don't cool down soon. Sitting in the stands at Pairc Tailteann, I nearly had to break up a row that was about to boil over.

Every late Dublin tackle or high challenge was treated by Westmeath fans as if it was blue murder and they ranted and abused the Dublin players accordingly. The more this went on, the more I could feel the Dublin fans around me get more and more pissed off. Sure enough, after one Westmeath abuse too many, one fan beside me laid into them for going on about Dublin tackling so much. 'There's two effin teams out there, don't ya bleedin know!' he screamed at the group sitting in the row in front of us who were abusing the Dublin players.

But of course the Dublin challenges were a hundred times worse than what any Westmeath player could do. Only a few scores on the pitch refocused minds, but a few minutes later an apple was launched from behind the goal at a Westmeath forward taking a free. Just when we could win the moral argument, I thought, some gobshite goes and does that. No wonder the rest of the counties hate us.

Despite doing well in the first half, there's a spark missing from this Dublin team tonight. It's as if they are half afraid to really let rip in case of a badly timed challenge. Knowing the rest of the GAA world was looking on can't have made things any easier and you just felt they were all waiting for another Dublin slip-up. The Dublin team, it seemed, were walking a tightrope with no fire in their bellies.

Westmeath lifted their game for the second half and Dublin had no answer. The subs bench was threadbare and nothing could be done to stem the maroon tide. By the time the final whistle went and Westmeath celebrated their five-point victory, I was gone out of the ground heading for the car. With defeats like these all you want to do is get out of culchie land and get home as quickly as possible to nurse your sorrows.

The row from the match left a bitter taste and I hoped it wasn't to be a prelude to the Championship to come. Dublin needed to circle the wagons, develop a siege mentality and say, fuck the rest of the GAA counties and fans. The events of the last week would either kill us or make us stronger. Pillar Caffrey has eight weeks to find that out.

Roll on the Championship. Dublin will be a wounded beast with something to prove, come June. I just hope the fight hasn't been taken from them altogether. I can feel the heart beating faster when I think of those summer Sundays in Croker to come.

# MAY
## SLOW DAYS

**MAY**
**1**
**Thursday**

I'm still revelling in the glow of United reaching the Champions League final and smacking my lips at the thought of Munster against Toulouse in the Heineken Cup a few days afterwards. I sometimes fantasise about what it would be like to live a life where money is unlimited and has no effect on your life. I would be booking five-star all expenses paid trips to Moscow and Cardiff now and putting my signature to my own corporate box in Croke Park. My father telling me what Brendan Behan's mother, Kathleen, once said, that you should only be a socialist when you can afford it, sticks in my head.

Away from the day-dreams and the what-ifs, this year has the feeling of being on a precipice at times. I think of the lines from one of my favourite poems:

Come to the edge, It is too high.
Come to the edge, We might fall.
Come to the edge, And they came.
He pushed them, And they flew.

We're entering May already and the year promises so much. And not just in sporting terms. Our house is due to be finished in June and we can finally stop living out of our suitcases. I'm about to leave my job to find a new career and I feel like I'm driving without brakes at the moment. It's all happening and by the summer I'll either have won the equivalent of the Champions League or be hearing the sound of second place. Oh, and our wedding is due to take place in August, just when the All-Ireland semis are taking place. That one I'll cross at a later date!

It's also Trapattoni's first press conference as Ireland manager and as he was unveiled before the Irish media in Abbotstown you could tell they were impressed just by his slick Armani suit. We think we're all that with our latte-loving lifestyles, but in truth we're mostly just hicks dressed up in BT's clothing. The Europeans on the other hand know how to do style. And multiple languages. Trapattoni answers questions in a strange cosmopolitan mix of English, German and Italian that served as a gentle reminder that we're still just from a wind-swept island at the back arse of Europe.

It's busy on all fronts this month — except one of course. The Dubs' football campaign doesn't start until 8 June against Louth and we've got to endure these lazy May days for a whole 31 days plus before we'll get any more action from the Dubs. This is like purgatory for the fans, waiting in frustration while all else around them gets into the swing of things. Soccer, rugby, work and the new house should be more than enough to keep me occupied, but there's only one date that's firmly pencilled in: Sunday, 8 June.

**MAY**
**3**
**Saturday**

Leinster win the Celtic League and I don't care. What does it say about me as a Dub born and bred when Leinster winning a League title has the same effect as if it was the Ospreys? Munster on the other hand are a different story. Their Heineken Cup final is coming up in a few weeks and I'll be glued to the box watching it. Hell, if I could afford it I'd be flying over on an all-expenses weekend. Then again, if Leinster were in the final I'd be still watching it and getting excited about it. Truth is, as a sports fan I only get a real kick from the big competitions. The Champions League and Heineken Cups of this world are what I'm into. But then again, is that a definition of a real fan when I can get worked up about seeing the Dubs in the O'Byrne Cup and Football League? I'll follow rugby and soccer with interest, but it's only the Dubs who can get me to drive around the country and beyond on a Sunday afternoon.

**MAY**
**5**
**Monday**

If this was a blog, it would be titled, 'Mental Health Break'. It's a Monday; there's not much in the sports pages, so instead I feast on this snippet of a story that I came across in *The Irish Times*:

*The Leinster minor hurling championship clash between Meath and Laois scheduled for Páirc Tailteann, Navan, on Saturday evening was called off in bizarre circumstances. Laois arrived at the Meath county ground at 5 pm but after waiting three-quarters of an hour for admittance learned the game had been switched to Boardsmill, 20 miles farther on.*

*Laois management, after consulting with officers of the Meath hurling board, refused to travel to Boardsmill, arguing their players had been on the road since 1.30 pm and it was unfair to expect them to travel farther. After consultations with the Leinster Council the referee left for Navan, only to learn the Meath team were refusing to travel. Meath chairman Barney Allen spoke with his Laois counterpart, Brian Allen, and agreed to instruct the Meath officials and players to go to Navan, where the game would start an hour late.*

*Having waited in the Navan O'Mahoney's ground until 6.45 pm, the Laois team and management were informed Meath would not in fact be travelling. Laois learned from locals that Páirc Tailteann had been closed for reseeding ever since the National League final between Dublin and Westmeath.*

*The matter will be dealt with by the Leinster Council this week.*

I mean, where would you get it? If it was the FAI, people would be saying how typical; when it happens in the GAA, people smile and say, 'How wonderfully Irish!' At least I face this particular Monday with a smile on my face.

**MAY**

**6**

**Tuesday**

My good humour from the day before carries over as it's the last day of Bertie's reign. He'll be back of course with some more tomfoolery in front of the Mahon Tribunal. But how will people look back on his time as Taoiseach? As the man who oversaw the transformation of this country into an economic miracle? The man who came, saw and conquered, leaving behind a first world economy with a third world health, transport and broadband system? Or the man who was an apt leader and symbol for what we have now become: shallow, vacuous, obsessed with money and celebrity, without any guiding principles, only to keep on trucking and making money?

I think in the long run Haughey will be seen in a better light and the bould Bertie will be remembered as the Taoiseach without clothes.

The only thing is, I couldn't ever have imagined Haughey going to Parnell Park to see the Dubs in the O'Byrne Cup. I suppose when it's one of your own who's found out, it's all the more galling. We might even chip in together as Dubs fans and get him a Parnell Park pass. After all, he's used to the ould whip-arounds.

**MAY**
**8**
**Thursday**

The worst kept secret is officially out and Declan Kidney has been appointed as the new Ireland rugby manager. It's amazing to see how well developed Irish sport is becoming. First there was the visionary appointment of Giovanni Trapattoni to the soccer team, and now, arguably the most successful Irish sports coach ever, Declan Kidney is getting his just rewards. I think we underestimate just what he and Munster have done in winning the Heineken Cup and now reaching their fourth final. To be European champions in any sport, never mind one that is so professional and has huge financial backers behind some of the other clubs, is an unparalleled achievement in Irish sport. From Munster to Ireland though, is it some kind of step down, I wonder. A bit like going from the Dubs to M%$th!

The news of the Burma typhoon puts sport into perspective, however. Up to 100,000 dead and a country that is so impoverished and closed off to the outside world that even aid workers can't get in. You hear Bush talking about giving countries freedom and democracy and wonder why he couldn't have been bothered to do the same for Burma. Now call me cynical but I'm thinking it might have something to do with oil. Speaking of which, there'll be less and less driving around the country to see the Dubs if the price of oil keeps on going so high. Caffrey's men had just better not get involved in too many replays down the country this summer.

**MAY**
**9**
**Friday**

The avalanche of newspaper pull-outs signals the imminent return of the Championship. It's not much of a bang to start with though. The clash of Longford and Westmeath is the pick of the bunch among New York v Leitrim in Connacht and Cavan v Monaghan and Tyrone v Fermanagh in the Ulster Hurling Championship. Some people are saying the GAA should kick it all off with a high-profile game and I tend to agree. There's so much media coverage and hype in the run-up to it, but it all falls flat when there's no game to match the hoopla.

At least we get to have a look at our most likely opponents in the Leinster semi-final — Westmeath. They beat us handy enough in the Division 2 League final, and while that was a Dublin team missing about eight players and a team edgy and fearful because of the fall-out from the Meath game the previous week, I'd still be worried. People are presuming four in a row in Leinster is a done deal and that it's all about the Sam. But Leinster does seem to be stronger now with Westmeath, Laois and Meath all coming strong.

It's not too long now before the Dubs will be in action

themselves. I've been checking the post assiduously every day since the start of May and each day has brought the same emptiness. There's no sign of my Parnell Park pass arriving. It looks like I've missed out again this year and another season of fretful panicking lies ahead of me. If you're not in you can't win and all that. Tickets for Dublin v Louth will be OK to get hold of, but it's really from the Leinster final on that things get tough. If you're not in a club it's even harder. Sending in your application is like walking into a sweet shop and buying your bar of chocolate. You hand over your money and as you unwrap the bar you just don't know whether you'll see that Willy Wonka glint of gold or just the dark chocolate instead. So I've sent the application for membership of the scheme to Parnell Park along with the cheque. That was over six weeks ago and from what I've been reading online, the memberships have been filled or are being filled.

It was a long shot anyway. And I've found in my life that longshots just never come off.

**MAY**
**11**
**Sunday**

With more of a whimper than a bang, we're off. The start of the Championship has finally arrived, but it is a bit of an anticlimax. A Dublin game or a Tipperary v Cork clash would really get things going. Instead though, and I'm ashamed to admit it, it's also the final day in the Premiership and I flick over to Sky Sports. After the entire season it all comes down to Wigan v Man Utd and Chelsea v Bolton. If United win then the title is theirs again. It's the perfect finale for the most hyped league in the world and Sky Sports are loving every minute of it. I flick back to RTÉ and somehow Westmeath v Longford doesn't seem so out of place. The flash bang wallop coverage of Sky is what the Premiership has become. Let's hope the GAA never tries to do the same.

United win the title and the first of my sporting hopes for the year has been achieved. Next up is the Champions League final, then Munster in the Heineken Cup before finally being topped off with Dublin winning the Sam. Now that's what you call the perfect year.

 To get an idea of just how valuable the GAA has now become, the results from an auction of GAA-related memorabilia held yesterday point to an interesting trend. An All-Ireland winner's medal from 1887 went for between €20,000–30,000; Kilkenny's first All-Ireland winning medal from 1904 was going for up to €17,500; an original ticket from the Bloody Sunday match between Dublin and Tipperary sold for €7,600; while the earliest known hurling final programme from 1913 for Kilkenny v Tipperary went for €3,600. Just like the 1916 Rising and 1921 Independence memorabilia, the market for GAA artifacts is growing in value. There are a lot of people out there, it seems, who are willing to fork out thousands to own some little piece of our beginnings.

From beginnings to futures, economic times will not be all bad, it seems. The ESRI is predicting medium-term growth of 3.75 per cent per annum between 2010 and 2015 — we just have to ride out the choppy few years until then, we're being told. For mortgage holders like ourselves, any economic news can be stomach churning or a ray of hope. The good news has been in short supply recently, so we'll take this news happily.

Let's hope we can all ride out the coming storm for the next few years.

**MAY**
**15**
**Thursday**

Good enough for Meath. Their five players who were banned for eight weeks after the Parnell Park punch-up have had their bans upheld. There was talk last week of them getting off on some sort of technicality, but thankfully they don't have a Frank Murphy in their midst up there.

Meanwhile the real world still revolves and the daily death-toll from the earthquake in China keeps on rising. It's now up to 15,000 and could reach a much higher figure. It's hard to come to terms with the fact that the Olympics will be taking place in the country in just a few months, but barring a disaster of apocalyptic proportions the show will go on. A cousin who was in China recently told me how, while on a business trip there for a few days, he got to visit the Olympic Stadium in Beijing and witnessed a practice run of the opening ceremony while walking around the stadium. It was, he said, a spine-tingling moment and says the Beijing Olympics will be incredible. One part of me still hankers after the romantic notions of the Olympics, but then the other half of me sees what a commercial money-making racket it really is with all those doped-up athletes. I prefer to turn back to the GAA Championship and feel pity for those affected by the earthquake who will never see anything to do with the Olympics.

I check the dates of the Olympics and realise it lasts for two weeks in August and coincides with the Football Championship quarters and semis. A free all expenses

Once more into the breach. New year, new beginnings.

Over before the whistle blew. Dublin v Monaghan, abandoned.

A bright start to the year. Alan Brogan lifts the O'Byrne Cup.

Not giving in. The Blue Book readers in action against Meath in the National Football League.

Slowly out of the blocks. The Dubs get the summer off to a winning start against Louth.

Easy warm up. Dublin's Leinster Championship opener against Louth proved a facile affair.

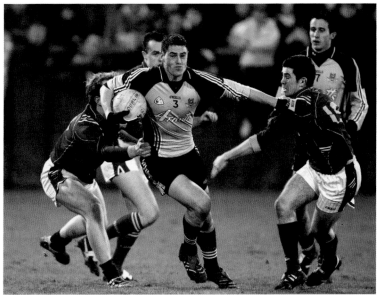

Dublin's full back answer? Ross McConnell would be dropped against Wexford later in the season.

Westmeath were to prove a more difficult proposition in Leinster, but the Dubs still prevailed.

A great season from Shane Ryan, but this proved to be Dublin's last win of the 2008 season.

Easy, easy . . . the Dubs' 23-point victory over Wexford promised so much.

High hopes. A fourth Leinster title in a row and the Dubs were on a roll.

Thirty-one v One. All-Ireland quarter-final v Tyrone.

Brian Dooher, one player who single-handedly took Dublin apart.

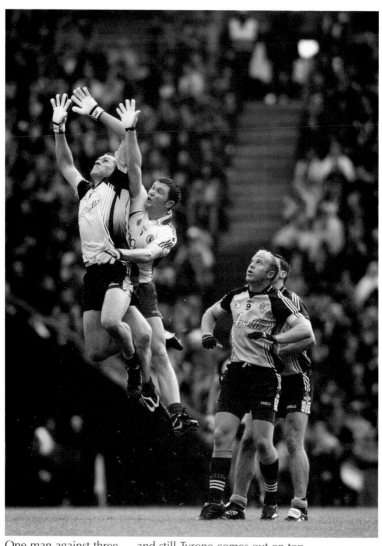

One man against three — and still Tyrone comes out on top.

What now? Dublin's management team looks for answers against Tyrone.

In the rain and the cold. Dublin's darkest day: the quarter-final
embarrassment against Tyrone.

Pain and despair. In the aftermath of defeat.

A Dublin legend, but the last season for Sherlock?

'The best Dublin midfielder since Brian Mullins,' said Paul Caffrey. Was this Whelan's final farewell?

Where did it all go wrong? Paul Caffrey couldn't deliver an All-Ireland title and resigned in the aftermath of the humiliating 12-point defeat to Tyrone.

All for one and one for all. The Dubs together and their Blue Book came to naught in the end.

Never mind the seniors. An All-Ireland title did come to Dublin this year, courtesy of the Juniors.

paid trip to the Olympics or a ticket standing on the cramped, sweaty and smelly Hill to see the Dubs in an All-Ireland semi? Not even a contest.

I also make a mental note remembering that I'm getting married on 21 August and will be on honeymoon a few days later. Damn, it's happening at the same time as the football semis. All sorts of crazy ideas are going through my mind: if we were in Europe, maybe I could fly back for a day to catch the game. I might have to pack my Dubs jersey in the suitcase just in case. I see trouble ahead with this almighty clash. I decide to set this particular problem aside and cross it another time. I know what will win out, but the thoughts of missing the Dubs in a semi depresses me — although we are counting our chickens thinking it's a foregone conclusion that the Dubs will reach a semi. I'll see how Leinster goes and maybe start panicking when August looms closer.

MAY
**17**
Saturday

It's FA Cup final day and who cares. Portsmouth take on Cardiff City and I'll be out and about, not watching it. It's a far cry from the days as a child when you would be ready early in the morning for the extended build-up to the game on the BBC. From midday on they would be previewing the match and you couldn't get enough of it. This was the highlight of the year for soccer fans. Of course, when the teams came out and 'God Save the Queen' was sung, the TV would be muted by my family and I would sit staring at the screen in strange fascination at those strange words being mouthed in front of me.

The one Cup final that will always stand out for me was the 1985 match between Man Utd and Everton. United had become my team from two years earlier when they beat Brighton & Hove Albion to win the FA Cup. But I was also drawn to them because it was the team Kevin Moran played for. I had grown up seeing matches of that Dublin team from the 70s. Moran swathing through the opposition, hair flowing behind him, unstoppable, was the stand-out vision for me. He was tough, fast and skilful. He was everything I wanted to be. The warrior hero was my idol (Bryan Robson was another Man Utd favourite of mine) and it was no surprise that I ended up becoming a half back in Gaelic football and a full back in soccer.

But of course the 85 Cup final goes down as the only time a player was sent off. Moran received a straight red for a late challenge on Peter Reid and this was a time in football when such things barely received a yellow. To get a straight red in the Cup final was unheard of. I was told, of course, it was a case of anti-Irish bias, and for years I was convinced that only Irish players in England were sent off. That day was both painful and magical for me as a 7-year old. When Norman Whiteside curled the winner into the bottom corner of the net, I was in footballing heaven.

Since then, Cup final day has always held a special allure and mystique for me. I remember Coventry's surprise win in 1987, Wimbledon's massive upset winning in 1988, United's first trophy for Ferguson in 90, Spurs' victory in 91, and then the frequent United final appearances in the late 90s and early 2000s. By that stage I was watching Cup finals in the pub, and remarkably, 'God Save the Queen' was still being muted. Today, though, it's Portsmouth v Cardiff. And I'm out in the city doing house stuff!

**MAY**
**18**
**Sunday**

How does he do it? It's the second weekend of Championship football and finally it awakes from its slumber. And how! In an incredible afternoon of football Mick O'Dwyer's Wicklow beat Kildare by four points (0-13 to 0-09) in the first round of the Leinster Championship. Who would have thought Wicklow had it in them? Who would have thought the old dog O'Dwyer could conjure up another footballing miracle with a small county in Leinster. It's Wicklow's first ever win in the Leinster Championship in Croke Park and judging by the dancing and jumping around by O'Dwyer afterwards, he's not done yet.

The Championship feels like it has finally kicked into gear and people will be sitting up and taking notice. Nothing like a surprise win to get people's attention. O'Dwyer's capacity to perform miracles with the smaller counties is unsurpassed. He did it with Kildare and Laois, and now Wicklow. And what is his X factor? The Wicklow players after the game spoke of his passion and enthusiasm for the game and it is amazing how positivity can work wonders.

There is something about the man, though. I met him once while working on a Kerry GAA special and we had him, Jack O'Shea and Eoin Liston in the TV studio with us for an afternoon. After just a few minutes in his company you wanted to stay there all day listening to him and basking in his infectious warmth and nature. Nothing in life would ever get him down, you'd think. He reminds me of that outlook we all had when we were younger, before jobs, mortgages, bills and getting older became our chosen mills around our necks. O'Dwyer, by contrast, is one of those rare people who has managed to hold on to his magic, youth and exuberance and we all, fans, journalists and players alike, should gladly bask in that if only for a few moments, just to remind us what life could be like.

O'Dwyer's style is in marked contrast to Kildare's new manager, Kieran McGeeney. The Armagh man was taught a lesson in his first Championship outing and the styles between the master and the apprentice could not be more different. McGeeney is in the Roy Keane mould of intensity of application and focus; there is a seriousness of dedication to his approach to life and sport that makes him stand out among people. But how many of us can be carried along by such a work ethic and aspire to be like McGeeney? We would much rather be the children following the Pied Piper from Waterville.

I had met Kieran McGeeney once before. He seemed like he was chiselled out of rock he was so lean and muscled. You would bounce off him even wearing a suit of armour, it seemed. And you could tell by the way he spoke and carried himself that here was a man to admire and respect. Here was a man who, at the time, was working in Dublin and travelling up to Armagh twice a week to train. He would catch the 4 pm train to Dundalk, from where he would be picked up and brought to training for 8 pm. It would be two hours of hard graft before changing, grabbing a bite to eat and getting the lift back to Dundalk to catch the last train to Dublin. He would fall into bed about 1 am. This he did twice a week during the week and then travelled back up on Friday for the weekend for either a match or more training.

And if he wasn't travelling and training in Armagh? The other nights McGeeney was training by himself, lifting weights, doing specific exercises and following a dedicated regimen. This was a man who told me about the bar he had on a wall at the bottom of the stairs in his house. Every time he passed by it to go upstairs to the bathroom or whatever, he would make himself do twenty pull-ups. Every time. No matter what. And you knew he meant it when he said he did it religiously, even if he was dying to go to the bathroom.

But are these the qualities you want in a manager? Brolly and O'Rourke made good points on RTÉ after the game, pointing out how much Wicklow seemed to be enjoying playing. Kildare, on the other hand, were more fearful than anything else. Knowing you would have to face the wrath of a steely, determined manager produced only nervousness and anxiety. Maybe the day of the wrathful manager throwing cups of tea and scaring players into winning is gone. Even Keane has had to change his ways at Sunderland.

For now, it has been a cruel learning lesson for a winner such as McGeeney, but he has come up against an old master in O'Dwyer. Seeing what the Kerry man has done with smaller counties, it makes you wonder what might have been had O'Dwyer ever taken charge of the Dubs. There was talk of it a few years back and O'Dwyer wrote in his autobiography recently that if he had taken the Dubs they would be All-Ireland champions by now.

There has always been talk of how Dublin people would react to a Kerry man in charge of them, but I tell you if we were winning All-Irelands, the Hill would be singing Kingdom songs till the end of the year. It's amazing how success can neutralise any former prejudices. Look at how we embraced Jack Charlton, and now Giovanni Trapattoni. The fickle Dubs would be no different. Of course we would be just as quick to turn on any Kerry man who wasn't succeeding with us, but then again you don't have to be from Kerry to suffer abuse and bile at the hands of Dublin fans. Just ask Mickey Whelan.

If Pillar Caffrey fails to land Sam this year, the Dublin County Board will have to start looking outside the county. An outsider's view might bring some perspective on ourselves in the capital and wake us up to just how good or bad we really are. It's funny though how, as Dublin fans, and before we've kicked a ball in Leinster, we're half thinking about the future and our failings. Just once it would be nice to be proven wrong. After all, when you see what Wicklow can achieve, maybe Dublin should start to believe in themselves more.

**MAY 21 Wednesday**

Part two of my perfect year has come true — and in unbelievable fashion! Man Utd win the Champions League on penalties, consigning Chelsea to another failure this season. Not a good night for the nerves though. I was watching the match in a bar in Marbella, of all places, while trying to decipher the Spanish commentary. And, surprisingly, it doesn't get any easier the more beer that has been drunk.

We were in Marbella for a wedding for three days and thankfully the wedding was on the Thursday, not the day of the game. But watching a game in a bar with just a few casual Spanish onlookers and with your nerves on edge is not a good place to be. The cool beers were going down too easily. I was the only one ordering large (pint) beers, I noticed, and by the fourth the barman was buying that one for me. Things are certainly different in Europe!

There was the match and beers I know. Then there were the penalties — and some more beers. Then there were the celebrations where I befriended a Chelsea-hating Arsenal fan who decided we should have tequila shots in honour of United winning. The rest, I'm afraid to say, is a blur. Did I imagine it or was Dustin the Turkey singing 'Irlande douze points' in the Eurovision semi-final in a shopping trolley with camp singers and dancers prancing around the stage and wearing tricolour wings? The lines between surrealism and reality are blurring all the time. Dustin in the Eurovision I can probably believe more than United beating Chelsea on penalties.

 Oh, sweet Jesus! Oh Jesus Christ! Oh, God! Waking up dehydrated and hung-over in 100 degree heat is never a pleasant experience. I piece together the night before and remember United winning the Champions League, a Spanish bar, and tequila . . .

**MAY 22 Thursday**

I spend most of the morning curled up in a ball and in the doghouse with the missus. The wedding is at five this evening and I pray I'll be able to stop swaying in the heat by then. If this is what it's like when United win, what on earth will it be like if the Dubs win an All-Ireland, I wonder. My whole body shivers at the thought of the aftermath. I go back to sleep dreaming of being on the Hill as Alan Brogan hammers the ball into the back of the net to beat Kerry and win the Sam Maguire.

**MAY 23 Friday** Finally get back to terra firma. It's crazy but after only two days away I was pining to be back home, to have a proper cup of tea and a big fry-up. Over two sausages, two bacon, two eggs and plenty of tea and toast, I catch up on any of the GAA news I may have missed while I was away.

Ger Brennan, the Vincent's All-Ireland winner, has opted out of the Dublin panel this year, it seems. According to the report, Brennan had become frustrated at the lack of game opportunities he was getting. While Bryan Cullen is at No. 6, Brennan was always going to be playing second fiddle, although there is an argument that says he should be out on the wing in place of Paul Casey.

I just wonder if Dublin has become a bit like the Eddie O'Sullivan era where players were so ingrained on the team that they were untouchables. We all know how stale Ireland ended up and there has been little freshening up of things since Caffrey has taken over. Hopefully the way Ireland finished up under O'Sullivan won't be a portent of things to come for the Dubs.

I also read that the ESRI and the Irish Sports Council are reporting a 'relative decline' in the numbers playing Gaelic games compared to other sports. Not surprisingly, the GAA come out fighting, saying there are record numbers playing club hurling and football.

I can understand the ESRI coming to such a theory though. While you can get inculcated into the GAA scene at school, by the time you're heading for college or work it's very easy to slip out of the game entirely. I did it when I was 16, preferring to play soccer, though it's something I've always regretted.

Interestingly, the report found that while more people in Ireland are playing sport than ever before, most adults are now opting for individual sports such as aerobics or jogging. We're fast following the American example and will soon be 'bowling alone', as the American political scientist, Robert Putnam, wrote. We're fast becoming a society and world that prefers only our own company. We choose to text or email rather than talk or meet face to face and we'd rather spend an hour in the gym than an hour training with a team. The only bit of mass communion we get these days is going to matches and cheering on a team. It's a scary thought that the only human interaction one gets in the year is with Dublin fans on the Hill.

**MAY**
**24**
**Saturday**

I'm not quite out of the doghouse after my exploits in the aftermath of United winning the Champions League, but I'm out of it sufficiently to get to spend the afternoon watching Munster in the Heineken Cup final today.

Will my luck continue, I wonder. I'm two out of two so far and have only Munster and then the Dubs to complete the perfect sports year. I've been in Tipperary and Cork these last few days and it's incredible to see how much this Munster team means to the people down here. Flags and banners are everywhere and as we arrived into Cork Airport from Malaga, scores of fans in their Munster jerseys were heading over to Cardiff for the game.

Munster is a place apart in Ireland. It could probably and quite easily break away and form its own country and they'd be all the happier for it. Most people down here are rarely in Dublin — usually just for All-Ireland finals it has to be said — and don't see the need to be close to the capital. They have beautiful scenery, fertile land, successful stud farms, GAA teams, rugby teams and Shannon and Cork airports that will take them anywhere they want to outside of Ireland. Dublin? It's just that big noisy city full of jackeens, they tell me. Sure, why would anyone want to live up there? It's quite an eye-opener for a Dub realising that we're not as important as we think we are, and what's worse, the rest of the country actually doesn't give a toss about us.

And why would they? Munster are champions of Europe. They beat Toulouse in a pulsating match to win the Heineken Cup for the second time. They are a class apart.

One downer to the day: the Eurovision is on this evening minus Dustin the Turkey's 'Irlande douze points'. Europe doesn't know what it's missing. Europe doesn't get Ireland and we like to poke our fingers in the eyes of Europe — a lingering omen for the forthcoming Lisbon Treaty perhaps?

| MAY **25** Sunday | *Leinster Hurling Championship quarter-final, Westmeath 0-11, Dublin 3-21, O'Moore Park, Portlaoise* |

Is today the official start of the season for Dublin fans? The Dublin hurlers face Westmeath in Portlaoise today in the opening round in Leinster. Win today and the Dubs will face Wexford in the semis. Win that and they would have a Leinster final against Kilkenny. Croke Park would be full that day, I guarantee you, with Dublin fans. But today I have been coerced into kitchen shopping for our new house which will shortly be finished. Actually, our house will be finished about four weeks before our new kitchen arrives, so it looks like our place will become take-out central for the first month.

Good relationships are all about give and take, of course, and knowing which battles to fight and when. We men all know who is boss and we try and trade off days like this for future days out in Croker. This weekend I decided to trade today with being able to watch Munster in the Heineken Cup yesterday. So it means the opening Dubs game of the summer goes on without me. Am I any less a fan for it? There might be a thousand Dubs fans there maximum, so I know I won't be in a minority. And if I can make it to their semi-final and final in Leinster, it will have more than made up for it.

I manage to catch some of the highlights that evening after a thoroughly exhausting day learning about mdf, hdf, formica, teak and granite. Who knew what went into a simple kitchen? The Dubs win handy enough, although not as easily as the final scoreline suggests. Dotsy O'Callaghan was the key figure for the Dubs, scoring 1-05 including the goal that put daylight between the teams. I remember him as a footballer for the Dubs a few years back and thought he could be our next Dessie Farrell. Small with a low centre of gravity, he could have been a tricky corner forward for us. But like so many players on the fringes, they just seem to drift away, although this time at least the footballers' loss was hurling's gain. Next up is Wexford in the semi-final and to measure any kind of progress in Dublin hurling, beating Wexford has to be achieved. I definitely won't have any kitchen shopping to do that day.

**MAY**
**26**
**Monday**

Holy shit! The good vibes just keep on coming. I don't know what I did or who I rubbed, but some magical genie is looking out for me at the moment, and long may it continue. I got a phone call this morning that I never expected. You can have your Lotto anytime, but when Seán O'Mahony from Parnell Park introduced himself, my heart skipped a beat.

In his soft Cork lilt, Seán said he had my application and was wondering if I still wanted the Parnell Park pass? Want it? I practically jumped down the phone thanking him for it. What did I have to do? When? Where? What? How? Who cares! I've just won the Dublin GAA fans' lotto. I'm now guaranteed to get tickets for Dubs games in the Championship. Guaranteed!

I give Seán my effusive thanks a million times over and he finally gets me off the phone telling me to come and collect it in person later in the week.

I hang up and collapse exhausted into my seat grinning stupidly from ear to ear. I had given up entirely on getting the pass this year. I had been told there was a long waiting list and when I hadn't heard anything by the start of May, I thought it wasn't to be. I had in fact completely forgotten about it and was resigned to another summer of losing my dignity scrambling around for tickets.

Now for once I could keep some of that dignity and not

be annoying long-forgotten friends and those who are barely friends for tickets. I could relax and not be worrying in the weeks before a game knowing all I had to do was meander up to Parnell Park the Tuesday before the big game, hand over my pass and say, 'One Hill ticket for the All-Ireland final please, my good man.'

I don't think I'm exaggerating when I say that Seán's phone call has actually changed my life. For ever.

I'm afraid of seeing any crows or breaking any glass at this stage. I don't want to jinx whatever run I'm on now. And to top it all off, I managed to get last-minute tickets to see Billy Connolly tonight. If Carlsberg did Mondays . . .

**MAY 27 Tuesday** The sun was barely over the horizon and I was outside the gates of Parnell Park ready to collect my pass. Just in case Seán was going to have a change of mind, I made sure it wouldn't be happening this side of breakfast anyway. I find Seán and he brings me into his office. For a moment he can't find my application and I have this horror scene in my mind where P. J. Gallagher and his *Naked Camera* crew come in saying it was all a joke. Thankfully, Seán finds my application and cheque and hands over my little pass. I thank him a million times again and skip out of Parnell Park.

When I get to my car I look down at this little piece of gold. It reminds me of a Dart ticket. It's about the same flimsy thickness and has a big *Daily Star* ad on it and just my number. That's it. This little card is what Dublin people would sell their children for. I wasn't quite at that stage — probably only because I don't have children — but now I can't quite believe it. I will be getting Dubs tickets without having a heart attack this season.

These last few years I have scrounged, begged and pleaded and managed to not miss a game as the Dubs made their way to quarter-finals and semi-finals. Please! Please don't let this be the year when they get knocked out in the qualifiers and me left all dressed up with a Parnell Park pass and nowhere to go.

**MAY**
**28**
**Wednesday**

Seán Moran's always excellent GAA column in *The Irish Times* on Wednesdays has a piece that sticks with me today. He writes about the findings of last week's ESRI report and coincidentally highlights Robert Putnam's 'Bowling Alone' analogy as well. He makes a good point though, that while we are choosing to pursue increasingly solitary activities such as jogging or the gym, the importance of clubs shouldn't be underestimated in helping to socialise children and even bring some stability to children's lives in socially disadvantaged areas. In many cases coaches and volunteers are acting as part-time social workers.

In this light the ESRI report should not be seen as an indictment of the GAA for falling numbers, but rather as a wake-up call to how much value GAA clubs give to communities. Government funding should reflect this and it should not just see clubs as a sporting outlet. As anyone who has played sport knows, clubs and teams are about so much more

When the right people come together with the funding, the will and the collective drive, anything can be achieved. The Special Olympics was one example and the success of Dublin hurling at under-age level is another.

It's exciting as a Dubs fan reading the piece in the *Irish Indo* highlighting the recent achievements by Dublin's juvenile hurlers: two Leinster minor titles in three years, a feat not achieved since the 1940s; two Feile wins for two different Dublin clubs in three years; an All-Ireland U-21 final appearance; Ballyboden reaching last year's Leinster club final; an All-Ireland senior colleges title for the amalgamated county team; three Leinster colleges titles in the decade under the same banner; and most recently a Dublin North colleges side beating the famous hurling nursery, St Kieran's of Kilkenny.

When a Dublin North under-age team beats a team from St Kieran's, you know things are on the up. There's a player I've been told to look out for in future years, a Ciaran Kilkenny from Castleknock, who is being tipped for future hurling stardom. I'm only 30 now, but realistically in the next 20 years we should be seeing a Dublin hurling team challenge for All-Ireland honours. What a sight that would be, to see a Dublin v Cork/ Kilkenny/Tipperary/Waterford in an All-Ireland hurling final in front of a blue Croke Park.

Fair play to Michael O'Grady who is spearheading things in Dublin. It just shows you that with money, the right people and the will, you can do anything. Let's just hope the footballers don't suffer as a consequence.

**MAY 29 Thursday** Ireland played Colombia this evening and got their first win under Trapattoni. We played Serbia in a 1-1 draw in Croke Park last week as well, but I think I barely noticed. I used to be a soccer nut, but I have become increasingly blasé about Irish soccer. The drab and losing regimes of Kerr and Staunton had a lot to do with that, but so has the world where Irish soccer players come from now. The second generation Irish from the UK have barely anything in common with us over here apart from the English language. Watching Phil Babb give his analysis on Ireland, and you realise he has about as much affinity with this country as Paul Gascoigne. I was half expecting him to say, 'Eire done well' and 'aren't Eire great?'

Even the players who go over as teenagers and make it in England have little in common with us Irish fans any more. They are millionaires living in bubble worlds in England whose lives revolve around getting everything done for them at the drop of a hat. Compare and contrast them with Munster players or GAA players and it's obvious why you would feel closer to our home grown teams.

I can't wait for Trapattoni to get us winning again and if we do qualify for a World Cup or a European Championship, I will be going as crazy as anyone else. There was a time though when I would religiously go to every home international game. But following them feels a bit like following an English Premiership team. I can't recognise who these players that are supposed to represent my country are. They are not from my world and have become more like economic mercenaries who will choose club commitments over country. Except the country lads of course, players like Kevin Doyle, Shane Long and Stephen Hunt. These are all lads who, when you see them talking about playing hurling games after training, haven't lost touch.

**MAY**
**31**
**Saturday**

Wake up with a sore head from too much wine last night and am greeted with the sobering headline on the front of *The Irish Times* that says: 'House prices plummet'. You know things are bad when *The Irish Times* starts using language like 'plummet' in relation to house prices.

Ah well, the high of the last two weeks had to come to an end sometime, I suppose. Reality always has a funny way of intruding on you and reminding you it's not all about match tickets, Champions Leagues and Heineken Cups. You know you've grown up when you make sure to read about rate increases, bank rates, the ECB policy and house prices. There's nothing like a couple of hundred grands' worth of debt to focus the mind when the housing market starts to fall. When ECB policy meetings and newspaper headlines can cause minor heart attacks, is it any wonder grown men like myself wrap ourselves up so much in the escapism of sports? Better that than drink and drugs, I suppose. Wine doesn't count though, does it?

I tear my eyes away from previous bank statements and mortgage rates to read that the Meath players who wouldn't accept their bans from the Parnell Park punch-up have been finally told to piss off by the DRA and take their punishment like men. It's still not enough to lift me out of this housing-plummet blues, so myself and the missus go see the new Indiana Jones movie. It's Indie all right — the hat, the whip, the wise cracks, but it's not the same. Maybe it's because I'm 20 years too old for it now. As we leave the cinema I notice that the audience are all 30 and 40 somethings. There are no kids, teenagers or even 20 somethings — the age we were when we first feasted on Indiana. It seems we're all caught in this time warp of catching up on our youthful fancies.

What was supposed to lift my spirits has only made me ponder some more on getting older. Next thing is I'll be getting out the old *Star Wars* and *Tron* movies.

I go online and see that Wicklow's dream Leinster campaign has ended. Laois beat Mick O'Dwyer's men in the evening kick-off by two points, 0-15 to 0-13. Fairytales have to end sometime, I suppose, and Wicklow go back into the Tommy Murphy Cup now. The summer of shocks and upsets is over for another year for them, but for what the win over Kildare did for them, if only for the briefest of moments, then Mick O has done his job. Another dream shot down in flames. Life wasn't this shitty when you were a kid, was it?

OK. Mental health break required. Reservoirdubs.com always comes up with the goods when I need it. Sure enough, I read one story from a Dublin fan about paying to listen to a game on the radio in the US:

> *By Jaysus we've come a long way since August of '83 when we paid $5 into the Horse and Jockey in Woodside in Queens NY to listen to the replay aginst Cork on the fucking radio!! The place was belly button to arsehole. Loads of Dubs. We were only there for the weekend from Boston and ran into a whole crew of lads we played with or against back home. Some walloping was done that day.*
>
> *Yer man, the boss had a microphone hooked up to the telephone. He rang the brother in Ireland and the brother put the phone up to the radio and off*

*you go! It's great to be able to see the games now. Not too many Dubs. Daddy Seán Myler from Churchtown who played his football for Peadar Macken's back in the day is 80 and he's there every week. I couldn't be bothered me bollix to go and watch the likes of Galway v Leitrim. It would only put me in a bad mood. There's always good banter with a shitload of counties represented on a regular basis. G'wan the Dubs.*

# JUNE
## IT FINALLY ARRIVES!

**JUNE**
**1**
**Sunday**

It's the first big Championship weekend. First Clare beat Waterford convincingly in Limerick and question marks over Waterford's hunger and drive have really come to the fore now. They looked like a team that don't believe in themselves any more. This game was also the first broadcast by TV3 as part of the new rights deal and in fairness to them, while all week GAA fans were holding their breath expecting the worst, it all runs smoothly. Having well-known and well-polished experts such as Liam Griffin and Nicky English gives the coverage kudos from the outset. The jury's still out on Matt Cooper as presenter though. It's strange and diverting watching the Championship on a station other than RTÉ, but that's the future and reality of TV rights these days. Once TV3 produces it in a competent manner the fans will be more than happy.

I go online to catch the Meath-Wexford game (God bless the internet, rte.ie and video-on-demand) and as Meath are ten points up with 20 minutes to go, I go back to my work. I've been asked to work in RTÉ today and there's a chance they might want me for the duration of the summer every summer. My first instinct is to say yes for the money and the opportunity. And then I realise — every Sunday! That means Dublin games would be ruled out unless there was some way I could work around it.

But are you going to ask your new employers from the outset for a couple of Sundays off just so you can go and see the Dubs?

After all the good news and events of the last few weeks my stomach drops like a lead balloon. This is the worst situation to be in. Here's a great opportunity staring me in the face, and all I can think about is how not to miss the Dublin games. I've a meeting next week with the company and I will find out whether they want me every Sunday or not. I don't know what to think. I want it and I don't want it. I need the money and yet — signing away my Dubs season? Can money buy that? Time will be ticking very slowly between now and the Wednesday meeting.

I continue my work and flick back to Meath-Wexford. I have to do a double take looking at the score. There's 71 minutes gone and it says Wexford 2-14, Meath 2-13! But when I last looked it was Meath 2-08, Wexford 0-04. This is unbelievable. The ref blows his whistle and it's all over. Wexford have come back from a ten-point deficit and beaten Meath in the process. My sinking feeling about working for the summer has disappeared. Meath beaten by Wexford! I'm kicking myself for missing it, but I'll make sure to catch the *Sunday Game* later on this evening. I'll record this one and watch it and watch it again and again for the rest of the summer if I can't get to a Dubs game.

**JUNE**
**2**
**Monday**

It's a bank holiday Monday and I really should have better things to be doing, but I start the day off on a good footing by watching the *Sunday Game* highlights of Meath v Wexford from last night. The point from Mattie Forde to win was just sublime and watching him and Ciaran Lyng pinging the ball from either side and on the run has got me scared if we meet them in Leinster. But aside from the players, what could be really dangerous for Dublin or anyone else who meets them is their new young manager Jason Ryan.

Appointed last November, aged just 31, Ryan was a former Waterford footballer who could be a new type of manager coming into the game. We have seen the rise of the 'professorial' type of manager in soccer in England, the kind that doesn't have to have played the game at a high level but has studied it intently, such as Wenger and Mourinho. Ryan is only in his first season in charge of an inter-county team and already they have won Division 3 and are still unbeaten for the year. It's some record and might just prove that you don't have to have played at a high inter-county level or won All-Ireland medals to succeed in modern day sport. It's only one win, over Meath, but Wexford could be the ones to watch in Leinster and beyond.

**JUNE**
**3**
**Tuesday**

Surreal non-sports moment this evening. Got dragged along to the *Sex and the City* movie (it's actually SATC, don't you know!) with the missus. Sat there in an old-style Tipperary cinema that even had an upstairs like in *Cinema Paradiso*, watching the travails of four white, female, upper middle-class New Yorkers, and even found myself laughing in parts. Of course, as the male usher joked with us as we walked in saying, 'No men allowed in here', I had to tell him loudly enough for the rest of the cinema to hear: 'I'm not gay you know. Not gay.'

By the end of the night I could tell a Dolce from a Vera Wang any day of the week. The Hill should straighten me out soon enough though. If I start admiring their blue jerseys then I'll be getting worried.

**JUNE**
**4**
**Wednesday**

It feels like summer and the Championship has at long last arrived. The Dublin team to face Louth on Sunday has been announced and it's like the first salmon appearing in spring or the first snowflakes in December. This news is like our own summer sunshine. We can now feel the game is just around the corner. We can actually picture the players on the pitch and lining out in their positions. After the false dawn months of the O'Byrne Cup and the National Football League, after the endless chatter and arguments about who should play where, it has all come down to this.

And as it turns out it's not that different from last year after all. Four players — Ciaran Whelan, Bernard Brogan, Paul Flynn and Diarmuid Connolly — were unavailable because of their suspensions from the punch-up with Meath in April, but there are only two new debutants for the Dubs, Eamonn Fennell and Paddy Andrews. Those two were enforced anyway as Fennell comes in for Whelan and Andrews for Brogan. The other two changes are at corner back where Paul Griffin, who had been in Australia and had only recently returned, is replaced by Seán O'Shaughnessy, and one free-taker, Mossy Quinn, who is preferred to Mark Vaughan.

Is Caffrey that confident in his squad that we need only make such minor changes? Does he really believe this team can improve from last year so much and beat the likes of Kerry again while being virtually unchanged? I can't believe it's been a whole year and that the Championship is back. But another part of me feels like it's *déjà vu* seeing that teamsheet. If previous summers were unsuccessful, how then can persisting with the same players change things in any way? The excitement at the team being announced gives way to morbidity and pessimism. But I shouldn't get carried away with myself before the Championship has even begun.

Change mightn't be in the air for the Dublin team, but it is certainly hitting US politics in a big way. Barack Obama clinched the Democratic nomination for the presidency last night and his mantra 'Yes we can' is an infectious one of hope after the eight years of misery and mistakes the George Bush years have brought. Whether America has the courage to vote in a black president remains to be seen though, and one gets the feeling that outside of the east coast and west coast, the rest of America in between sees Bush as one of their own. It's a dangerous place to be entrenching itself in religious, economic and foreign policy terms and while the States builds a moat around itself, the rest of the world and the Obama voters look on in worry. November could be truly momentous if Obama does get in and it's amazing to see how his campaign and message has infected younger generations in Ireland as well. It's win or bust for America this year — a bit like how Pillar Caffrey would look on things as well.

**JUNE**
**5**
**Thursday**

It's kind of typical the way my life seems to be panning out at the moment. I win the equivalent of the Lotto for a Dublin fan by getting a Parnell Park pass and the first opportunity I have to saunter down at my leisure to Donnycarney to get my hands on a Hill ticket for the Championship, I'm working down the country. Yes, I'm out of Dublin this week and there's nothing I can do about it. I'm sitting in a country pub nursing a pint, feeling sorry for myself and looking morosely at the green pass that's on the table. It's looking back at me as if to say, you went through all this and you're not even going to use me? As Forrest Gump was wont to say: 'Shit happens.' In the end I have to get a friend to buy Hill tickets for us.

Oh, and just to rub salt into the wound, I've been asked to work again this Sunday from 6 pm. The Dubs throw-in is at 4 pm, so I'll have to get to the game extra early and park the car somewhere around Ballybough. I'll have to leave the game before the end and make sure I'm not caught in the crowds before zooming off across the city for a few hours' work. And all the while the rest of the Dubs will be carrying out enjoyable post-mortems in some beer garden underneath a summer sun.

I still don't know whether the summer Sunday work gig is to be a permanent thing and I won't know for another few weeks. But when you've a mortgage to pay and you work for yourself, there is no such thing as 9 to 5, Monday to Friday. You take what you can and suffer the consequences. The excitement has subsided now. But I know that just being on the Hill for that first Sunday, if only for an hour, will make it worthwhile. Breathing in the atmosphere deeply and letting it waft over me, the summer will have finally arrived.

I'm checking out for Dublin stories daily in the papers and online and one fan on reservoirdubs sums it up well: 'I cant wait, am talking to a mate by phone twice a day every day about the louth game. on Res Dubs each day in work as a guest, looking at the framed dubs poster on the kitchen wall for inspiration, reading old match programmes, watch dubs v kerry 1977 semi twice a week, you name it im feckin doin it. i hate these last few weeks leading up to the first game.'

**JUNE 8 Sunday**

*Leinster Football Championship quarter-final, Dublin 1-22, Louth 0-12, Croke Park*

For some reason, every morning of a Dublin game as I get up, wash and get ready to travel to that day's game, I'm always reminded of the scene in Joyce's *Ulysses* where one of the characters (Buck Mulligan is it?) stands in front of the mirror shaving while intoning to himself. There's something pleasurably ritualistic and familiar about each of these Sunday mornings. They are rare in the scheme of things for the duration of the year, but over the past decade they have become rhythmic and familiar markings. The same hopes and fears greet me on each of these mornings. What will the day bring? What will happen and how will it pan out by day's end? Will we be in good or foul humour? The uncertainty of the day and match ahead is in stark contrast to the familiar rituals of the morning.

But this morning as I wake up to get ready is slightly different. For one thing, I have work to go to after the game — no post-mortem drinks this evening for me. And secondly I am in Tipperary and driving two and a half hours to get to the game. Things never seem to run too easy these days. One would have thought I would at least have been in the same province! The radio stations in the car don't carry much by way of pre-match analysis, so I have to content myself with some more guff on next week's Lisbon Treaty vote. The political talking shop never ends and it sometimes feels that sport is more relevant these days. How can anyone like or identify with the self-interested politicians and bureaucrats that abound on the airwaves? At least I'm guaranteed an easy run on the roads this morning — what other lunatic would be driving from Tipperary to Dublin for the first round of the Leinster Championship against Louth?

Three hours later and I'm standing at the corner of Summerhill and the North Circular Road. I inhale deeply and let all the sounds and smells soak in. The Dubs in the Championship and it finally starts for real today. After all the false starts, warm-ups, league layabouts, fisticuffs and pub talk, here we are at last on Sunday, 8 June 2008. It's another year already. The last time I walked down this street wearing blue was last August and I was panting and out of breath, racing to Gill's to get my hands on a ticket for the All-Ireland semi-final against Kerry. The streets today are only half as busy. There's barely a crowd gathered and once again the fair weather tag will be thrown at the Dublin fans. I wonder how many of them are choosing to stay at home or go to the pub to watch instead the European Championships which kicked off last night.

For the soccer fanatic there'll be three weeks of non-stop football to look forward to. It's second only to the World Cup in terms of exposure and matches and comes like manna from heaven for the die-hards. But strangely, for a self-confessed sports nut, I'm not as enthused about these Championships. International soccer is losing its lustre. The players care more about their clubs and it shows in the international games. When a team like Greece can win in 2004, then the coaches are truly taking over the game and strangling the life out of it. I'm all for Europe and will be voting yes in next week's Lisbon Treaty, but there's only so much of Europe I can take. Do we really care about Austria v Croatia or Switzerland v Czech Republic? Wake me up when we get to the quarter-finals please.

Today's game should be a gimme as far as games go for the Dubs, which probably accounts for the 30,000 fans awol for today's game. But this is the Dubs' chance to blow off the cobwebs and shake out their legs for what one hopes will be a long stretch of games in Croker.

For the fans it's the chance to commune once more on the Hill. She's been left derelict and bereft of her beloved Dubs for too long. The rugger buggers have had their fun this year, but once more the Hill will belong to Dublin. It's like revisiting a long-lost friend's house or returning to an old childhood home. It's both our home and our church; it's our local and our own front room. Most importantly it's ours and we're returning for another summer of Sundays.

Louth won't prove too troublesome and so I'm relaxed and at ease. Tickets were easy to come by — no need for the Parnell Park pass to be used just yet — and the build-up was more reminiscent of a League game than anything else. Here on the North Circular as I make my way to Gill's, the streets are laid back and easy. Today is a day to be enjoyed. The rest of the summer will bring more serious issues of its own. There are plenty more days to be worried and stressed. But today is not one. Or shouldn't be anyway.

Meeting friends in the bar, we have time to watch the Munster hurling clash between Cork and Tipp in Pairc Uí Chaoimh. It's a match I would have gone to if it hadn't clashed with the Dubs. Dublin in the football and Tipperary in the hurling, as I tell my friends (and future in-laws). If the GAA is quintessentially Irish, then Munster hurling is the DNA in all of us. We must at one time have all come from Munster.

Today in the pub on the North Circular, the Dublin fans cheer wildly for Tipp. Not a blue supporting blue thing but more an 'anyone but Cork' situation. Add 'anyone but Meath' to that as well while we're at it. Cork or Meath — who would be more hated in Dublin terms? It's a tough one but Meath would probably shade it because of its geographical proximity. Cork thinks it's the real capital, of course. Dublin knows the truth and gets secretly irate at the uppity attitude 'down there'. We're like two brothers close in age and always vying for top spot. Only one can be the elder though and Dublin can look down its nose at the Rebel county's stance. It's the second half in the hurling and Tipp are starting to pull away from Cork. Another point goes over for the Premier county to loud cheers in Gill's. 'Kick the shit out of them Cork hoors' comes a voice from behind us.

It's a Dubs fan resplendent in his jersey, cowboy hat, gold hooped earring and a pint bottle of Bulmers in front of him. And he's hitting about 60 years of age at least. As I turn to look at him, he catches my eye and tries to strike up a conversation, 'Where's your jersey? And wha' part of Dubbalin are you from, den? Southside probably wha'?'

I'm just wearing a shirt and jeans today, having ditched the Dubs top because I've to go to work afterwards. I've also driven two and half hours up from Tipp this morning and am in no mood for this 'Dubbalin' bullshit. I turn away and go back to watching the hurling. Our 'fan' turns to one of my mates nearby and wants to know 'what's up with yer man?' My mate tells him that I've actually driven all the way from Tipperary this morning just to be at this game and would he politely piss off. Tipp score another point and are on the verge of beating Cork for the first time in Cork in 82 years. Our pal behind us goes on supping his Bulmers and probably wouldn't know one end of a hurley from the other. Outside of the Championship, his Sundays are probably spent drinking the same Bulmers but wearing a Celtic or Liverpool jersey.

Yep, you know the Dubs are back in the summer when you meet your first fucking idiot Dubs fan. And it only took one hour. The Hill between now and the rest of the summer will be full of them. So why do we bother still? If you can get past the dopes and mouths, a good portion of the Hill are just ordinary Dublin fans and people. A lot of fans have given up the Hill for the stands and it does take a certain amount of sado-masochism to want to stand there and be crushed while the sweaty, drunken bodies around you shout obscenities towards the pitch. But when the Hill is in full voice or when a Dublin goal goes in in front of us, there is nowhere better to be. When you hear the chants and songs emanating from the Hill and making their way around the stadium to you, all you can think of is how much you would give to be standing there in the middle of it all. The Hill, when Dublin is playing, is the heartbeat of the ground. It leads in the chanting and songs; it picks the team up when they're trailing; and it leads in the wild celebrations when the team wins. It's no coincidence that the players march up to the Hill before every game, as if in homage and as if they're drawing sustenance from the thousands standing before them.

That's the romantic notion and idealism of the Hill anyway. You're reminded all too often however of the gritty realism as our Bulmers drinking fan in the pub starts mouthing off to some other fans near him.

Five minutes to go to throw-in. We knock back the last of our pints and make our way to the ground. The ritual of showing your tickets, having walked down through Summerhill and on to Clonliffe Road, never tires. You get a sense of the atmosphere and get caught up in the chanting. As you queue at the turnstiles you hear the roars from inside as the teams make their way out on to the pitch. Next time, you promise yourself we'll leave earlier and not be rushing. But sure what's the rush, the rest of the Hill asks, especially as they're good enough to delay throw-ins for us and all?

I'm surprised at how packed the Hill is. It is only Louth after all, and normally it wouldn't be until the Leinster final before it starts to creak at the rafters. Today it's the first round and we can barely squeeze our way up the steps. Halfway up and behind the goal there's no room, but we find a half open space to cram ourselves into. The next 70 minutes will be a constant flow of being pulled and pushed as the crowd sways and you think — not for the first time — of the comforts and benefits of a seat in the Hogan Stand. I'm not even talking corporate box or Premium level — a plain old foldy-down plastic seat will do me just fine, just something solid and unmovable. That and somewhere that doesn't smell like an Amsterdam coffee house. The smell, not just of hash but freshly imported grass, wafts across the Hill. Breathing in, one can't help but start to get stoned. It's grass all right — strong, pungent and highly potent. I'm even beginning to get the munchies just standing here. The Croke Park pitch is taking on a whole new perspective as I stand there inhaling.

The game starts but drags ever so slowly. And it's not the grass that's making it seem that way. It's the first match of the Championship for the Dubs and you'd think they would come bursting out of the blocks and quickly into top gear. Instead they're playing as if it's a challenge match in Swords in the middle of winter. Half a yard off the pace and shooting wides that your granny would be slotting over, the Hill groans loudly at every missed effort and unforced error. If Louth were any way decent they would be burying us, but instead they too kick most of their easy chances wide.

We're all soon losing interest on the Hill. Soon the chants of abuse at some players in blue can be heard (this must be a record — only 30 minutes into the season and already the fans are abusing the players). We all start talking among ourselves — from team selection to the Munster hurling final — and only occasionally look up to see another wide sail by. How I would love to have been in Pairc Uí Chaoimh today to see that Tipperary win. On days like today Gaelic football is the poor cousin of hurling. Hurling is a neutral's favourite whereas Gah on opening rounds against Louth is something to be endured. But that's what being a fan means, isn't it? It's not being one of the 30,000 missing, watching soccer or doing whatever today.

The ref blows for half-time and we console ourselves with the fact that the second half surely can't be as bad as the first. 'And you drove from Tipp for this shite?' someone asks me. 'Don't fuckin remind me,' I say. It was nearly five hours ago that I was filling the car with petrol and looking at all the Tipp jerseys around me as they headed off to Cork. I can safely say I was the only one travelling from south Tipp this morning heading for Croke Park. For a game against Kerry or an All-Ireland final, one could understand, but for this fare against Louth? For now I'll put it down to a genetic defect and inherited insanity (from your mother's side no doubt, as my father would say). But ultimately if Dublin get to another All-Ireland final — or even a quarter-final or semi — being a Dubs fan one can't be too choosy or hopeful. I couldn't stand in good conscience on the Hill knowing I wasn't there for earlier games in the Leinster championship. Even today there are friends of friends who haven't come to the game, but you're guaranteed they'll be shouting the house down if/when the Dubs start inching closer to a final.

It's like in rugby. I'm a supporter and follow the team, but I couldn't in all honesty look for a ticket for a Six Nations game against England or France, knowing full well I couldn't be bothered with a clash with Scotland or Wales. Who am I to take a ticket off some more deserving fan? A friend who goes to the rugby games applauds me for my stance but then in the next breath asks, 'and do you really think they're all real and deserving fans at the games?' To that I have no answer. But for the Dubs my guilty conscience wouldn't let me wittingly miss a game. Work, family affairs and, oh yes, the little matter of my wedding in August might be grounds for non-attendance, but then only just.

The Dubs finally kick into some sort of gear (certainly not fifth anyway) midway through the second half — and just as I have to head off to work. For the next 20 minutes I get text updates of goals, points and some semblance of excitement. In the meantime I'm heading down Clonliffe, a lonely body leaving the action early. This won't be happening come the third Sunday in September I tell myself. No matter what.

The first Sunday of the Championship is soon over for the Dubs and what an anticlimax it's been. Things can only get better. But at least we're off and out of the blocks. This is what we've been waiting for all year.

**JUNE**

**9**

**Monday**

It's the usual Monday morning post-mortems in the papers for the Dubs — not good enough/poor/undeserving/need to improve. When the Dubs play everyone wants a piece and has an opinion. The GAA needs the Dubs and the media need the Dubs. We are the Manchester United, the New York Yankees of our sport, and that's just the way it is. But it would be good to see the current set-up embrace it more. We are in the spotlight because we are the capital, because of our history and heritage, and it should be something to be proud of and celebrated.

Instead the management and players treat all around them with suspicion and paranoia as if everyone is out to get them. Great teams and great clubs don't behave like this. The Dubs have an exalted position that needs to be cherished. We are not just any county team playing in the Championship. We are Dublin, one of the greats. It comes with extra pressure of course, but when you play for a special team, there will be special treatment.

So, it's only the first round and it was only Louth, but already the media coverage is all engulfing. You could get angry about it and rail against the anti-Dubs brigade in the media and the rest of the GAA, but you're better off seeing it as the flattery the Dubs deserve. If it's good or bad, it doesn't matter. It's nice to be special. It would be even nicer though to back that up with some All-Ireland titles.

After tossing the morning papers to one side I decide to do a bit of Wikipedia wandering and find out some historical Dublin GAA facts for myself. Did you know, for example, that — aside from the golden period in the 70s when we won three All-Irelands — our average All-Ireland wins have been one a decade going back to the 1920s? There was the one in the 1990s, one in the 80s, one in the 60s, one in the 50s, one in the 40s and none in the 30s. Of our 22 All-Ireland titles (which still places us second on the list behind Kerry), half of them were won between 1891 and 1908 with another three won in the 1920s (when we won our only three in a row: 1921–23). That means since 1923 we have won eight All-Irelands in 85 years! That's one a decade and that includes three from the golden age of the 1970s! And if you discount them, it means we've won five Sam Maguires since the 1920s, excluding the 1970s.

These are sobering statistics to be reading this morning but enlightening none the less. They're worth remembering as the Dubs start out on yet another Championship tilt with an All-Ireland or bust tag behind them. On the law of averages we should be winning an All-Ireland before 2010 — you have to go back to the 1930s to find a decade when we didn't win one — but that only leaves this year and next for them to achieve that. We're down to the last two rolls of the dice.

Speaking of rolls of the dice, Ireland votes on the Lisbon Treaty this coming Thursday and between *The Irish Times* poll from last Friday which had the No's leading 35–30 per cent and yesterday's *Sunday Business Post* which had Yes leading 42–39 per cent, it could be a close call for the government and the politicians. I can't see us rejecting the treaty — we learnt our lesson after Nice it seems — but the downturn in the economy, rising anti-immigrant sentiments and the sheer ineptitude of the political parties in this campaign means it will be a lot closer than it should be. If we keep rejecting treaties and causing problems for the EU, I'm sure they'll just end up taking our vote away. Who said democracy was good for us anyway? Just ask the GAA Congress.

| **JUNE 12** Thursday |
|:---:|

It's voting day for the Lisbon Treaty and the eyes of Europe and the world are on us. Fingers and toes are crossed in Brussels and Kildare Street. Don't fuck this one up, they're saying under their breath. I've decided I will vote yes after all — more out of consensus than anything else, I think. As I stand at the voting booth in my local library, my pencil hovers over the ballot paper for a second. I shrug my shoulders and tick yes. You can't beat the bureaucrats, I think to myself. Anyway, I've more important things on my mind. These matters are *faits accompli*, but the Dublin hurlers' chances of beating Wexford on Saturday to reach a Leinster final are not.

You can read into it what you like, but it's a strange coincidence that the vote for the Lisbon Treaty coincides with the twentieth anniversary of Ireland's historic 1-0 win over England in Stuttgart in Euro 88. Of course the papers, the TV and the radio are giving it wall-to-wall coverage remembering the day and all that. I remember watching it with my father and there not being a huge amount of coverage on the day. It was only after our win that suddenly people sat up and took notice. Now, sport is mainstream and no longer seen as something for the inarticulate and uneducated. Sure they're even saying Euro 88 and Ray Houghton in particular were responsible for kick-starting the Celtic Tiger! I'll leave those theories to the rock n roll economists, but I do know that it feels like another time and another place, as if we were all more innocent and childlike then. That same year the world was outraged when Ben Johnson won his 100 m in Seoul and then tested positive for steroids. How dumb we were to think it was just Johnson and not realise that most of the Olympic athletes were probably at it.

Back in 88 George H. Bush was elected President of the United States and the same year also saw the Irish government announcing health cuts. Maybe some things haven't changed that much after all. We haven't been back to a European Football Championship since then and it's even harder to believe that the Dubs have had only one All-Ireland to celebrate in all those 20 years. As the saying goes, the more things change, the more they stay the same.

**JUNE**
**13**
**Friday**

Things may actually have changed, changed utterly after all. It's Friday the 13th and Ireland has voted No to the Lisbon Treaty. This is an incredible result which I never saw coming. And neither did the government, the politicians, the EU or the rest of Europe for that matter. Suddenly the EU is in crisis and up in arms. How dare we ungrateful Irish, who received billions from Brussels, after all these years have the temerity to say no to what the EU wanted. We were only being allowed to vote on condition that we voted the way we were supposed to. Didn't we know that?

It seems like we haven't quite given up our rebellious streak as a nation just yet. Most of the no votes, it turns out, came from rural and working-class areas, whereas middle-class urban areas voted yes. Seeing the surly reaction from France and Germany on the telly now makes me proud of the vote. Good enough to stick it to the big shots in Europe. I flick over to *France News 24* to catch their reaction and they are asking a Libertas spokesperson why the Irish are so anti-European. To which the spokesperson replied, why did you not say the same when the French and Dutch voted against the Nice Treaty? The silence in the French studio spoke volumes. Suddenly my faith in the Irish people has been restored. There's nothing like an unexpected result to give everyone a jolt and make us all sit up and take notice. We've been awoken from our slumber now and made to realise that people can make a difference, no matter what the EU bureaucrats say. When politics gets revitalised like this, it can give even sport a run for its money. I'm sorry now I voted yes.

### Leinster Hurling Championship semi-final, Wexford 2-13, Dublin 0-19, Nowlan Park

**JUNE 14 Saturday**

It's D-Day for Dublin hurling. After years of development, money being poured into the game in the capital, under-age, minor and U-21 success, all that is needed now is a breakthrough at senior level. The Dublin hurlers need to be reaching Leinster finals to prove they are the second best in Leinster. Media commentators are talking about a revolution about to take off, but I'm not so sure. When you see Cork, Tipp, Waterford or Clare battling against each other, you can see it is in their blood, part of who they are and what they stand for. There are plenty of Cork people who are fanatical about hurling but would have little interest in how their county does in football. Hurling is their identity. It just doesn't have that same cachet in Dublin. Football is who we are, as it is in Kerry or Tyrone or Armagh.

But Dublin fans do want to see the hurlers doing well and want to see them playing in Croke Park. However, you get the feeling that until they're actually competing and beating the likes of Clare or Waterford, then they'll look on merely as distant spectators away from the grounds. So is this my roundabout way of trying to explain why I'm not in Portlaoise to see Dublin take Wexford in the Leinster hurling championship semi-final? Family stuff — a 40th birthday party this time — has intervened. It does however seem easier to have these things intervene when it's the hurlers who are playing.

In between helping out with the barbecue and the drinks, I catch snippets of the game online. Going in 0-11 to 2-01 up, the Dubs should have been further ahead and there is a fear that by not taking their chances they would come to rue it in the second half. Sure enough Wexford reel Dublin in. It's nip and tuck for the last few minutes and Wexford level it before being awarded a free in injury time. Thankfully it sails wide and the Dubs live to fight another day. Croke Park beckons for them in the replay, but it will be interesting to see how much stomach Dublin fans have for a Leinster hurling semi-final in their home town. This should be a sign of just how far the hurling revolution still has to travel in Dublin.

**JUNE**
**15**
**Sunday**

There are a couple of matches of note on today and I'll catch them on the *Sunday Game* later on tonight. In fairness though, I'm not expecting any shocks or upsets between Kerry v Clare and Cork v Limerick in the Munster football championship or between Kilkenny v Offaly in the Leinster hurling. It's becoming a problem for the GAA now, the one-sided and predictable nature of games, and it will keep fans away if things don't improve.

On the radio after the game though, I do catch word that Kerry captain Paul Galvin was sent off for an altercation with the ref. Unfortunately it seems to be the only incident of note from the entire day's games, although word is that Cork were very lucky to get past Limerick.

I make sure I'm in to catch the *Sunday Game* this evening and, sure enough, the Galvin sending off is pathetic and stupid. It seems as though he was getting involved in tussles with his marker, went to complain to the linesman, who then reported it to the ref. The referee gave them both a yellow, and with that Galvin was off for receiving his second yellow. But seeing him slap the book out of referee Paddy Russell's hands was unbelievable, before he then ran over to give the linesman an earful. Even his team mate Tomás Ó Sé got pushed away by Galvin as he tried to calm him down. It was reminiscent of Roy Keane raging and out of control and you'd sometimes wonder about Irish sportsmen, given Keane as their sporting role model.

I remember an interview Tom Humphries did with Paul Galvin a few weeks ago in which he spoke of his reputation preceding him and all that; but in his first outing as the Kerry captain, to get sent off in such a way is unforgivable and idiotic. At least for once it's not Dublin players getting it in the neck for their lack of discipline.

The Galvin sending off does though distract attention away from Limerick who should have beaten Cork in Munster's other game. Limerick were three points up with just two minutes left when, incredibly, they conceded two soft goals to let Cork slip in as three-point winners. After the strike and refusing to play under Teddy Holland, a first round loss to Limerck would have put the footballers under huge pressure. What, after all, people would be asking, was the strike all about if they couldn't even beat Limerick? Between that and the Cork hurlers being beaten by Tipp, suddenly Cork players are having to justify their strike action this year. Every defeat or near miss just gives more ammunition to their detractors. It's Kerry v Cork in the Munster football final in July then, but it's hard to see anything but a Kerry victory. Whether Paul Galvin will be there to lead Kerry out will be the question.

**JUNE 16 Monday**

Sure enough, it's Paul Galvin getting full coverage in the papers this morning. It's nice to see it's not just the Dubs who have to face the brunt of the media pack. Quoting the rule book, we're being told that the minimum ban Galvin faces is twelve weeks, which would rule him out until the All-Ireland final. Galvin comes out and apologises for his actions, but it all smacks of damage limitation and a PR exercise. RTÉ's Cork reporter, Paschal Sheehy, was contacted and told Galvin wanted to speak, and his apologies are across the news this evening.

The more you see the incident, the more idiotic Galvin appears. Fans are saying that if it happened in rugby the player would be banned for life, while other Dublin fans are making the point that if it was one of ours, he'd be locked up in the Joy for that. Kerry players, officials and ex-players however are coming out and, while not condoning his actions, are quick to defend him. The wagons are being circled and it must be because Kerry are only expecting the worst from it all. And good enough. The last thing you would want to see is this belligerent attitude to referees that we see every week on the

Premiership. The GAA needs to foster a rugby-style code of conduct that sees players, whilst they might be kicking lumps out of each other on the pitch, nevertheless respect the officials no matter what. Zero tolerance should be the GAA's policy.

I don't know which is more interesting at this moment: the fall-out from the Galvin sending off or the fall-out from the No vote to the Lisbon Treaty. One has more relevance and importance to my daily life, whilst the other is just about the future of Europe. Maybe we should just come out now and say, 'Yep, you're all right. We're actually just in it for the moola and since there's no more of it to be had, and we have to put up with Johnny Foreigner as well, we're not into this Europe malarkey any more and will be pulling out, locking our doors and going back to kicking lumps out of each other on the GAA pitches instead. So, thanks for the good times. See you in the next European Championship.'

Would make an interesting press release from Brian Cowen, don't you think? And we could get Paul Galvin to deliver it at the steps of the EU parliament. If any officials took umbrage, sure Galvin would sort them all out real quick. Hopefully we'd all get a longer than six month ban from Europe after that.

It's the CCCCCCCCC decision on Galvin today and it's even harsher than anyone expected — 24 weeks — which means he's out for the rest of the year. Everyone was expecting 12 weeks, but 24, phew! The GAA is laying down the law in relation to conduct towards their officials. This will be a big blow to Kerry's plans for the All-Ireland, but rest assured there will be appeals all the way to the DRA. I wouldn't be saying this if it had been a Dublin player on the receiving end of course, but fair play to the Central Competitions' Control Committee (CCCC).

It's been easy to get caught up in the Galvin affair and forget that the European Championships have been on for nearly two weeks now. We're not there and without England there, having watched them fail gloriously, has made it all a lot less fun. It's become a bit of a purists' tournament in the absence of any British or Irish team and the quality of Holland and Spain in particular makes you think it could be one of those special championships.

A word of hope for us Dubs fans who think the Kerry domination will never end. Tonight Italy beat France 2–0 to qualify for the quarters and send France home. This French team has finally come to an end. After winning the World Cup and Europeans their time is up and someone else has to take their place. Like New Zealand in rugby and Liverpool in soccer, all empires must come to an end. The sooner Kerry's does the better for us all.

This is the life, I tell you. We're in the middle of the Championship season and also have a European football tournament to help get us through June; oh, and we've also got the Olympics to keep us company in August in between Championship Sundays.

Not only that but Euro 08 has been one of the best I can remember (apart from the Platini-inspired France of 84). There's football on once if not twice most nights and there are the weekends of the Championship. I'm close to being divorced and I'm not even married yet. I think she's getting a glimpse of things to come from August onwards, and she's not liking it. Of course I tell her that as I work in the sports media, it's all for work purposes so there's not a lot I can do about it really. I don't know how long this will last before I'm told to get a job on something like the *Late, Late* instead.

Germany beat Portugal 3-2 in the quarter-finals and at long last Ronaldo is out of the tournament and we won't have to put up with his petulant goings-on on the pitch. Though I'm a United fan, I can't stand his showboating and indulgent style of play. Real want him for €100 m? Go right ahead and sign on the dotted line is what I say. And good riddance! I'll take a Kaka and a Robinho for that amount, thank you very much. Ronaldo is just symptomatic of modern sport and modern sports stars these days. It's all about him, the money and the attention, and the sooner we don't have to be dealing with him playing for the club the better. Hard to believe that he is being valued at twice what Real paid Juventus for Zidane. Ronaldo is a constant reminder of the road that professional sport has gone down and it is only going to get worse the more they pump money into the game in England, Spain and Italy. Is it any wonder Irish fans are turning more and more towards the GAA and away from the Premiership stars.

I have a theory on this disaffection towards soccer and it's called 'Dublin are the new Celtic'. My theory is that during the Troubles, despite our (by and large) condemnation of IRA violence, there was still a certain identity and affinity with the anti-Englishness of what was at stake. We mightn't have given a damn whether the Six Counties stayed as part of the United Kingdom or not, but we certainly couldn't bring ourselves to like the Ulster unionists and loyalists. We couldn't bring ourselves either to support the IRA, but we could sing ballads about the Irish Republic and in sporting terms that meant supporting Celtic.

For Irish, Ulster and Scottish fans, wasn't Celtic v Rangers just the conflict mirrored between two clubs on a football pitch? Rangers symbolised loyalism and unionism, whereas Celtic were the club for nationalists and republicans. It wasn't morally OK to support the IRA, but it was all right to cheer on Celtic in the Old Firm derbies. Never mind the saying that war was politics by other means; for Northern Ireland, Scottish football was the substitute for politics and sometimes war. The wearing of a Celtic jersey was a mini statement of sorts but one that was as acceptable as singing 'The Fields of Athenry'. It gave us a safe identity and association with Irish nationalism and notions of Irishness.

But with the Troubles all but over and power sharing between Sinn Fein and the DUP up and running, what place then for Celtic v Rangers? If you weren't actually into Scottish football, then its potency as a clash representing other ideals had gone. Suddenly you didn't have to hate Rangers and the Celtic jersey didn't have the same identity as before. For if the IRA had stood down and Sinn Fein were in power with the DUP, what then did it all stand for? Internationally, Ireland and Celtic means nothing and now that the province is at peace, Celtic is just another football club in a backwater league.

The Dublin jersey seems to be now taking its place. The last ten years of change and multi-culturalism has seen a new and different city and county arise. It's one where Africans, Asians and Europeans mix as freely as native Irish people; you're as likely to see black and Asian faces and to hear Polish or Mandarin being spoken on Henry Street. And into this mix has come an identity crisis for Dublin people. What does it mean now to be a Dubliner if it has become an eclectic melting pot of races and nations? Is Dublin Henry Street or Grafton Street? Arnott's or Brown Thomas? Or is it the new Parnell Street or the multinational suburbs? Is it the Spire or is it the GPO? Is it Polish shops or is it Carroll's?

We're stuck between two stools, it seems, between developing as a multicultural modern city a la London or New York, as against knowing who we were and are as a city and as a people ourselves. We might have had badges of identity for what it meant to be Irish — Guinness, *Riverdance*, traditional music — but we never put symbols or meaning to what it meant to be a Dub. Now in this changed city all we feel that is left is the Dublin GAA team, the jersey and Croke Park. It all comes back to the local now, and to be Dublin means the Dublin GAA team. For the Dubs are now the only outward identification of something that is intangible in identity terms. To be a Dub means wearing the county jersey and going to Croke Park in the summer.

And so, where the Celtic jersey now has little or no meaning left any more, wearing the Dublin jersey has become the new identity. In looking to cling on to the local, the Dublin and even other GAA jerseys have started to become imbued with a certain amount of local nationalism and identity. It's easy to know what it is to be a Kerry or Tyrone person or Clare or Waterford folk. To be a Dub has become a harder question to answer over the last ten years and the county jersey offers a simple answer.

**JUNE 21 Saturday**

The purists' dream has died once more as the Dutch football team exits the European Championships. Marco van Basten's team were threatening to rival their Euro 88 counterparts, but this time, in a reverse of the final 20 years ago, it was Russia who came out winners 3-1. That's the thing about sport. Rarely is there a fairytale ending any more. Money and tactics will win out — Greece beating Portugal four years ago to win Euro 04 for example. And this year? It looks like the Russian oligarch money that has been pumped into Russian football will pay dividends. In today's sporting landscape money can buy you success. Just ask Roman Abramovich at Chelsea. It's interesting to see how the Russian oil billionaires are using their wealth — at the behest of Putin — to revitalise Russia's standing via sport. They already have the 2014 Winter Olympics at Sochi; Zenit St Petersburg won the UEFA Cup; they're rumoured to be bidding for the 2018 World Cup; and it's only a matter of time before a Russian football team becomes Champions League winners. Sure they even hired Timbaland to produce their victorious song in the Eurovision! A Russian win at the Europeans would top it all off nicely for them.

I wonder is that what sport will eventually become — a playground for the billionaires to flex their egos, might and national pride. Maybe it's about time our billionaires got in on the act and we saw the likes of Denis O'Brien, Seán Quinn and Tony O'Reilly pumping vanity money into Irish sports teams. We hear a lot about Irish wealth and development, so why not see it tried and tested on the playing pitch.

## JUNE 22 Sunday

## Leinster Hurling Championship semi-final replay, Dublin 1-15, Wexford 2-15, Croke Park

I probably shouldn't be admitting this in a fan's book about following the Dubs. While it is about following the football team, the hurlers deserve to be part of the story as well and, truth be told, my commitment to their cause has been tested in this Championship. I've had excuses such as family birthdays, work, house renovations, and I did truly plan on getting to Croke Park today, no matter what.

It's the Dublin v Wexford Leinster semi-final replay and all the stories in the run-up to today's game predicted how few fair weather Dublin fans would bother turning up to see their hurlers in action. Another cross for us fans to bear, but unfortunately most of the commentators were spot on. What's worse, I too was one of those fickle followers who failed to make it on the day. And my excuse? Although it hurts to admit this publicly, it was Dolly Parton.

I was reminded this morning over breakfast — just as I had casually mentioned to my better half that I would be moseying on down to Croker for an old game, don't you know — that I wouldn't be doing anything of the sort. Had I forgotten my brain or something? Hadn't I bought her tickets for the two of us to see Dolly Parton in Nowlan Park this evening?

Shite! That's right. I cast my mind back to Christmas when they were bought as a present. Didn't see that one coming, I have to admit. In future all Christmas gifts will have to be bought with an exclusion zone of May to September built into them.

Who would have thought it? Not being able to see the hurlers in Croker because I had to go to Kilkenny, to Nowlan Park itself, not to see any hurling but to watch Dolly Parton doing 'Nine to Five'. When you're caught on the hop like that there's only one thing to do and that's surrender immediately and hope she remembers how noble and generous I was in giving up this Sunday for Dolly. I'm storing these days away for bigger ones needed later in the summer, I hope.

So, despite having a great chance of reaching their first Leinster final since 1981 with a squad as good as they've had in years, and with the rest of Dublin waiting, just waiting for them to make that breakthrough, the hurlers then go and come up short once again, beaten convincingly. I don't know what was more galling: failing when it was wanted so badly or the embarrassing support given to the Dublin hurlers by our fans. Just 25,000 turned up in Croker today for the double-header of Laois-Wexford in the football and Dublin-Wexford in the hurling. And probably just 5,000 were Dublin supporters. The Hill was a sparse, ghostly reminder each time the camera moved towards that end. There were pockets of blue, but more, much more concrete swathes to be seen. You could nearly hear the echoes of the fans bouncing off the empty steps, eerie reminders of how shallow the support for Dublin hurling is.

But who am I to talk? Before the game was even finished (I caught the end on the radio in the car) we were heading out of the city to go see an American country and western singer. Choice or not in the affair, it was still painful to know I was part of the faceless stay-away hordes. I didn't want to believe it could happen but here was proof enough, if it was ever needed, that hurling just isn't in our blood, that we are a football county first and foremost. Come back to me in 25 years' time if the hurlers are winning All-Irelands and prove me wrong, but in the meantime the image of the empty Hill stayed with me as we drove to Nowlan Park.

And for the record, arriving in Kilkenny for the gig, I have never seen so many blonde wigs and fake boobs at one venue since one horrendous Friday evening spent in the Ice Bar at the Four Seasons in Ballsbridge three years ago, when I spent the whole night averting my eyes and trying hard to stare at the floor instead.

Forgive me, father, for I have sinned. It's been three months since my last Dublin hurling game.

**JUNE 23 Monday**

While the year of the Dublin hurling revolution has to wait once more, the real story of the Championship has been the Wexford footballers making it to their first Leinster final since 1956. What's more remarkable is that they have done it with a coach who is still not even a year in the job, has yet to hit 32, and was once a Waterford footballer. What was that I said about there being no fairytales in sport any more? If Dublin get past Westmeath, we'll know more about the long-term fate of fairytales come 20 July.

In the hurling, of course, the Dublin fans get a pasting for their poor support yesterday. I'm one of the guilty parties in this so I'm going to keep my head down, but I will say one thing. Why is it OK for other counties to have mediocre fan support some days and not Dublin? Kerry fans only travel in great numbers for All-Ireland finals. Same for Kilkenny. The fair weather fan is not just confined to Dublin, but there seems to be some sort of expectation that we should be turning out 50,000 plus for every game, no matter what.

On a more positive note, Clare's defeat of Limerick has their fans harking back to a return to the 1990s. Imagine another Banner county revival. Jesus! I don't know whether the capital would be ready for another influx of those Clare hoors on All-Ireland final day. They're still cleaning up the puke around Dorset Street and O'Connell Street from their celebrations in 95 and 97; and I can still hear their daft 'whoo-hoo-whoo-hoo-hoo' chant ringing in my ears as I walked past their hordes clustered around the chippers in the aftermath, eating sausage in batter as if it was an exotic dish brought in by newly arrived immigrants.

**JUNE 24 Tuesday**

'We blew the boom,' declares the *Irish Independent* headline this morning. The ESRI has come out and declared we're in a recession. About time somebody had the balls to do it. The curmudgeon in me is glad. Not that I'd go back to the bad old days of the 1980s, but when you hear of women in Galway pulling each other's hair out to get their hands on the new, exclusive G reg

SUV, and when you go into the Ice Bar on a Friday night, it's time to say stop and call a halt to proceedings.

I just hope we're not too late and haven't all become complete wankers over the last decade in the process. Will we find it hard to give up our panninis and lattes and go back to sausages and rashers? Will we actually be able to drop the now all too prevalent arrogance and ignorance that pervades our psyche that says to one and all, 'Fuck you. I'm unhappy so don't think I'm going down alone with it.'

I know it's bad when I drive around Tipperary, Kerry or Galway and find people on the country roads driving up your tail, rushing to overtake, and all in a rush to get to nowhere. Before we were in no rush to get to anywhere at all. Now we don't know where we'll be going in the future and I hope some sanity will return. 'It's all rush, rush, busy, busy, drive the big car, pay big prices for everything', was how one French angler described the Ireland he now saw to me. 'In future I think I maybe go fishing to New Zealand now instead' he said, shrugging his shoulders. You and me both, Pierre. You and me both.

**JUNE**
**25**
**Wednesday**

Let the real games begin. The naming of the Dublin team on the Wednesday before the match signals the start of the build-up for us Dublin fans. We've Westmeath to face in the Leinster semi-final and from here on in there's plenty to be discussing.

This evening's team news is a bit of a shocker from Pillar Caffrey as he has dropped Paul Casey from the half back line. Dubs fans have been moaning about Casey for the last few years and even Dubs favourite Charlie Redmond had come out saying it in his newspaper column the other week. So now it seems that Pillar has taken note of what Charlie has written! It's an interesting call from Caffrey especially as he has been so reluctant to change things around, and why change now that the Championship has already started?

But the big talking point has to be the omission of Hill favourite/focus of abuse — delete where necessary — Ciaran Whelan. Whelan had been suspended following his scuffle against Meath in Parnell Park of course, and while Eamonn Fennell had a storming match against Louth, one would have thought Whelan would have easily reclaimed his place. By leaving Fennell in the side in place of Whelan and by also dropping Casey, is this a new Caffrey we're seeing? Is he admitting that some changing of the guard is necessary in his last chance at Sam?

One would have thought Dublin fans would have been up in arms at the dropping of Whelan, but chatting to fans and going online to the forums shows most Dubs to be happy enough with the arrangement and hoping to see Whelan come off the bench as an impact sub with 20 minutes to go. That might be all right against Leinster counties, but can we really afford to be leaving our All Star with just 20 minutes' game time against the likes of Kerry or Armagh?

I can't see this arrangement lasting although I would like to see Whelan and Fennell both in midfield together, similar players as they are. It's only the second game of the Championship, but the question marks about the starting 15 and our spine still remain. We've never been settled through the middle from the backs all the way through to the forwards, and the pundits have long been saying it's our downfall. Wonder what Caffrey will decide to do. Hang on, I'll go see what Charlie Redmond has been writing.

**JUNE 27 Friday**

The GAA aren't showing Paul Galvin any sympathy in his appeals process. Today the Central Appeals Committee (CAC) upheld the six months ban and now all that's left to him and Kerry is the Disputes Resolution Authority (DRA). Going by previous bans they too should uphold the sentence which would leave Galvin out for the season. Harsh though the ban is, fair play to the GAA for sticking to their guns in relation to crossing the line with their officials. The question now is, how will it affect the Kerry camp and could Galvin's loss be a chink in their armour for later in the season?

**JUNE 28 Saturday**

Normally Galway v Antrim in the qualifiers wouldn't merit a mention, but today sees the Championship debut of Joe Canning and anything the Portumna man does these days is covered by acres of newsprint. For a 19-year old he's handling the whole situation with the maturity of someone ten years older and you just hope it lasts. He's a special, special talent, the sort who would even make non-hurling fans sit up and take notice. If Canning does well, then hurling will do well. Maybe more so than the Dubs. Perhaps it's not the Dublin hurling revolution we should be trumpeting, but the Canning one.

A bit like Tiger Woods in golf, Canning could be the torch paper that lights up the general sports fan's interest in hurling and bring the GAA to a whole new audience.

Imagine the rugby or soccer types gawping in awe and wonder at his skills on the pitch in the maroon for Galway. Actually, on second thoughts, maybe we should keep him wrapped up and away from the spotlight after all.

## JUNE 29 Sunday — Leinster Football Championship semi-final, Dublin 0-13, Westmeath 1-08, Croke Park

The second big day of the summer dawns. It's Dublin v Westmeath in the Leinster semi-final. And I'm not even nervous or perturbed. But I should be. Westmeath gave us a pasting in the Division 2 League final and Dublin have been stuttering of late. And Whelan is on the bench. Will he be needed to save the day late on? We hope not, but it's Dublin and you just never know.

Again it's not a sell-out — 60,000 pack into the stadium — making you wonder why the other 20,000 should be let in for the Leinster final or the All-Ireland series. It's not helped of course by the fact that the provincial championships just don't mean as much nowadays. Munster hurling and Ulster football excepted, the back door system means that for counties the provincials aren't the be all and end all any more. However try telling that to the Wexford fans who are in their first Leinster final for over 50 years. But for Dublin who are going for four in a row, who cares? Leinster is merely an obstacle to be endured and overcome before the real season begins. But if we don't win it, then Dublin are in 'crisis', 'downfall', or just plain 'crap'. It's a no-win situation for them, but thems the breaks for being one of the big boys. So let's get this provincial road-block out of the way as soon as possible and start to test ourselves against Kerry and the likes.

The crowds around Fairview and Meagher's are as busy as ever — at least this end of Dublin isn't holding back on their support. It must be the southside element that's staying away. I'm sure the pubs the far side of Summerhill are empty and waiting to open their doors, but not until August.

We get the last pints in and head for the Hill crossing over Luke Kelly bridge. It's 1.45 and we're early for the game at 2 pm. But when we get to the Hill and squeeze ourselves on to the steps midway behind the goal, the teams don't arrive out until ten past. It's another delayed throw-in. But this time the Hill is jam-packed on time. A lot of the Hogan and Cusack stands are not full yet and it's the feckin prawn sandwich brigade who are holding things up as they throw back another canapé to be washed down with their aperitif. I've said it before and I'll say it again, the GAA is going down the wrong road. If they're delaying games now because of the crowds in the stands while the Hill looks impatiently on, then there's no hope left at all. But I'm sure the fans on the Hill will be blamed for it anyway in tomorrow's papers.

The downpour on the way in doesn't improve our humour and the ominous-looking black clouds lying in wait just behind the Canal End are the last thing we need today. And, just as the ball is thrown in, some punter standing near me on the steps and wearing a Dubs cap wants to know how long will the game be on for! I take a deep breath, mutter something under my breath and hope those black clouds come, hover right over my friend here and tell him what I think. It seems not all southsiders stayed at home today.

Westmeath start brightly before Dublin get a few points of their own on the board. But it's another unimpressive opening from the Dubs. As another Westmeath attack comes towards the Hill, my hand goes into my jeans pocket to make sure the small betting slip is still there. Twenty quid laid on at 10/1 says Westmeath will be leading at half-time and Dublin will win at full time. It's my little dark secret — well nearly. I make the mistake of telling two of the lads I'm with, and now every time Westmeath score they both turn around and say 'You must be pleased', while when Dublin score it's 'Not cheering now are you, eh?' I'm soon getting strange looks from other fans on the Hill wondering what the hell is going on.

I just stand there grim faced. I nod and tell them to turn around and 'watch the fuckin game'. But I am secretly thinking, 200 quid I could be collecting here today. What would I do with 200 quid?

And then Dublin score in injury time in the first half and the teams go in level at the break. 'Not to worry, eh?' the two mates chime in. 'It would have been nice getting your hands on that money.' Yes, I think, and it would be nice for you to get out alive if you don't keep going on as if I'm cheering for the Dubs to lose. I'm not quite as crazy as the fan I saw earlier on walking in through the turnstiles and on to the Hill wearing a Meath — not Westmeah, but Meath — jersey. I think I may have heard his stifled cries coming from the back of the Hill a while ago.

It's another muted Hill at half-time and even the deadened atmosphere continues into the second half. It's only livened up by the yo-yoing substitution of Ciaran Whelan who seems to be on and off the pitch every few minutes as a blood sub replacement for Shane Ryan. 'Leave him on for fuck sake', shout a few on the Hill — the impact Whelan is making is obvious for all to see. Today Whelan is a hero to the Hill.

Worryingly, in the first half Bernard Brogan pulls up with a hamstring injury while chasing a ball down the sideline and it looks like he'll be out for a month at least with that one. Jayo is having an off-day and Keaney doesn't look like he has started the season — never mind the game — yet. Ross McConnell was hauled off at half-time with David Henry put in as full back, and you have to ask why change things so drastically now? Why at half-time of a Leinster semi-final are we tinkering with our full back position? Could this not have been done sometime between January and May? There's still nothing settled in the minds of the management it seems, and it's unsettling the Hill as well as the team.

But in the end we just about have enough. Westmeath kick enough wides to let us out of jail and we manage to kick a few late points to pull away. In fairness we never looked like letting them steal a march on us during the game, and while it may have been tense, Dublin's experience sees them through in the last five minutes. It's this rather than talent which will get us only so far. But it's cuteness we will need for later stages.

We leave the Hill not satisfied but glad the job has been done. Is it getting over the line that matters or doing it in style, we wonder. As ever the questions over the full back position are still there, as is the question of whether Whelan will be starting next time around.

We face a resurgent Wexford in July, but for now that's weeks away. The season is stop-start this time of the year and there has been nothing to get excited about so far. The post-mortems in Chaplin's on Townsend Street move quickly on from the Dublin game — there's only so much you can get excited about in a game against Westmeath — and we're soon engrossed in the clash between Armagh and Down on the telly.

I spot Con Houlihan sitting at the corner of the bar. The big hulk of a man has aged, but he still looks as shy as ever behind those furtive Kerry eyes of his. He has seen many GAA days and many good ones for Dublin football as well, but today his back is turned to the match on the TV. Even for Con this time of year seems to be an exercise in false skirmishes. There's nothing to be getting excited about just yet, his body language seems to be saying. And as ever, he's probably right. Soon the plates of sandwiches are being passed around and for a minute you'd forget you were in Dublin at all.

**JUNE 30 Monday**

As ever, the light relief from a sore head the next day can be found online. Someone was quick off the mark about the Dubs fans turning up late for yesterday's game and has come up with the new Ticketmaster page for the Leinster final tickets (notice the instruction on the bottom right-hand corner of the image and the sarcastic comment on the top left):

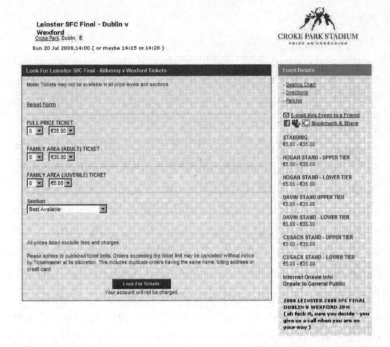

The Leinster final is a good three weeks away and in the meantime I have a wedding to organise, a house to renovate, and to somehow try and talk up this Leinster final. Who would ever have thought that going for four in a row would be such a hard thing to get excited about? I wonder what the GAA equivalent of Viagra would be.

# JULY
## MISSING IN ACTION

**JULY**
**4**
**Friday**

The GAA disciplinary process is turning into a farce and making a mockery of itself. Colin Moran has been banned for four weeks by the CHC (if you think you know what CHC should really stand for, answers on a postcard please). This is trial by TV now. Moran's ban — for a shoulder challenge that turned bad when his opponent slipped and fell into Moran's shoulder — only came about when the 'experts' on the *Sunday Game* that night decided to pick out this moment and declare that it should have been a sending off. Lo and behold the GAA ask the ref to think again about the incident and he decides to change his mind and agrees with what the *Sunday Game* panel decreed.

And now here we are with Collie Moran set to miss the Leinster final because of what a TV show thinks and because of the spineless way in which the disciplinary body bows to media talk. What, we wonder out loud that night in the pub, of the hundreds of other incidents that go unchecked and unnoticed by the officials and the *Sunday Game*. Is it only when pundits highlight something that it becomes important? It's all a sad indictment of the way the GAA is going in terms of bowing to commercial and media entities every step of the way.

There's plenty to get us talking tonight after work. The brewing row between Tadhg Kenneally in Australia and the Aussie Rules agent Ricky Nixon, who is in Ireland to organise a recruitment camp and meet up with the GAA, has shown just how fractious this whole issue will be. Do we really want organised draft camps with Aussie Rules clubs and agents coming over here? Do we have to make it so easy for them to come over and tap up our best emerging talent?

Most of us agree tonight it shouldn't be so easy for them to come over, but then we ask, how do you stop them? And isn't it better to have it done openly and with some form of control than by undercover methods or by stealth of night? There are no solutions to be found this evening in the pub and there's a general lack of faith that there won't be any found in GAA HQ either.

Over a few pints we've managed to right the Collie Moran issue, denounce the *Sunday Game*, solve the Palestinian problem and ease global warming. But we can't come up with an answer to players going to the AFL. And there's barely a mention of the ECB raising their interest rates to the highest in seven years. Or that it's American Independence Day. Any mention of the Yanks invariably means Bush raises his ugly head, as well as that of their fucked-up housing and financial economies. Before Bush the Americans were always good for a laugh, but nowadays they seem to bring nothing but headaches; now, like religion and politics, they're best left off the table. Sport's intractable problems are always more interesting than the cold light of reality anyway. Plus, it's the weekend; let us leave talk of bills and mortgages for the working week. There's Kerry v Cork in the Munster football final and some hurling to look forward to on Saturday and Sunday.

Cork beating Kerry — again? Who would have thought it possible? I didn't bother watching the game — especially as I heard on the radio during the first half that Kerry were eight points up. Nobody comes back at Kerry from that margin. Or so I thought. After coming in from an afternoon excursion to God knows where, aka some home improvement store, I catch the incredible result and hear that Cork have come back from the dead and beaten Kerry by five points. Kerry only scored three points in the second half and it ranks as one of their worst implosions in their Championship history. But how much do provincial titles matter any more? Aside from the Munster Hurling Championship, nowhere else do they really matter; it's only in the likes of Dublin where hype and hubris are king and that 'lording' it in Leinster is seen as some kind of badge of honour.

No, Cork will take solace from this victory only in the fact that when it comes to the latter part of the All-Ireland, they know they can dig deep within themselves. For Kerry, losing Munster is no big deal — but losing it like this is. The provinces now are mere sparring grounds, a way to find out some more about yourself when it comes to the All-Ireland proper. Still though, for a Dub it augurs well if a Kerry team can capitulate like that. Cork may be Munster champions, but Kerry wounded is still a dangerous animal. Maybe, just maybe, chinks in their armour are appearing which the rest of us can exploit.

Just to prove how little the provinces now mean, Kilkenny win another Leinster title today as well. No news in that really. And no news in the fact that their whipping boys this time around — Wexford — were hammered 5-

21 to 0-17, a margin of 19 points. Just what is the point in these facile victories, everyone is asking. Is it that the rest of Leinster is so bad or that Kilkenny are that good? It's a bit of both, but it's also a fact that only Munster hurling teams can give Kilkenny a run for their money these days. So how to answer the provincial conundrum?

Should we revert to a Champions League style format and give weaker counties a chance to qualify by vying against each other? But then, why have a mini league when we already have the National League earlier in the year? So many questions and still so few answers. Minor tinkering with the competition over the last few years has neither done the sport any good nor improved the overall standards. The weaker counties are still getting left behind while Kilkenny just pull further and further away from everyone else. Only something radical can shake things up, it seems, and maybe the Champions League is the way to go. But then, does that mean you scrap the Munster Championship altogether? So many questions . . .

Kerry's collapse may have been the big talking point in the GAA over the weekend, but on a rare occasion this summer Gaelic games take second place this Sunday. Rafael Nadal beat Roger Federer in a five-set epic thriller in the Wimbledon final to win what is being described as the greatest tennis match of all time. It was scintillating, pulsating, nerve-jangling, heroic and all-engulfing. And I didn't see one minute of it.

As the match entered its fifth set and as the light faded, I sat at home blissfully oblivious to what was going on just a few channels over on the BBC. Many times in sport when it comes to favourites and inevitable outcomes, I bow my head to the expected result, get on with life and nod knowingly when I read later that yes indeed Kilkenny/Federer/Chelsea/Kerry have won. Kilkenny's facile Leinster hurling victory today is a case in point. Why waste a few hours of your precious weekend in a one-sided game that you know will end up with a runaway victory for the favourite? But this time I should have known better.

I stayed up all night to watch the Patriots make American football history back in February and was witness to an unbelievable game — one that many say was the greatest Superbowl ever. Today it was Federer v Nadal, seeds 1 and 2, and Federer was looking to make Wimbledon history by becoming the first man ever to win six in a row there. In the process he was up against his nemesis, Nadal, who had trounced Federer in the French Open final. This Wimbledon encounter was an obvious one in hindsight really. It was destined to be an absolute humdinger of a game. Instead, I paid lip service to it earlier in the morning, forgot about it totally later on, got caught up in Cork's win over Kerry, and then proceeded to only start channel flicking just as Nadal was lifting the trophy and BBC's commentators gushed about tennis's greatest ever night.

Ah shit! I thought. The match I forgot all about and now I'm hearing it was one to live in the memory. Watching the highlights later on still couldn't quell my disappointment. This was one sporting occasion I had missed and wouldn't be getting back anytime in the next 20 years. Does that mean then that I have to sit through every tennis final, every soccer match, every hurling and Gaelic football game, every week of every year, in the distant hope that this one might just be the classic?

Sorry. Sports nut I may be, but sports lunatic without a life, wife or friends I won't be. I'll continue to weigh up the odds, take my chances and in the cold light of day do whatever the better half tells me to. Play the greater odds for the easier life is my motto.

**JULY 9 Wednesday** Travelling and working between Dublin and Tipp, where the missus is from, has given my life a certain exotic glamour this year. Heading off into the sunset, leaving Dublin far behind me, always makes me feel warm inside, as if I'm leaving the stresses and strains of life. It's my city and my town, but I always like to leave it behind and be embraced by the peacefulness and familiarity of the countryside. In the eyes of my friends I've become a bit of a nomad; my Marco Polo-esque excursions beyond the Pale leave them shaking their heads in bewilderment, while others say, 'Jaysus, you lucky bastard!' Returning again unannounced a few days later and I'm greeted like a long-lost soul who needs to share his stories about the natives beyond the city walls.

In a way I've become an outsider in Dublin and I'm already an outsider in Tipperary. It's not that you're not wanted — more that you don't fit in any more. We're not easily boxed now. Are we Dubs or culchies? No one knows for sure and no one knows what to do with us. But not fitting in has always come naturally to me. I've always liked the 'outsider' tag, feeling you can't be easily categorised. When my family emigrated to

Australia in 1989, we were the talked-about ones in our suburb, the ones who had dared to sell up and start a new life. And then when we came back less than a year later, when my family didn't like the life or culture down under, we were talked about all the more. We were the ones who had thrown in the towel and come home. But my parents weren't afraid to say, 'We tried it and it didn't work out, so here we are back again.' I was also the one on our return who had the Australian accent — which I soon got rid of before it was beaten out of me. I always felt most at home in my own skin, beating my own drum. So now, once again, living between Tipperary and Dublin, I was an outsider again.

Until, that is, I pulled into Thurles train station this morning. Parking the car as I prepared to get the train up to Dublin for the day, I spotted the unmistakable blue of a Dubs flag flying from a car; and on the back window was an 'Up the Dubs' sticker. My heart leapt for joy and a big, stupid grin wrapped itself across my face. I suddenly felt my heart strings tugging for 'home'. I always saw myself as one of no fixed abode, but seeing this unexpected declaration for the Dubs down in Tipperary, I immediately felt lighter and happier.

This car belonged to an exile too. And they weren't afraid to hang on to their Dublin-ness or proclaim it loudly — not in a fucking-eejit-amn't-I-bleedin-deadly way, but in a way that I knew these were lost Dublin souls trapped beyond the capital like myself.

We'll keep flying the flag, I thought happily to myself. We'll keep flying the flag.

**JULY 11 Friday**

It's the theme of the summer: bad news, followed by bad news. The ISEQ plunges even more and I'm reading about losses of €3 billion; the government is announcing more cutbacks and uncertainty fills the air. No one knows how many jobs will be lost, for how long the recession will continue, and if we'll have homes to pay for before too long.

But sometimes the ridiculousness of it all can only make you laugh in a black comic way at how shit things are getting. The radar in Dublin Airport has broken down since Wednesday, resulting in thousands and thousands of stranded passengers and flights being delayed and cancelled. When asked how such a situation could happen, one Dublin Airport spokesperson replied, 'Sometimes these things just happen.'

Can't you buy a car sticker somewhere that says just that? Shit happens. But why is it that more of it seems to happen at the same time?

**JULY 12 Saturday**

*All-Ireland hurling qualifier, round 3, Cork 1-17, Dublin 0-15, Pairc Uí Chaoimh*

It's a bit like walking the last mile, knowing the end result as you travel the road. Cork is a long way from home and it will be an even longer one on the way back after defeat. I think it's a disgrace that the weaker counties don't get home advantage. This is how to promote hurling GAA style. I mean, a few plonkers like myself might travel, but no one else will, and why should they for a foregone conclusion. 'A complete total and utter joke', says one Dublin fan online and you know he has a point. The Dublin hurlers face Cork *down there* in the hurling qualifiers, but realistically the best we can hope for is sticking it to them and keeping our pride for the long journey home.

We should have been down there earlier in the year with the footballers of course, and how things have changed so quickly since the strike. Their hurlers are looking aged and past their best and it's their footballers now who seem to be on the brink of greater things. Their stance and refusal to play under Teddy Holland now seems to have quietened their many critics, but one gets the feeling that anything less than an All-Ireland, and the knives will be out for them again just as fast.

Friends of Dublin Hurling have organised transport leaving Dublin at 10 am and I'm told about a hundred fans are on board. It's the usual Dublin hurling die-hards who show their support for their team and they'll be trudging more lonely roads until the hurlers make some sort of breakthrough. It's just that we don't expect one today.

I'm travelling down from Tipp for the game and, unlike the other Dublin fans, have only an hour's journey to get me to Cork. I like Cork. I like its atmosphere and attitude that thinks it's so great. Unlike Dublin and Galway, it hasn't sold all of its city soul just yet. There are still small shops down narrow streets competing with the high street brand names and you get the feeling that Corkonians will always support their own just to show everyone else that they can.

It was a lovely evening for hurling down by the Lee and Pairc Uí Chaoimh was eerily quiet as just a few thousand turned up. But that's the way it is when you go to Dublin hurling matches. Playing in Parnell Park and other such smaller venues always makes for a better atmosphere and makes the game feel more alive.

But for those of us who did make the trip down — and the Cork fans who turned up as well — we were so nearly treated to an upset. Cork ran out 1-17 to 0-15 winners in the end, but that only tells a small part of the story. We were ten minutes into the second half and hanging on to Cork's coat tails trailing by just two points when Dublin goalie, Gary Maguire, bungled a clearance to Joe Deane (of all people), who netted easily and put Cork five points up. That sort of lead was always going to be too much for Dublin against a team with the guile, experience and scoring power of Cork, and it proved to be the death-knell for the Dubs.

Still though, we didn't disgrace ourselves. It could have been interesting — who knows — if only we hadn't conceded that sloppy goal. But you don't get away with mistakes like that at this level, and it's even something the footballers are learning when facing the likes of Kerry.

So that's it for another year for the hurlers — another year of what-ifs and maybes, another year when the breakthrough didn't materialise. They say under-age hurling in Dublin is blooming, and that it's just a matter of being patient and waiting until the younger generation matures. Then, they say, we'll see Dublin becoming a force to be reckoned with. But I often wonder, however, that when this mystical day finally arrives, how much further ahead will the likes of Cork and Kilkenny be.

The Dublin minors and U-21s both gave up their Leinster titles this year in dispiriting losses that suggest we still have a long way to climb to match what the likes of Kilkenny are developing at under-age level. The seniors' loss to Wexford in the replay followed by this defeat to Cork were merely the latest in a long line of kicks in the teeth this summer.

Will we be forever playing catch-up, I wonder. At least though, and like many other counties, we refuse to give up the fight. Hurling is a sport to be cherished and nurtured in the capital and, unlike Kilkenny, we are punching above our weight and improving in our weaker sport.

But it's no wonder Kilkenny are obsessed with hurling. Their footballers were beaten today by London (0-08 to 4-13) in the Tommy Murphy Cup. With results like that you would throw in the towel fairly quickly, one suspects.

It's no fun as a fan either. The Friends of Dublin Hurling board their coaches afterwards and face the long journey home. There's plenty to talk about and rue, but that's been the way of it for fans of hurling in the capital and it's something they're all used to by now. As the football fans wonder will this be the year, so too Dublin hurling fans speculate each season, albeit with different expectations, if this will be the year when the breakthrough happens.

For the hurlers it's another summer of disappointments and near-misses to look back on. Let's hope it's not a similar tale of woe for the footballers. At least we have another few weeks to dream. For the hurlers there's just the winter slog of club commitments and training to look forward to.

<table>
<tr><td>

**JULY**
**13**
**Sunday**

</td><td>

It's Munster hurling final day. Tipp are playing Clare down the road from us in Limerick, but I'm on my way to Dublin for work. It's been a summer of going against the flow, it seems.

</td></tr>
</table>

When I should be in Munster I'm on my way to Dublin and when I should be in Dublin I'm invariably on my way to Munster. I like swimming against the tide normally, but on days like this I must be the only one leaving Tipp for the capital. I stop off at a petrol station and look around me jealously as the forecourt fills up with fans in the blue and gold, all set for their trip to Limerick. Me, I fill up the engine (at €1.42 a litre I might add) and gaze wistfully at the phalanx of cars with their flags flying proudly and heading west to Limerick. I turn right instead and head on to the Cashel bypass. Dublin is only two hours away, but it might as well be a lifetime as I leave a promising Muster hurling final behind me.

And sure enough Tipp win their first Munster title since 2001 while I'm left watching it all unfold on the telly. It wasn't a classic or the humdinger of years gone by, but this Tipp team is worth watching and could be the story of the summer. Still unbeaten for the year, you get the feeling their biggest challenge was in the previous game against Cork. Coming through that, and beating Cork on their own patch, they must have been confident going in against a new Clare team. Their superiority showed early on and you can see this Tipp team gaining in confidence with each win.

Could they just be the team to halt Kilkenny's march

this year? The five-week lay-off for being provincial champions until their next game doesn't help and in the meantime the likes of Cork, Galway and Waterford will be building up a head of steam. But the lay-off doesn't affect Kilkenny and they won't accept anything as an excuse for performances less than 100%. So Tipp are Munster champions again and like any county that wins, the feel-good factor permeates throughout the villages and towns. Flags are flying high from houses, bridges, shops, tractors and castles; all the talk in the fields and in the pubs is about Tipp's chances. For the next few weeks at least even the rain won't seem to matter.

It's evening time before I leave Dublin and make my way back down to Tipp. Drive through Dublin and you might not know there's a Leinster final waiting at all. Cross through Urlingford and into Tipperary and the bunting and flags greet you. You're in a hurling county now and the difference after two hours in the car couldn't be more marked. Tonight in Tipp the pubs will be full with only one thing on their minds. In the capital the world turns relentlessly with or without the GAA. Down here in Munster it's part of the fabric of who the people and communities are.

**JULY**
**16**
**Wednesday**

'Will you be going to the game on Sunday?' I ask John, the 'Dubious Dub'. You've already been enlightened as to his thoughts on some elements of the Dublin fan brigade, but I like to tempt him occasionally to see if he can't be for turning back to blue again.

'So there'll finally be a full house on the day, huh? huh? huh? huh?' he blurts out in contempt. 'The pale jocks, shades and brand new Arnott's jersey brigade should be in full effect then. Likewise the little mullet-wearing knack-bags. And let's not forget the ignorant bogger who knows only a couple of terms such as "quarter pounder", "Dublin knackers" and "coppers"; he'll be sure to be in the house also . . .'

'That's a no I take it then?' I ask. John the Dubious Dub can be a welcome anecdote to the Dublinese bejaysus brigade that visit Jones's Road on match days. 'At least,' I say, 'I notice, in the interests of balance, you were equally scathing of the culchie as well as the Dub. Just don't come running to me in September when we're in the final and you've rediscovered your Northside chic.'

John snorts a barely stifled 'as fucking if' and I know that his move wesht has him gone truly all native. We should start calling him Dunbar after the Kevin Costner character in the film *Dances with Wolves* and we'll be expecting him to be wearing the maroon jersey and adding sh's to his ss's very shortly.

Still, it's always nice to be awoken with a jolt and realise the Dubs love-fest isn't all embracing. It's almost a glimpse into the culchie's world view of the Dubs.

John's bad mood I can't put down to the ECB hiking up interest rates — he's renting down in Galway — but I'm sure the economic doom and gloom is hitting even G4 down there. For us worker drones, we're facing increased mortgage payments from next month on. We're starting to hear of friends losing their jobs or failing to get one, having moved on. The good times are over and we're starting to stare into a bleak future. You know things are bad when I read that Lidl are to replace Habitat in College

Green. Things are really hitting rock bottom now. And even the Dubs are becoming culchies.

**JULY 17 Thursday** It's the week leading up to the Leinster final and there's a certain blasé attitude around the city. We're going for four in a row and we're well used to these provincial shake-downs in the summer. It's hard, the city seems to be saying, to get livened up for a local encounter against Wexford. The story really has been about Wexford and their first Leinster final appearance for 52 years. This is their ball while the old hands from the capital merely see this as another stepping stone to the All-Ireland.

It would be great to be in Wexford this week and be surrounded by the infectious enthusiasm and delight at the prospect of just playing in a Leinster final. The cynicism and know-it-all attitude in Dublin is too deeply ingrained in us to be lightened by an encounter against Wexford, but you can't help but be envious of their childlike giddiness about this game.

Jason Ryan's management and revolution with the footballers is the story of the summer as far as I'm concerned. His rise shows that you don't have to be an All Star, All-Ireland medal winner to have managerial success. Finally we're seeing that the introduction of modern sports management and sports science techniques by someone with an attention to detail can take a team places. Hopefully Ryan's prominence will lead to further openings for sportsmen of his ilk and that in future modern management will develop along these more studied lines. It's certainly something the Dubs will have to look at in future years. But that's talk for the winter when the games are gone; for now we're more interested in the team that Caffrey has finally named for Sunday's final.

The incredible thing is that Collie Moran's appeal against his ridiculous suspension is still ongoing and Caffrey still doesn't know whether he can have Moran in his squad. This is three days before a Leinster final and this confusion isn't helping matters and makes a mockery once again of the whole disciplinary process. Caffrey can't wait any longer and names his team late this evening.

There are five changes from the one that beat Westmeath. Ciaran Whelan returns to midfield replacing Eamonn Fennell; Kevin Nolan fills in for Moran; Kevin Bonner replaces Bernard Brogan who is still not fully fit; Diarmuid Connolly comes in for Paul Flynn; and most noticeably Paul Griffin takes over the full back spot with Ross McConnell dropped to the bench.

Tinkering with the wing forwards still goes on and it has been a constant theme over the years, but we still can't seem to produce high-quality wing forwards who can terrorise defences. Bernard Brogan has been the only bright star to emerge and his loss is significant; none of the replacements fill you with confidence that they can be slotting over the points in his stead.

Never mind the problems in the forwards, it's the defence that's most worrying for Dublin fans. Since Paddy Christie's departure we've struggled to fill the vital full back role and Ross McConnell was to be the latest player to answer our prayers. Tall and physically imposing, this converted midfielder was to be able to compete with the new breed of basketball-style full forward such as Kieran Donaghy. But McConnell has been inconsistent and has been shown up most noticeably against smaller, quicker forwards. It must be with this in mind that Caffrey has brought in the more agile Griffin. But to suddenly drop your full back at the Leinster final stage smacks of indecision still lurking in the Dublin management. How can you not be settled on such a vital position in the middle of July in the Championship season? Can you realistically be chopping and changing your key positions based on each different opponent that you face? None of the top counties does it. They are settled through the spine of their teams, confident in who they have and what they can do.

It's worrying and unsettling seeing the management still chopping and changing things at this late stage. And it's one of the key reasons why lingering doubts about an All-Ireland remain. We shouldn't still have question marks about our full back just three days before a Leinster final. Luckily for Caffrey and the management team, however, the Collie Moran mess is taking up most of the newsprint and the McConnell dropping gets tucked behind the DRA controversies. This is worrying though.

**JULY**
**18**
**Friday**

Incredibly, just two days before the Leinster final and a day after the Dublin team was named, the DRA finally come out and decide that Moran doesn't now have to serve the four-week suspension that was so stupidly imposed on him. It's too late for all concerned though. Caffrey says he's sticking with the team he's named last night, which means Kevin Nolan will make his Championship debut. Are Leinster finals the time to be throwing new blood into the fray, one wonders. And how will the full back fare? We'll know more on Sunday.

The interesting contrast to the GAA summer has been the on-off transfer saga with Ronaldo between Man United and Real Madrid. You couldn't get two more different worlds and personalities, between the preening prima donna Ronaldo and the GAA player. Seeing Alex Ferguson hanging on to the Portuguese's coat-tails, not wanting to let him go while the player said he wanted out, has been embarrassing for the club and for the fans. Ferguson has now changed tack, it seems, and told the Portuguese ponce that he's not going anywhere; end of story. It seems like Ronaldo will just have to put up with his £100,000 a week salary whether he likes it or not! When you see how money distorts and makes sport so ugly, you thank God for the GAA and its semblance of reality. But at least the Ronaldo saga is a welcome and entertaining diversion from the DRA, the CHC, the CCCCCCCCC, the Real DRA, the Continuity DRA and whoever else you can think of.

This has to be the strangest GAA summer for me ever. You couldn't make it up if you tried. As previously mentioned, I seem to be always in the wrong part of the country when the top games are being played down the road from me, and this weekend is no different.

It's round 4 of the hurling qualifiers with Waterford facing Offaly, while a cracker is promised between Cork and Galway. Both these games of course are being played half an hour down the road from us in Thurles, while I'll be in Galway at a friend's stag with a bunch of hockey players who think hurling is a bog game played by foreigners who don't live in south Dublin.

So once again as I hit the Galway road I'm staring ruefully at the cars with their maroon flags heading past me in the opposite direction. I must have done some horrendous things in a previous life to warrant all this bad fortune.

I get to Galway, check in, and have two hours to kill before dinner; and so I at least get to watch Waterford v Offaly which isn't a bad game and in which Offaly nearly threaten an upset. In the end though, Waterford have too much fire power and win by 2-18 to 0-18. Since Justin McCarthy was forced out by the players, they have turned things around in the Deise county and there are whispers around saying don't write them off for a tilt at the Liam McCarthy.

It was time then for Cork v Galway and as the players ran out on to the pitch, I had to finish my drink and head off to the restaurant. It was an enjoyable and civilised stag — we're all getting old and sensible it seems — and I was getting text updates from a mate on the Cork-Galway game. And what a game to be missing! 0-23 for Cork to 2-15 to Galway with Joe Canning scoring 2-12. And it was all taking place just 30 minutes down the road from us in Tipp. Jesus, I could have wept! I turned around looking for someone to talk to about this incredible game as well as the even more unbelievable performance from Canning.

'Who's Joe Canning?' one hockey jock beside me asked. 'Cork and Galway were playing? Was that the final?' another queried. Here we were in the heart of Galway city with the pubs full to the rafters with hurling folk and here was I stuck in a Mexican restaurant surrounded by unknowing and uninterested blokes. That was two classics I'd now missed this summer: the Federer-Nadal Wimbledon final and now Cork v Galway. Never again, I promised myself, would I be putting hockey stags before hurling.

**JULY**
## 20
**Sunday**

*Leinster football final, Dublin 3-23, Wexford 0-09, Croke Park*

I manage to get myself back to the hotel at a respectable time — 1 am is still respectable, isn't it? — and have an early start for Dublin in the morning. But I'm 30 and after a few pints and anytime after midnight, I may as well have been on the piss all day and night. The sore head and bleary eyes aren't cured by an early morning fry-up and buckets of coffee. But it's after ten now and I have a Dubs game to get to — I just don't make these things easy on myself. The rest of the lads are still suffering in their rooms after a night that went on till after 5 am, so I slip off, bottle of water beside me and hangover cap low over my weary eyes.

It's only three hours by car but it feels like it's taking for ever. Stuck on the single lane national road heading out of Galway is difficult enough without a pounding head. Again I think I must be the only one driving from Galway for a Dublin game. Not without pain, I arrive into Dublin well ahead of time and I'm able to park the car in O'Connell's car park behind Croker.

It's three hours before throw-in but already it's filling up with expectant Wexford fans. It's the great thing about the GAA, seeing the families and kids all up for the match. The sandwiches have been made and the flasks filled and the boots are being opened as the Wexford fans settle themselves in for a few hours of ham sandwiches and tea. It's a scene in marked contrast to last night's stag in Galway. I'm staying away from the drink for today. It's the first time I reckon that I'll be having nothing stronger than a Sprite before a Dubs game, but it actually does make a nice change. Seeing the Wexford families with their tea and sandwiches and you realise that Dublin games don't have to begin and end with pints in the pub.

The sun was out in O'Connell's car park and the atmosphere was one of enjoyment; it has been over half a century since Wexford were last here and they were going to make sure they enjoyed the day. Amidst all this merriment I slumped over the steering wheel, pulled my cap down lower and wished, not for the last time that day, that I hadn't been in Galway and had all those pints.

But this was the Leinster final. The Dubs were going for four in a row and I was going to enjoy it come hell or high water. To ease me along my way we avoided Gill's today and gathered in Jurys on Jones's Road. With Sprite to hand I watched parts of the Ulster final and parts of the British Open where Padraig Harrington was in contention. Two more markedly different sporting events you couldn't find anywhere, the staid formality of the British Open — or just the Open as they prefer — versus the gritty harshness of Armagh v Fermanagh in Clones in an Ulster final.

Like Wexford, Fermanagh too were playing for history, looking for their first ever Ulster title, and when they were seven points down it looked all but over for them once again. But they dug deep and clawed back the Armagh lead. Armagh's psychological dominance over teams has eroded in recent times and Fermanagh were not afraid to keep plugging away. They reeled Armagh in and might even have won it at the end, but they face a replay now and how many times do Armagh let you slip away a second time?

We headed for the Hill as the Ulster final finished and joined the crowds on the terrace. It was a nice short walk from Jurys to the Hill via the Nally and I was already spruced up after my soft drink sugar kick.

We found a good spot midway up behind the goal and near a bar so I could rest my tiring body which I knew would be flagging later on. The crowds were still spilling in by the time the game started and I had for company on one side of me a rather common sight on the Hill now — the Dublin fan who likes to show he's not really a blow-in and actually does know the names of the players. He might have known the names, but for the next 70 minutes he was calling the players by the wrong ones. Now he may have left his glasses at home — I don't know — but I'm thinking calling Jason Sherlock Bernard Brogan would be a pretty obvious howler. Not to mention the fact that Brogan was actually not playing but was sitting on the bench.

In this Dubs fan's parallel GAA universe, Conal Keaney became Ciaran Whelan (Caffrey must have decided Whelan was better off further up the field in the full forward line), Paul Griffin became Stephen O'Shaughnessy and the fact that Collie Moran was in fact playing as corner back as a replacement for O'Shaughnessy with David Henry as full back must have seemed completely bewildering to him.

What can you do though? You just smile to yourself and

wonder what games these fans do watch and what part of the team line-up they don't read. Don't read, won't read, can't read perhaps? Anyway, as the game went on, I tried subtly to help our friend out. Every time he'd shout out, 'Go on, Whelan', I'd in turn shout out, 'Nice one, Keaney' or something similar. It might actually have been registering because as the game wore on his shouts became more and more muted until finally I had complete silence beside me by the 50th minute. Either that or he just got bored.

By that stage Dublin had increased their three-point half-time lead to 0-16 to 0-07 and were pulling away from Wexford with complete ease. The Dubs had stormed out of the blocks at the start of the second half and Wexford just didn't have any answers. Ten minutes and three goals later, it was goodnight Irene. Dublin were now ahead by a massive 19 points. The Hill was now in festive mood and every pass, point or shot was greeted with a loud cheer while any Wexford effort was sardonically applauded.

It's hard to believe, but we were actually starting to get bored with it all. This was too easy and turned into a rout, ending up with Dublin winning by 23 points (3-23 to 0-09). Wexford had scored just two points in the second half to Dublin's 3-13. Incredible stuff. This was four in a row now in Leinster, but it shouldn't have been that easy.

It was hard to burst the party atmosphere that pervaded Croke Park at the final whistle — or close to the final whistle as some gobshites decided they'd have their on-pitch celebrations before full time. As the now obligatory pitch invasion took place, Alan Brogan lifted the trophy to loud cheers. But it was all too easy and didn't really mean anything in the end. We watched from the Hill — we had

run on to the pitch four years ago and that was enough —
smiling to ourselves but worried at the same time.

This Dublin team was not as good as the scoreline
suggested and Wexford were not that bad. But by
tomorrow morning the hype machine would be in full
swing and Caffrey's men would be All-Ireland favourites
once more.

Had the full back change really worked? Was David
Henry now the answer? Did our wing forwards impress
enough? How well is Cullen doing at centre back? These
were all questions that had been left unanswered and you
worried about future sterner contests. The Dubs, however,
can only beat what's put in front of them, and they're
passing all the tests at the moment, however poor the
Leinster fare may be.

It's an idle four weeks now for the Dubs until their
match in the All-Ireland quarter-final and you just hope
they won't be dining out on this victory for too long. The
real questions have still to be asked of this Dublin team.
My hangover meant I was off home to rest, but even so we
didn't feel much like celebrating this facile victory.

Still, it was a good weekend all round in the end.
Meath got thumped by Limerick in the football qualifiers
the day before and the Dubs fan beside me finally got one
name right in the end. 'Go on, Brogan' he shouted as Alan
lifted the Leinster trophy. Whether he knew it was Alan or
Bernard though was something I never found out. I was on
my way home to bed.

Or so I thought. I had the Sunday papers laid out before
me and with a glass of red wine in one hand I turned on
the Beeb to see how Harrington was doing. Incredibly he

was leading over Ian Poulter while his playing partner, Greg Norman, the fairytale hero of the tournament, had drifted back and out of contention.

Harrington was two shots up going to the 17th when he played a five wood approach shot from 249 yards to three feet. Seeing the ball sailing up and pushing on to the green, finishing just three feet short, you knew you were watching sporting greatness. He doesn't walk like one, talk like one or strut like one, but Harrington's shot on the 17th will be for ever remembered and played back in the sporting moments archive.

Never mind winning a golf major once, but to retain the championship while suffering a wrist injury in the run-up was one of Irish sport's greatest achievements. We were watching one of our own rise to the pinnacle of world sport in one of the hardest disciplines to master. Not bad for a former accountant and amateur.

Contrast Harrington with Ronaldo and you see everything that is wrong about football and right about golf. We can't blame money for football's corruption entirely — Harrington picked up close to €1 million for the four days' work at Royal Birkdale — but you realise and appreciate much more the sporting achievements of sportsmen like Harrington in the process. I went to bed smiling to myself that night. Dublin victory, Meath loss, Harrington major, hangover gone. I slept soundly.

JULY
21
Monday

The Dubs' historic Leinster victory rightly gets buried beneath the avalanche of coverage on Padraig Harrington. The President, Taoiseach, everyone gets in on the act and there is Harrington's beaming face with the famous claret jug on the front page of every newspaper. Success stories come round so rarely in Irish sport that we have to cling on to them when they do arrive. There's something very gratifying being able to revel in a global sporting achievement; not in an 'aren't-we-so-plucky-and-great' way, but rather in a knowing this is the real deal sense.

Harrington is no flash in the pan. Last year's British Open victory was celebrated wildly like an Irish venture at a soccer World Cup; this time it's different. Winning it a second time and we're basking in our obvious long-standing greatness. Golf? Oh yes, we all play the game in post Celtic Tiger Ireland. Me? I'm a three handicapper myself and well, everyone is pretty much the same in the country. I mean, we're practically born with silver putters in our mouths nowadays!

It's amazing how delusional and expert we can be. It's the great thing about Ireland. Someone else's success quickly becomes our own. We all won the British Open yesterday.

And thank God for Harrington's win. It was something to keep that preening, perma-tanned gnome, Nicolas Sarkozy, off some of the news coverage. The Napoleon wannabe was in town to patronisingly 'listen to our complaints about Lisbon' and to conduct a PR exercise for the rest of Europe — that and to make himself feel good. As he walked out of government buildings arm in arm with Brian Cowen, Sarkozy beamed to all around, one the well-groomed, tanned and teeth to drown out the sun by president, the other an overweight bogger who loves nothing more than a few pints, a bit of Gah and a few songs. And they say we're not stereotyped as a nation?

**JULY**
**23**
**Wednesday**

Just when you thought the DRA couldn't throw up any more shocks or surprises in relation to suspensions, news about the Paul Galvin affair came out this evening. A decision was originally supposed to be announced on Monday, but then it got put back to the Wednesday and all day the media have been on tenterhooks waiting and wondering.

L'Affair Galvin has been the main off-pitch talking point all summer and has been dragging on and on. Of course it hasn't been helped by Galvin fighting the six-month suspension handed down every step of the way.

Listening to the radio this evening, and another twist has been taken, it seems. The DRA have announced that Galvin in fact didn't get a fair hearing before the CHC as there were 'procedural irregularities'. The DRA statement ran as follows:

> *The DRA Tribunal is of the view that procedural irregularities occurred at the CHC hearing on 23 June 2008 which were in breach of his right to fair procedures and to a fair hearing.*
>
> *The DRA Tribunal has directed as follows:*
> *(a) that the matter be re-heard by a newly convened and differently constituted CHC as soon as possible; and*
> *(b) that Mr Galvin remains suspended in the interim period and is not eligible to play Gaelic games until the disciplinary process has been concluded.*

Clear as mud, eh? So basically Galvin has to go through

the entire process all over again, and until that happens he is still suspended. But reading between the lines and listening to media commentary on it, the word from the GAA appeared to be that six months was too harsh and that three months was sufficient. However, the DRA cannot reduce a suspension, only quash it or uphold it. The obvious answer seemed to be to rule the original hearing out of court, send the poor hoor back to the beginning where he'd get the three-month suspension, and then everybody would be happy.

And that, in the land of the GAA, is how things happen. Makes you understand why so much of the rest of the country is so fucked up when you see the thinking that goes on in sport's administration.

**JULY 24 Thursday** The front page of the *Irish Examiner* has a terrible story about the racist abuse of a Nigerian teenager (Teboga Sebala) playing for his U-14 GAA club in Carlow. I was going to say shocking, but then are we really shocked when we read about these incidents?

A father of one of the boy's team mates was quoted in the paper describing the incident: 'There were obscene racial comments like "kill the fuckin nigger" and the like. It was ongoing throughout the match and Teboga was visibly upset', said Mr Tomlin.

The *Liveline* brigade were in full flow that afternoon rightly condemning the actions of those at the game but then calling the GAA into question. There is a deep-seated racism in this country towards immigrants, be they African or Eastern European, and no organisation, especially one like the GAA, is immune to it. Dublin fans well remember the abuse Jason Sherlock got especially in his first years with Dublin, and which I'm sure he still gets.

And the Hill is no 'pure as the driven snow' territory either. In the half-time kickabouts with primary schools, it's always noticeable that the 'white Irish' kid gets the biggest cheer from the Hill. He's one of our own, they seem to be saying.

Perhaps it will take kids like Teboga Sebala winning an All-Ireland and lifting the Sam Maguire before we all come to fully accept the multi-ethnic and multi-racial make-up of Irish society now present. The GAA, however, shouldn't be blamed for the rest of the country's ills.

**JULY**
**27**
**Sunday**

It feels like we're only killing time for the next few weeks. Winning your province means you have a long lay-off before the quarters and there's a lot to be said for playing and coming through the qualifiers. For one thing, as a fan at least you get regular games to go to and sometimes with unique match-ups that you wouldn't get any other time. As a fan you want to be going to games with your county, but now we have to put up with watching the others go through it all.

So far for us Dubs it's been a far too quiet summer. We've had just three games in seven weeks of action, none of which was a classic or would whet your appetite much. It's a fine line for the GAA between overkill and under-appreciation, but so far this summer the Dubs are definitely getting bored. Things have been dragging and only a few hurling games have kept our spirits up.

Today it was the hurling quarter-finals (Waterford v Wexford and Cork v Clare). Again Thurles was the venue, but this time I was in Dublin and was not feeling anxious about missing out on this occasion. After all, I'm getting married in just over three weeks, so I reckon I should be focusing more of my energies on more important matters than the GAA Championship. Still though, that's two weeks in a row where I've missed the Cork hurlers, and it's two opportunities I've since rued.

Maybe it's because I was so underwhelmed when seeing them in action against Dublin that turned me off them; maybe I just thought this was a team over the hill and past it. What is it they say about never writing off Cork hurlers?

After a pulsating game against Galway last week, Cork once more had to go to the well and pull victory from the jaws of defeat. Eight points down and looking knackered, Cork somehow pulled themselves together and began the fight-back. And they did it. Emerging 2-19 to 2-17 winners, this Cork team looked shattered at the final whistle. After all, they'd been through two wars in two successive weekends and now had Kilkenny to face in three weeks' time.

This is a Cork team unrecognisable from the one that struggled against Dublin, but it also goes to show how beneficial the qualifiers can be. Cork are on a roll and finding strength from within; they're being tested every step of the way and finding the answers they need. It's a team that seems unwilling to bow to destiny; they refuse to give in and are once again giving us the tale of the hurling summer.

The hurling semis have now been decided and it's Cork v Kilkenny and Tipperary v Waterford. Kilkenny are still favourites, but you couldn't write off any of the other three.

In football we're getting closer to seeing who Dublin could be facing in the quarters and after this weekend's qualifiers it could be Tyrone, Kildare, Monaghan or Down. Throw Kerry, Mayo and Fermanagh into the mix and it's obvious that there's not a huge amount separating many of the teams. The presence of so many Ulster teams is a cause for worry, however. Dublin never fare well against the scrappers from the North and you'd be hoping we'd get a Mayo or a Kildare. Definitely not Kerry though. But at this stage can we be hoping to avoid any teams? The fact that we as fans are worried about certain counties shows we still don't have enough faith in ourselves. I hate to say it, but whatever the Cork hurlers have, I wish we could bottle it.

JULY
28
Monday

As part of my pre-wedding arrangements, my best man (and future brother-in-law) has organised for myself and himself to see Sunderland take on Cobh Ramblers in Cork in a pre-season friendly this evening. It was either that or golf, and after my last attempts on the golf course, I reckoned a football match was definitely the safer bet for all concerned.

Roy Keane was a hero of mine growing up and even until recently (Saipan and the fall-out and all of that) he was a major influence and someone I greatly admired and looked up to. We all outgrow our heroes eventually though, and Keane is now firmly in the 'he's just another human' category.

Since he's become a manager he's had to become a

different beast and wears different hats now. He is a complete contradiction in many ways to the player who railed against so many things. Nowadays he seems to be either believing his own hype or he has had a lobotomy. Keane the manager is not someone you would admire and aspire to be as a kid. Keane the player was uncompromising, stood up for what he believed in no matter what, and it was these qualities many of us greatly admired and secretly wished we could be like him.

Now we see he's merely flesh and bleeds like the rest of us, and it's a huge disappointment. Luckily I'm 30 years of age and so I don't rely on idolising Keane any more. I've just about moved on from our separation and think it was amicable on the whole.

I still fondly remember the one and only time I met Keane back in 2003 when he was on the ill-fated *Dunphy* TV show on TV3. Being in the green room backstage that night was one of the highlights of my life back then. You truly felt you were in the presence of star quality just being in the same room as him. As I hoovered the bottles of beer back to get some Dutch courage into me before I attempted to sidle up to him and ingratiate myself in his company, I realised I wasn't the only one star struck. Bill O'Herlihy, Alistair Campbell and all the grown men in the room were in awe of him. Me? I got tanked up on enough Heineken and somehow ended up beside Alistair Campbell with Roy Keane opposite me.

Campbell, seeing the glaze in my eyes, knew to make a hasty retreat and so I was left trying to strike up a conversation with Roy Keane who sat just a few feet from me. And like any footballer or fan, once you started asking him about soccer we were both on safe ground.

I don't remember much else of the conversation, only that I probably laughed a little too loudly at his jokes and agreed with everything he said. By the end of the night I got a picture taken with him where I was practically throwing my arms around him as if I wanted to give him mouth-to-mouth. I still have the picture and for a long time it was on my fridge at home.

But thankfully my grown man's infatuation faded and I could concentrate on more mature pursuits like getting married and buying a house. As we sat in Turner's Cross this evening, applauding Keane coming out on to the pitch ahead of his Sunderland team, all these Keane memories came flooding back. I hadn't thought about him for a long time and I realised then that my infatuation with him had ended.

Keane the player was a brief encounter in all our lives which affected every person in the country at one stage. Now he was Keane the manager and he was just a man. Sometimes, I realised, it's OK to let our sports heroes die — at least we have the memories.

For what's it worth, Sunderland beat Cobh 4-0 and it was a crap game. But I was glad to finally get closure on Keane.

**JULY**
**29**
**Tuesday**

My attention turns to the Premiership in England briefly today. Robbie Keane signs for Liverpool and is unveiled at Anfield in front of the British press. He's reportedly on €80,000 a week. Keane has hit the big time now, and the best of luck to him. But seeing him there in Anfield with Benitez by his side, and being on the back pages of all the British tabloids, you see how far his world is from anything that people in Ireland or the UK can associate with. He's on a pedestal now where his every whim is catered for, where stuff like household bills and dental appointments are looked after by the club. Just train, turn up, play and score, and here's €80,000 every week for your trouble. Nice work if you can get it. The problem is earning that kind of money in a culture such as that in English soccer. It has to affect you sometime.

Robbie Keane is Irish and Tallaght born, but now he may as well be from Mars. If I was a kid nowadays, I wonder would I still be looking to follow in the footsteps of a Kevin Moran? Would Bryan Cullen or Ciaran Whelan be my heroes or would I be looking at Robbie Keane, seeing the money, the cars and the bling MTV lifestyle and think, that's what I want when I grow up?

More and more it's about the money and true sports stars are harder to find. Come back Roy Keane; all is forgiven.

'Up she flew and the cock flattened her', as a mate of mine was wont to say. We still haven't figured out what it's supposed to mean, but it seems kind of apt today. Surprise, surprise but didn't Paul Galvin only have his 24 week ban reduced to 12 by the 'newly convened' CHC on foot of the DRA's directive last week.

The GAA tries to give credence and authority to its 'independent' disciplinary bodies. And yet the dogs in the street knew that Galvin was going to get 12 weeks once the DRA directive was handed down last week.

What's probably more annoying is that when you talk

to Kerry folk, they make the point that Galvin will be ready 'when we're in the final'. The presumption and arrogance of Kerry football folk that they will be in the final, come 21 September, is staggering. But when you've been there 55 times in 121 years, presuming you'll have a day out on the third Sunday of September is a pretty good forecast most years. But they've been stumbling of late. Cork's Munster final victory was a serious blow to their pride, while the Galvin affair hasn't been helpful either. Rumours of training ground bust-ups abound as well. These might only be stories to try and unsettle the Kerry camp, but we'll take anything ahead of their tough tie against Monaghan on Sunday.

Their aura of invincibility has been thawing this summer and the chinks in their armour are giving the rest of us cause for hope. Now if Monaghan can go one better than last year then we'll all be a little lighter of heart, come Monday morning. Never, ever, write off those Kerry hoors, however. Sure they might even find a way to postpone the Championship into December and at least Galvin would be fit enough for them by then.

**JULY**
**31**
**Thursday**

Clare is in uproar. The GAA, it seems, doesn't like to stray too far from the limelight and the back pages. A Munster U-21 hurling final between Clare and Tipperary last night ended in incredible circumstances and has lain further derision on GAA officialdom. From what I've been reading in this morning's papers, the gist of it is that the teams were tied going into injury time. Clare had a free within pointing distance when the umpire called the referee's attention to a minor infringement by the Clare goalie moments earlier. It seemed his foot had gone outside the square during his puck-out and it was this infraction that the umpire was notifying the ref about. End result? Ref cancels the Clare free and gives Tipp a 65 for the infringement. Tipp score and win the game.

Pictures this morning are of the Clare fans baying for the umpire's blood. He had to receive a Garda escort off the pitch and out of the ground. It's more 'the crowd goes wild' scenes. The GAA mob knows no bounds! If it was Dublin fans frothing at the mouth and on the hunt, we'd be hooligans bringing soccer elements into the game; when culchies do it, it's how very country of them! The look of fear in the umpire's eyes was very real in the pictures and hands, claws and fingers can be seen reaching out to get a cut at him. Hell hath no fury like a GAA mob.

I've no sympathy for the umpire or the ref though. Over-officiousness at such a critical juncture in the game was imbecilic. It was a case of following the letter of the law versus the spirit of the game. Why was the goalie not pulled up for other previous infringements, one wonders. And why wait till injury time of a drawn game to decide to pull him up on this one? What does be going through their heads at all, you would wonder.

Whatever about the umpire, a GAA mob on a rampage is something to behold. We hear and read about stories of fans, coaches and players chasing refs off pitches; of barricading officials into their corrugated changing rooms; or even worse, locking them into the boots of cars. I mean, you couldn't make it up, could you? If *Après Match* or the D'Unbelievables tried it, we wouldn't believe them. Put a few culchies on the side of a pitch, dress them in local colours, pour a few pints down them then let them loose at the closing stages of a close game, and hey presto! Watch mob rule and chaos unfold before your very eyes. But it's the GAA, so how very Irish! We'll have to try selling it to the Yanks.

# AUGUST
## RAINY DAYS TO THE END OF THE ROAD

**AUGUST**
**1**
**Friday**

This weekend is the August bank holiday weekend already. The summer is flying by and we're still peering out our windows at the rain, waiting for the season to start sometime. At this rate we'll have forgotten what the sun and heat feel like. We'll become the Irish version of that Scandinavian region that has six months of darkness; instead we'll have six months of pissing rain followed by six months of darkness. If it keeps up like this we'll all be migrating in our droves again. The commute from Marbella for Dubs games would be a killer though.

We're getting to the 'it's-starting-to-count' stage in the football championship. Wexford v Down, Mayo v Tyrone, Kildare v Fermanagh and Kerry v Monaghan all face off to decide who will play the provincial winners in the All-Ireland quarters. I'm starting to feel the stomach nerves playing up now. By the quarter-finals you'll be meeting a top team either way, and as it's knock-out it's last chance winner takes all. One bad day for the Dubs and we're out; season over; summer gone; dejection for another year. One mistake is all it takes to potentially ruin the summer of nearly 100,000 people. So no pressure lads. Just keep running the bollox off yourselves between now and the 9th. We're only three games away from Sam. You can nearly feel it now. It's not good for the nerves. When will this summer ever end?

**AUGUST**

**3**

**Sunday**

It's the unfortunate thing about Kerry these days, it seems. When they get outside of Munster nothing will trip them up. They are becoming the Kilkenny of Gaelic football. Whatever is thrown at them they just eat it up, spit it out and move right on.

Today they played poorly and still overcame Monaghan by three points. What was a near miss last year became, this year, a problem that just had to be overcome. And they did. With no fuss, no recriminations. Good, bad or indifferent, Kerry just get on with the job and then get ready for the next task at hand — an All-Ireland quarter-final.

Thankfully it's not against the Dubs. The draw was made this evening for the quarters. Also in the hat were Wexford who looked impressive scalping first Armagh and now Down. (Were they really that bad in the Leinster final and were Dublin really that good? Probably not is the likely answer to both questions, which means the Dubs still have some improvements to make.) Tyrone had a fine win over Mayo, although beating them by only a point, while Kildare beat Fermanagh in what was a crap game with the first score coming only after 25 minutes. If Kildare and Wexford are top eight sides, what does it say about the state of Gaelic football this season?

Pulled out of the hat to face the Dubs were Tyrone. With that there was probably a collective 'ah shit' from the Dublin fans across the city. They beat us in 2005 at the same stage and while some people were stupidly writing them off early in the Ulster campaign this year, Mickey Harte's men have been on a roll of late and will be a tough, tough assignment. After such an easy victory over Wexford, and poor opposition offerings from Westmeath and Louth, are Dublin ready for this challenge?

Having said that, beat Tyrone and we face either Wexford or Armagh — more than likely Armagh. And if we get all the way to the final, then it will probably be Kerry. Three tougher games you won't find this summer. To win All-Irelands you have to prove you're the best and beat all comers. It's just that the doubts are still there about this Dublin team. Could we beat any of those three counties on the day playing our best? Absolutely. Can we beat all three of them one after the other needing three huge consecutive performances? I can't see it happening. But nobody said it would be easy. Let's just see how we fare against Tyrone first.

We have to wait for two weeks now for the Dubs-Tyrone clash, but at least it will be a stand-alone game with Croker full to the brim with Dubs. And for the first time I won't be worrying about getting tickets. I have my Parnell Park pass tucked safely away — my pass to my blue heaven. One less thing to worry about.

**AUGUST**
**6**
**Wednesday**

Most of the sports pages this week are dominated with the weekend's Cork v Kilkenny hurling semi-final as well as the three football quarter-finals. One gets the feeling that this could be the end of the line and the end of an era for this Cork team. It is probably the last season for the likes of Diarmuid O'Sullivan, Donal Óg Cusack and Seán Óg Ó hAilpín, and the question now is can they give it one last hurrah? They've dug deep and come through against Galway and Clare, but against

Kilkenny? The Cats are so clinical, almost machine-like in the way they dispose of any opposition, that you'd fear for Cork. This could be one last attempt too many. For one thing, you don't go seven or eight points behind against Kilkenny and live to come through it.

Dragging myself away from Gaelic games, I turn my attention to the one black spot on the Irish sporting calendar — the League of Ireland. It's good though to see the League of Ireland nearly getting some good news. With all the financial troubles of the clubs hitting the headlines this summer — in marked contrast to the feel-good vibes from the GAA Championship — it was compelling watching Drogheda's second leg in the Champions League qualifying round against the mighty Dynamo Kiev this evening.

Trailing 2-1 from the first leg and facing Kiev away from home, no one gave the Drogs a chance in hell against the former European powerhouse. And yet Drogheda came about six inches from beating them and reaching the final qualifying round before the glamour of the Champions League group stages.

With just two minutes left in the game, Drogheda got a late equaliser and only needed one more to go through on away goals. It would have been an unlikely and unforeseen conclusion to the leg, but incredibly, deep into stoppage time, Drogheda's Shane Robinson had a shot from the right which beat the keeper, hit the post and then rolled agonisingly along the goal-line before being cleared.

Then just when we thought the drama was over, with nearly the last kick of the game, the ball broke clear to their Aussie, Adam Hughes, who ran on to it just six yards out. The keeper was stranded out from his goal with only a defender covering the goalmouth. It seemed harder to miss, but miss he did and the ball went sailing over the crossbar.

And that was it for Irish soccer's European hopes. A win in Kiev would have given the League such a boost that it was hard to believe it so nearly happened, but ultimately it didn't. Hard luck endings have been the story of the League and once again a nearly, might-have-been match left all concerned wondering what if. Would this have been the catalyst to revive interest in the League again, one wonders.

As the GAA hurtles onwards so successfully in spectating, commercial and media terms, the League of Ireland appears to be dying on its feet. Irish people don't want to know about shoddily run organisations or teams that can't succeed. Munster and Leinster can do it in Europe so why can't soccer, many want to know. The League's continued failings speak volumes to the floating fan about mediocrity and failure. But things do seem to be changing, and for the better.

If the clubs can keep chipping away and improving all the time, I'm sure we will soon see them competing in the final qualiying rounds and then the next stage will be the Champions League group stages proper. If we can get one or two Irish teams qualifying for those on a regular basis, then you will see the fans coming out in their thousands to support the League clubs in their European endeavours. How long it will take though to get to that level, God knows; and will there even be a League by that stage?

However, sitting down in front of the telly to watch Drogheda's exploits, not expecting much and then being thrilled and on the edge of your seat, meant so much. It meant you would gladly support an Irish club team competing strongly at the top echelons of European soccer. You could be proud of Drogheda's achievements and for one evening at least ignore all the bad stories emanating from the domestic League. For on this night a strong Irish club team proved that the League of Ireland could have a product that could compete successfully with the GAA during the summer.

Europe and more than the local is something the GAA can never offer its fans and rugby has stolen a march on soccer through the success of Munster and Leinster. It really is the last chance saloon for the League of Ireland as to its long-term success and place in the Irish sports fans' hearts. Tonight they were only six inches from winning over some of the doubters and proving that Irish soccer can be something to be proud of.

And, oh yea, Ronaldo confirmed today that he's staying at United. Who cares? Give me an Irish team getting to the Champions League group stages any day. But give me Dublin winning an All-Ireland first.

**AUGUST**

**7**

**Thursday**

OK, it's nothing to do with the Dubs or even sport for that matter, but I must mention the story in today's *Irish Times* that says a new holiday resort is being built in . . . Iraq.

'. . . *swans gliding on a lake in front of red-roofed houses, snow-capped mountains rising in the distance . . . and not a soldier in sight'*, states the

*Irish Times quoting from the brochure, with the developer saying that the resort at Talin will be a 'fully gated community with security fence, checkpoints, high-tech screening at entrance gates, numerous internal monitoring points and around-the-clock security patrols.'*

At this juncture I, of course, refuse to mention any comparisons between parts of Dublin and this development. That would be just too easy.

Back to sport and tomorrow sees the opening ceremony of the Beijing Olympics. It's being touted as the biggest, the boldest, the bravest, the brightest and the best, but then again aren't they all? Having said that, with 1.3 billion people at their disposal and able to call them into action at a moment's notice, one gets the feeling that tomorrow is going to be pretty spectacular.

It's hard to get too excited about the events themselves though. Who knows who's on drugs and who isn't? After my childhood scarring when I found out that my hero Ben Johnson was in fact a drug cheat, I've never had any faith in athletics or even gymnastics or swimming. If the likes of Marion Jones can so publicly and so daringly con the world with her Olympic golds in Sydney in 2000 and only 'fess up' when all the evidence is stacked against her, you realise that probably most of the elite athletes will stop at nothing to win.

One authentic triumph that could come from the games is an American swimmer called Michael Phelps. He does seem to be the real deal and is aiming to eclipse Mark Spitz's 1972 record of seven golds at one Olympics.

Reading about his amazing stats and unique physiology that practically makes him a human fish, Phelps is one winning story we might just be able to believe in. As for the Irish, I presume it will be more hard luck stories. We might get a few personal bests and national records if we're lucky, but it will more than likely be failure. Not heroic, just failure.

But I'm settling in comfortably for the next two and a half weeks. Between Olympics coverage all day as well as the return of the Premiership, international soccer and the latter stages of the All-Ireland Championships, I could quite comfortably not leave home for the month of August. And of course if I absolutely had to leave home, I can still get as much Olympics coverage as I want online or via my mobile.

We should start including more hours in the day for special occasions like this one. By the end of the month I will be versed again in the intricacies of such minority sports as clay pigeon shooting, synchronised diving, the pole vault and other such sporting wonders. Whoever knew that so many people the world over dedicated themselves to such lonely and unwatched pursuits. It should make even League of Ireland fans feel loved.

**AUGUST**
**8**
**Friday**

Yep, it was spectacular. We went crazy ourselves when we put on a bit of a concert, a parade and a little fireworks display for the Special Olympics. Beijing on the other hand spent $100 m on the Opening Ceremony alone and mobilised, it seemed, half of their population turning them into flag-waving, drum-beating, all-smiling participants in probably the most synchronised show of history, light, colour, flair and fireworks the world has ever seen. All I could think of while the pageant went on was the Will Smith movie, *I, Robot*, where the robots all move in perfect harmony and unison. This was the human, smiling version, but as in the film, you couldn't help but wonder about the dark things lurking underneath the gleaming surface.

You also watch something like this and realise we could never, ever, in our wildest dreams, achieve anything close to what the Chinese did. Even if we had the money, the resources and the numbers, we'd still mangle it, be out of step and have rain pissing down on all concerned.

If not in my lifetime, but probably in the next few generations, China, I'm pretty sure, will be the centre of the world. This Opening Ceremony was so perfectly produced and executed that it was scary. You don't know what's going on behind those smiling faces and we probably don't want to either, but the future is Chinese and we'd all better start being part of their new world order.

Midway through the extravaganza a strange thought struck me. It wasn't about world peace (although that would come later when news about Georgia broke); it wasn't my pending marriage; nor was it the western world's complicity with the Chinese superpower. No, for some reason, and out of the blue, I realised with a shock and a fright that Dublin's potential All-Ireland semi-final was going to be played on 31 August. The rescheduling of the Dubs game to a later stand alone date meant that the Dubs were playing the second semi-final — just when I would be on the other side of the world on my honeymoon on a little island in the Gulf of Thailand where I was pretty sure they had never heard of Gaelic football.

If it had been the first semi-final on the 24th, I would have been just about OK. We are flying out to Thailand on that day at nine o'clock in the evening and I had got a special dispensation to go to any games that afternoon once I was in the airport in plenty of time. But this was bad news. This was all presuming the Dubs would be in a semi-final of course, but contingency plans must be made, especially if you're going to be in the back arse of Asia.

A few minutes on Google and wouldn't you know it but there's an Irish bar in the Thai island of Ko Samui. Called Tropical Murphy's and serving draught beers, Guinness and fry-ups, it sounded like my idea of holiday hell, but needs must and if it's the only place to catch the Dubs when I'm thousands of miles away, so be it. It would certainly be a first for me watching the Dubs in an Irish bar on an island in the middle of the Gulf of Thailand.

I could breathe a little easier now knowing that a plan B was in place. Plan A was of course beating Tyrone to get into the semis in the first place. But for now, I returned to the *I, Robot* human exhibition of flag-waving and drum-beating and perma-smiling while Russia's Vladimir Putin looked on in a similar smiling and waving fashion. In just a few hours the whole world would be finding out what was lurking beneath his Olympic grin.

**AUGUST**
**9**
**Saturday**

'Russia declares war on Georgia' ran the newspaper headline this morning, but it felt like the end of the world had come to Ireland instead. Rain, darkness and flooding, and this was all at eleven in the morning. I catch glimpses of Wexford's remarkable win over Armagh and realise now that if Dublin can beat Tyrone next week, then you'd have to fancy our chances against Wexford in the semis, which means we'd be into an All-Ireland final and then . . .

Kerry's demolition of Galway in the later game brings me back down to earth. The Kingdom were simply awesome in some of the worst conditions I've ever seen for a match. It wasn't rain; it was a deluge that you would see in a hurricane. Here was proof, if you needed any more this summer, that the weather was being turned on its head by global warming. Rain, hail or shine, this Kerry team is simply not for beating. They meet the winner of Cork v Kildare and you'd fancy them to be in another final and going for three in a row. Could it really be a Dublin-Kerry final that people are starting to whisper about? Knowing Wexford are in the semis makes it hard to stop wandering thoughts . . .

**AUGUST 10 August**

Today I join the convoy of Cork cars headed for Dublin as I get tickets for the day's Cork double-header between the footballers against Kildare and the more mouth-watering hurling semi-final against Kilkenny.

I'm sitting with Cork friends and fans and arrive just in time for the footballers' quarter-final. There's a sizeable crowd in Croker, but I'm told there'll be thousands more coming in when the hurling gets going.

There's still a large number of GAA fans who wouldn't regard Gaelic football as a proper game at all. I got some first glimpses of this antipathy towards football on St Patrick's Day at the All-Ireland club finals. But to see this attitude from fans towards their own county players was a first for me and an eye-opener. I'd say there are fans who couldn't care less if their footballers won an All-Ireland, but they would go to the ends of the earth to catch the juniors playing hurling for their county.

The Cork footballers duly beat Kildare — but only just — and get a semi-final appointment against Kerry. Cork are a good footballing team and up there in the top rankings, but having disposed of Kerry in the Munster final, it's scant reward for having come through the quarters, only to face their old rivals again. Not only that but they're facing a Kerry team that will be smarting from the last defeat, and one that actually gives a damn this time. Poor Cork, it's no wonder some people are starting to question the back door system.

The football is over in Croker and suddenly the ground swells by thousands. 'Bring on the real game' I hear from some Cork fans arriving into their seats. They're not one bit bothered that their county footballers are into an All-Ireland semi-final. All that matters is this game against Kilkenny. Theirs is a world only inhabited by men with hurls and sliothars.

I haven't told my Cork friends, but I don't give Cork a chance in hell. They won't be able to come back from the dead against Kilkenny and I think it's the end of the road for this Cork team. So much so I've put €20 on them to lose by between seven and nine points at 9 to 1. Sitting amidst so much red, I keep this bit of information to myself.

Cork are up for it. But so too are Kilkenny. And Kilkenny are the more composed and better organised. On every part of the pitch they're first to balls coming in;

running off the ball they're running Cork ragged; and they're picking scores off from sidelines, 65s, even from their own half. Anywhere Cork look for a weakness, there is none. The death-knell for Cork comes as early as the 32nd minute when Eoin Larkin nips through the Cork defence and fires the only goal of the game. But it was enough as Kilkenny opened up an eight-point lead by half-time.

This was not Clare or Galway that Cork were facing, and there would be no way back for the brave Rebel hurlers. Only three years ago the whole country was talking about Cork going for three in a row. But Kilkenny stopped them that day and are now going for their own treble. How quickly sport changes and can knock you off your perch. Cork are seen as yesterday's men now; Kilkenny are the stars of the present and the future.

Kilkenny are methodical and clinical in how they succeed — if they were a country they'd be China. When Cork did win, they did it with a certain panache, passion and raw edge. That fire in the belly stuff you can't buy or breed and while Kilkenny's high standards of excellence can only but be applauded, for this hurling neutral at least we'll miss the intensity and characters that Cork have given us over these last few years. For them it's now the end of the road and the sad last picture as I left Croke Park was that of the Rock, Diarmuid O'Sullivan, on his knees on the Croke Park turf and in tears. This was one man's sporting life come to an end and it was hard for him to see anything but misery in the present.

You'd think the day would have ended happily with the hurling semi-final, but getting home (bone dry remarkably as the weather thankfully held off for the afternoon) and turning on the telly, I was to catch the USPGA final round. It was the last golf major of the year and unbelievably Padraig Harrington was once again challenging for the top honours. Here was a man who up to just a few weeks ago was a top golfer who had won one major and many probably figured that, like many before him, he would stay as a single major winner. Golfers that achieve two majors are incredible; those who accomplish anything more than that can be counted in historic terms.

And yet here was Harrington, having just come off defending his British Open major title, contending for a third major and his second of the season. It was incredible stuff to be watching one of our own looking to go down as one of the game's greatest ever golfers. Adding to the storyline was the fact that it was Sergio Garcia whom Harrington beat in the play-off last year to clinch the British Open, who was vying with him for the USPGA title.

Harrington conjured up a magical 66 for his final round — this despite finding sand then heavy rough on the 18th before nailing a 15 footer for par. That was enough to break Garcia's spirit. The Spaniard bogeyed the 18th, leaving Harrington the winner by two shots. Two majors in a row and his third in a year! This was incredible stuff and the clock was ticking to 2 am Irish time when he finally lifted the Wanamaker Trophy and registered himself as possibly the greatest Irish sportsman of all time.

The best thing about it is that Harrington has shown that you don't have to be obnoxious to be successful;

talent and an immense and disciplined work ethic are what have put him on top. He stands in marked contrast to an earlier hero of mine when I was growing up — Roy Keane — whom I admired for standing up for what he believed in, no matter what. Now, here's Harrington, a true gent and nice guy, achieving what few people in the world — never mind Ireland or Europe — have done. I'm going to have to seriously reassess my value system in the wake of Harrington's achievements. Where once I admired ballsiness and guts, now I'm thinking that a work ethic should be greatly admired as well.

Having said that, and this may be heresy in the wake of the Dubliner's triumphs, isn't there something just too nice about Harrington? There's a certain edginess, for example, to Garcia that many people admire, and I wonder would many kids want to be more like Garcia than Harrington when they grow up. Maybe if Harrington said 'fuck' every now and again or even told a reporter to fuck off once in a while, it would make him seem more rock n roll. We don't want him going all John Daly on us, but a little bit of naughtiness might be good for his marketing, I reckon. Bleary-eyed, I hit the sack after 2 am, falling asleep to images of Harrington, unshaven and cursing, tearing up the fairways of the K Club on his Harley whilst knocking back a bottle of Jameson whiskey.

**AUGUST 11 Monday** I hear a great story on the radio this evening from that successful Irish sports journalist, David Walsh, of the *Sunday Times*. Over in Beijing for the Olympics, he told how he and a few other Irish fans and journos were gathered in O'Shea's Irish pub in Beijing. First off they were watching Cork and Kildare followed by Cork v Kilkenny; then, seeing how Harrington was doing, they had to stay on for that. Of course, because of a time difference of seven hours, it was nearly one in the morning by the time the hurling was over.

The numbers were dwindling steadily as time ticked on through the night, but Walsh and a few die-hards stuck it out and finally emerged from O'Shea's into the Beijing sunlight at nine o'clock in the morning. It was an epic all-nighter by the sounds of it and Walsh recounted how talk had turned to discussing Harrington's place in the pantheon of greatest Irish sportsmen and greatest golfers. It sounded like my kind of night — staying up all night to watch sporting history, not because you had a choice, but because you had to. Halfway across the world you have to find an Irish bar to watch the GAA and because it's an Irishman challenging for a golf major, you have to stick around, even if it means staying in the bar until the next morning when the rest of Beijing is busying itself with Monday morning work. It sounded like sporting bliss and I wonder if I'll get to experience something like it if I get to see the Dubs in the All-Ireland semi in far away Koh Samui.

Walsh is actually on the radio to talk about the wunderkid, Michael Phelps, whose two golds and two world records in the swimming pool are setting this Olympics alight. He is going for eight and looking to become the most successful Olympian ever in the process. Watching him each time is like watching that rare thing — someone transcending their sport, pushing themselves to higher and higher limits so that their achievements are incomparable to past or present, only to the future. In the same way that an Einstein comes along only once in a lifetime, so too does a Michael Phelps.

What's more, he's humble and unassuming with a gangly look and awkward smile that doesn't even hint at the extent of his potential. Such talent can only be harnessed to such high levels by an inner drive and intensity that is unique and incomparable, and seeing how such a talent can have the whole world talking about and watching swimming events is a measure of the man. He might also just relight my faith in the Olympic Games.

**AUGUST**
**12**
**Tuesday**

It's Tuesday and it's the week of a Dubs game. That can only mean one thing. With my Parnell Park pass tucked away in my wallet, I head in on the bus to collect my ticket for next Saturday's quarter-final clash against Tyrone. No worrying about tickets; no fretting about asking people for them; no making last-minute plans or wondering if I might not get to see the game. Nope. Not for me that messiness and uncertainty.

I walk into Parnell Park and join the queue outside the portacabin; I'm one more lucky soul to be here safe in the knowledge that I have a ticket waiting for me. Five minutes later and I'm headed out of the grounds with the Hill tickets pocketed. This was the most stress-free, hassle-free way I've ever experienced of getting a ticket, and long may it last. I want us to go all the way to the final just so I can take part in this calm and secure ritual, knowing that half the city outside the gate is frantically harassing and haranguing others to get their hands on tickets.

Leaving the ground I spot Ciaran Whelan pulling in. Wearing his Dublin T-shirt and probably collecting his own allocation of tickets, I feel a tinge of jealousy. What I'd give to be in his position, preparing for an All-Ireland quarter-final. I never knew Whelan although he was just two years ahead of me in my primary school. I was on the juniors while he was on the senior team and I'll never forget the day that three of us from the juniors were called into the senior panel when they reached the schools final in Croke Park. There we were getting to enjoy the day and be part of a final in Croke Park.

From the dressing rooms to the pitch to lifting the cup on the steps in Croker, it was the closest I ever got to sporting greatness. In my mind we were kings of the world for that day and it is still a day I have never forgotten. With Whelan leading the team, we of course won. Even in primary school he was a stand-out talent that you just knew would be starring for Dublin in a few years' time.

Seeing him pass me by in Parnell Park, I couldn't help but think what if I'd stuck at it? Would there have been any chance that I could have ended up like him? It's probably the single-minded determination and singularity of purpose that Whelan has had for the last decade that I admire most. What I'd have given to have been one of the rare breed that can dedicate himself so completely to his chosen sport, hobby, craft or art.

I know countless lads who were equally talented in various sports, but they never pursued it with the vigour needed to succeed. You realise quickly that in sport, as in life, only the few who focus singularly on the thing they want to succeed in, will do just that. It may take five, ten years to get there, but get there they will, no matter what. I last saw Ciaran Whelan close up that schools day in Croker 20 years ago and in all that time he has still been doing what he knows and does best. He has dedicated his life to it and is still pursuing his goals with that hunger inside him.

Twenty years on and I am still searching for that focus, that goal, that singularity of purpose. In many respects I am lucky that at least I know what it is — writing — but in many ways I have been lacking the guts to follow that dream to its end, no matter what. Seeing Whelan drive by made me realise how far we had both come in so many years, but I wished I could have been the one wearing the Dublin T-shirt and preparing for an All-Ireland quarter-final.

**AUGUST**
**13**
**Wednesday**

If you wanted any reminder of how much the Dubs mean to people, I got it today as I sat upstairs on the bus on the way into town. Staring out the window day-dreaming and barely noticing the scenes passing me by, the bus stopped at the traffic lights beside Balgriffin cemetery. I looked out across the wide expanse of graves; some were simple affairs while others were more ornately decorated and had no expense spared on them. There were flowers, toys, teddy bears and lights at all the different headstones, but one grave caught my eye.

It had a simple wooden cross, signifying that the grave had been freshly dug, and there beside it, stuck in the ground and flying proudly and high above the cross, was a Dublin flag. The three castles set against the navy blue background stood out in the graveyard and was a sight to behold as it stood sentry beside the wooden cross.

What Dubs fan, I wondered, had passed away recently. How old were they? Had they seen the Dubs win in 1995? Did they remember the 1970s or even earlier? Their family obviously knew how much the Dubs mean to him/her and the Dubs flag flying there was a way of keeping their favourite team close by. In this week of all weeks I hoped the flag would prove a good omen for us and that we'd have all the help we could get.

The lights turned green and the bus pulled away and I was left looking back at the flag flying on its own in that graveyard. It reminded you how much the team meant to the fans.

**AUGUST**
**14**
**Thursday**

The Dublin team was named last night and the tinkering goes on. Ross McConnell comes back in at full back and they reckon it will be his job to man mark Tyrone's midfielder turned full forward, Seán Cavanagh. Collie Moran has returned to wing back in place of Kevin Nolan while the rest of the team has remained unchanged from the Leinster final. Kevin Bonner keeps Bernard Brogan out of the team and there's still no place for former stalwart, Paul Casey. Eleven of the team that faced Tyrone in 2005 at the same stage are in the side with only McConnell, David Henry, Diarmuid Connolly and Kevin Bonner the new faces.

It seems like a solid enough Dublin side, but I still can't believe the chopping and changing going on in the full back line. McConnell was dropped for the Leinster final because of a poor showing against Westmeath's Denis

Glennon in the semi, and now he's back in to counter Tyrone's big man up front, Seán Cavanagh. Does that make McConnell a better player since the Westmeath game or is it a tacit acknowledgment that only a physically comparable player can take on Cavanagh? Why are we so worried about the strength of the opposition when surely we should be taking the game to Tyrone?

I can understand the logic to it and why Caffrey would match Cavanagh with McConnell, but can you drop a player one game and expect him to be at his peak the next? The rest of the team has a solid and stable look to it. Our corner backs, Henry and Griffin, are a safe pair of hands; Cullen is playing well at centre back and having Collie Moran back in as wing back with Barry Cahill on the other side gives us plenty of depth in defence and hopefully going forward as well; Whelan and Ryan are working well together as a midfield pairing and Ryan is having one of his best seasons yet.

It's in the forwards where I'd be worried at this level. Sherlock is having a very quiet season and I think is now better as an impact sub giving us a great 20 minutes rather than an average 70. I would have brought Bernard Brogan on in place of Bonner as Bernard and his brother Alan are the only real cutting edge forwards à la Colm Cooper that we have. Diarmuid Connolly has still performed better for St Vincent's than for his county; Conal Keaney doesn't do much as full forward especially when you compare his contribution with the likes of Kieran Donaghy or Armagh's Ronan Clarke; Mossy Quinn again doesn't give much penetration although is safe and reliable from free kicks.

Breaking it down, we don't seem to add up to much with the sum of our parts, and looking at it you'd think we don't have enough game-breakers whilst still being suspect in the full back line. Compare that to Tyrone who have the likes of Brian Dooher, Seán Cavanagh, Tommy McGuigan and Conor Gormley and you start to worry. Now maybe I am being the typical pessimistic fan before a match, but when you take away the hype you have to wonder. Either way, it's going to be a tight game with little between the teams. This one could go either way.

**AUGUST 16 Saturday** — *All-Ireland Football Championship quarter-final, Dublin 1-08, Tyrone 3-14, Croke Park*

'Met Éireann is forecasting a severe weather warning for Saturday, 16 August. Be warned.' It sounded like Armageddon was coming. And it wasn't the clash with Tyrone we were talking about. Rain this summer was nothing new of course and certainly not a surprise that it was being predicted for the weekend. But, we wondered, would we be expecting a deluge of biblical proportions, of the sort we saw during last week's Kerry v Galway game.

Waiting for Noah and his Ark to come sailing around the corner was not what summers supporting the Dubs was meant to be about. Standing on the Hill watching the boys in blue in the Championship is supposed to be about sunny Sundays with the sun beating down on us in short-sleeved shirts. It's about coming prepared when that meant wearing a hat and sunscreen while watching the hardchaws and blow-ins turn pink and then blistering red as they stood hatless and topless beneath the searing sun. By full time their sunburnt backs would be a source of great fun to other Dubs fans who would, while walking down the steps of the Hill, be 'accidentally' pushed into the red raw bodies of the wannabes who would wince, yelp and jump in pain at any and every touch on their skin.

But that was summers gone by and this was now. This was summer 2008, the summer of the deluge, one that no one in the country would ever forget; it was a summer of flooding and downpours, when barely a day would go by without the heavens opening.

Hearing the severe weather warnings being issued for the day of the game meant we would come prepared. This was no ordinary Irish rain we would be expecting. The sunhat and sunscreen would be replaced by rainjacket and boots, and canoe and paddle if needs be.

Getting up this morning for the game and my pre-match ritual was already being interrupted. Rummaging through the wardrobe, I couldn't for the life of me find my raingear. For somebody who fishes and someone who lives in Ireland, you'd think raingear would be close at hand. But no joy this morning and not for the last time I cursed the Irish weather and wondered when I'd ever move to the south of France and not be a victim of the fickle Celtic weather gods.

One quick call to my folks and I had procured some of my father's raingear. With his big black boots a size too big for me and his long knee-length boating jacket too wide for me, I cut a comical figure dressed for the circus rather than a blue Dub getting ready for the Hill. At least, I figured, I wouldn't be the only one looking ridiculous today. Today was about staying dry, supporting the Dubs and not catching pneumonia in the process. A sneezing, sniffling groom is not what the bride-to-be would be wanting as she walked up the aisle to me next Thursday.

I had a hard enough time convincing her of the absolute necessity for me to go to the Dubs game so close to our wedding. Between organising the ceremony and the reception, as well as the house renovations, me sneaking off at this juncture for 'just a game' was tantamount to grounds for a pre-marriage divorce, if such a thing exists.

Thankfully it doesn't (yet) and in the guise of book writing, here I was dressing myself as best one can for standing under a monsoon for nearly two hours. Glancing out the window as I tried on my scuba outfit, I saw that it was not yet raining. But it was coming. The deluge was on its way. The darkening sky and looming storm clouds gave a menacing tone which betokened foreboding.

There was trouble all right. Whether it was the coming storm or the pre-match routine being disrupted, I don't think I was ever as nervous about a game. This was Tyrone after all, a team that had 12 All-Ireland winners in its team, most of whom were around in 2005 when they outplayed, out-thought and out-fought us in Croke Park only three years ago. And all we were reading about in the run-up was how Kerry v Dublin in the final was on the cards. There was just one small matter of Tyrone in an All-Ireland quarter-final first.

I was cold and nervous this morning as I got ready for the match. The weather outside wasn't helping, but neither was the thought of facing Mickey Harte's men. If the heavens opened, the rain, the mud, the slipping and sliding and the late challenges would turn the match into a scrap, and a scrap in the rain is the last thing you want against a hungry and determined Nordie team.

I walked to the DART station — AA Roadwatch was advising against driving because of potential flooding on the roads — still bone dry, and it was strange to watch many of the Dublin fans standing there on the platform also in their raingear and all of us expecting the worst. For the football or the weather? It was hard to tell which from their pallid faces.

Everything was out of sync — from the clothes, to the weather, to even our pre-match drinks. For some reason, today we were meeting in town, just off O'Connell Street, before making our way to the ground. Nothing about the day so far felt right.

As I stood on the packed DART with Dublin fans all around me, I decided to catch up on some pre-match newspaper previews. It was hard though as the noise from the Dubs fans made you stop and listen and wonder in curiosity at what you were hearing.

There was a group in their 20s standing near me and they were all bedecked in their blue jerseys, Dublin flags and headscarves. True to form, they were also knocking back cans of Bulmers and talking in the flattest of Dublin accents.

But we were on a train from Drogheda and I guessed that these were the new Dubs, the exiles from the suburbs in Meath and Louth forced to live far from the city as house prices saw neighbouring counties become Dublin territory. The further they went, however, the more they had to prove their Dublinness, it seemed. Their flags and clothing were their marks of worth. One bloke standing next to me, the loudest, was chatting to young howyas near by. 'You'se goin to de game, yea? Can't bleedin wait meself. It's goin to be fuckin deadly.'

'Ah yea,' said the girls, 'the Dubs are fuckin deadly so dey are.'

'And so is Bulmers!' said the bloke. 'So is fuckin Bulmers!'

I was expecting Ding Dong Denny O'Reilly to pop out at any moment, but he didn't and I felt compelled to keep listening.

'The weather's goin to be fuckin crazy later on, did yis hear?' said the bloke.

'Ah, yea,' said the girls, 'bleedin mental all right. So wha about you? Where's your raingear? Or are ye too hard for it on the Hill?'

'Ah no, I've me tickets for the Hogan Stand, ya see . . .'

I had to turn away before they caught me listening and with a smirk on my face. The hardchaw, if you don't mind, was going to the Hogan Stand. The 'aren't the Dubs bleedin deadly' brigade always come out in full force on match days in the summer. But the Hill it would seem is just too much for some Dubliners. Their one day out in Croker couldn't be spoiled by having to stand or get wet for 70 minutes. Jesus, I realised, I was starting to be like my mate John, the Dubious Dub.

But more and more Dublin fans I meet these days are drifting away from the Hill into the stands. 'Are you still goin to the Hill?' they ask in wonderment. 'Jaysus, I don't think I could do it any more,' they tell me, 'what with all the dickheads, the bottles being thrown and the standing . . . Nah, I'm getting too old for all that. I'll take my seat in the stands from now on, thanks very much.'

I try to convince them that it's not all bad; that the atmosphere when the Dubs are on song is better than anywhere else in the ground; that there's nothing quite like the mass of heaving, cramped bodies as you struggle for space and somewhere comfortable to stand without being jostled and pushed every few seconds; or being stuck in the middle of the Hill away from the steps and exits and dying for a piss, and you know you'll never find your spot and your mates if you leave for the toilets; and if you do leave, it will take you about half an hour just to get past the other bodies, all the while pushing and jostling to get by. Yes, there's nothing quite like a day out on the Hill.

Am I getting too old for this, I wonder, as I make my way to the ground. Am I just trying to hold on to some long-lost romantic notions from my childhood? Should I just accept that I'm a grown adult with mortgages and bills to pay, and that I should be taking my place like the rest of the civilised Dublin population in the stands? More and more of the Dublin fans I know are doing that; they're now having to take wives/girlfriends/kids to the games and won't get away with bringing them to the Hill. Slowly the numbers we know on the Hill are dwindling.

Our pre-match drinks crowd is shrinking as well. The days when we spent hours in the pub beforehand dissecting the game to come and catching any of the earlier matches on the telly are coming to an end. Instead, many of the lads are lucky to be able to slip out for the two hours of the game before nipping back home to get on with the rest of the household stuff that herself has planned for them.

Yes, we're all getting older and moving on, and so the group is splintering and going its different ways. We're living in different parts of the city as well and can't all meet up in the same places or congregate afterwards for post-match pints. In a way we're all getting more serious about life and our place in it; we're thinking about responsibilities and career paths and then we're looking at those around us wondering is this what we want as well. And the following week another one drops off the radar and we hear stories that he hasn't been to a game in ages, or that she's from Kilkenny and will only let him bring her to their hurling games.

Are we just being juvenile in holding out for our days on the Hill? Should we just leave the history and the terrace to the younger ones, let them have their days on it now and move quietly on our way? A few of us are stubborn enough still to say no and want to have our cake and eat it. We want to soak up the unique atmosphere that only the Hill can offer, but at the same time we can look around us and wonder about some of the Dublin fans and their antics. It's part of it all. You have to take the rough with the smooth, and it's what makes the Hill experience what it is.

It is true though that the older you get, the less inclined you are for the warts and all match day experience on the Hill. We want our comforts more and more and will complain about loud music in a nightclub or if we don't get proper service in a restaurant. The Hill though is where all pretensions must be left aside. The only baggage that's brought on to the terrace is that of the Dublin fan wanting to be more Dublin than the other guy, but in a way they're a dying breed, becoming more insulated as time goes on and as the city changes ever more.

There's a lot of fucking eejits, that's for sure, and it's the biggest factor in people's decisions to leave the Hill for the Hogan. The tolerance levels drop considerably once you hit 30, but in fairness there's an awful lot of gobshites in the stands as well. It's just that on the Hill they seem a lot more concentrated. But if you can get there early enough and find a good position away from the steps and the entrances, you'll find that the early birds are more often than not the real die-hard fans. They're not the ones hoping to get another round in five minutes before the throw-in; they're not the ones who aren't too bothered if they miss the first few minutes or don't know who's playing full back on the team. They're the GAA fans who will invariably be there for the minor game and can tell you the promising players to look out for.

So if you can get there early, get a good spot in the middle near the real fans and do your best to be as far from the fucking eejits as possible, then you might experience the Hill as it should be experienced, a unique sporting spectacle. Otherwise you're in danger of spending an afternoon beside a group of drunken teenagers who think chanting the soccer song, 'Who are ya? Who are ya? in an English accent while giving two fingers to the other county's fans in the Cusack Lower is what being a Dub is all about.

The reason I was thinking about the Hill on our way to

the ground was because as we walked through Summerhill down to Ballybough, the predicted severe weather was unleashed. The heavens opened and the monsoon descended. No matter how dressed up we were for the rain, nothing could have prepared us for the deluge that fell upon us as we tried valiantly to keep the rain out of our eyes, ears and everything else.

We and the thousands like us faced into the rain, and it felt like we were soldiers being forced to endure the extremes of weather as part of our long march to dry land. But we weren't being forced to do this and there was a sort of camaraderie among the fans as we all got drenched.

At least most of them knew they would reach the safety and dryness of the Hogan, Cusack and Canal End when they got there. For us few madmen, we had the prospect of standing underneath the open skies for the next two hours to console us. There was nothing for it but to accept our fate and realise that it was going to get worse, much worse. All the raingear was doing was prolonging the inevitable and already you could feel the wet seeping through. This was no ordinary rain; this was rain that no wetgear would hold at bay. This was not rain one was meant to endure standing on an open terrace watching a football match.

At first you tried to avoid the many deep puddles that were forming, but then very soon the entire footpaths were like tributaries of the Liffey and we were sloshing our way slowly over the Royal Canal. The downpour was incessant and the darkening of the sky made it all the more surreal. It was still only 3 pm, but it may as well have been nine o'clock at night. The cars trying to get through were fighting a losing battle and most drivers just abandoned ship and hopped out, realising this was rain you wouldn't defeat.

At the barriers to Clonliffe Road I pulled out my sodden ticket for the stewards. It had been in my trousers pocket and was nearly turning to mulch already. The ink was starting to run and fade and I was worried I wouldn't be allowed through for possessing a forged ticket. Getting a ticket was no problem on this occasion, however; the touts who stood on the street corners soaked through were desperately trying to get rid of Hill tickets but couldn't find any takers.

Walking down Clonliffe Road, the squelching of my boots accompanied the sounds of the rain hitting off cars and roof-tops. My jacket had been keeping some of the rain out, but my cap was soaked through; my boots were just about doing the job, but my leggings were like wet cardboard and stuck to my legs every time I moved. I could feel the cold and the wet as it seeped into my skin, dropping the temperature in my body by a few degrees. And we still have to stand on the Hill for a couple of hours, I thought to myself.

For a while anyway our concerns had been with the rain and the wet and we'd nearly forgotten that there was an All-Ireland quarter-final ahead of us. Walking on to the Hill just in time for the anthems, the rain suddenly became less of a factor.

This was a first as well — there was plenty of room for us all. This wasn't like other summers gone by when squeezing on to the Hill became as much a health hazard as anything else. This time the fair weather fans must have stayed away as there were plenty of empty gaps and we could choose any spot we wanted and claim it as our own. We took a spot to the right of the goal on the lower end of the Hill and settled ourselves in, as much as drowned rats could.

The excitement of the throw-in got us warmed up though, and seeing the players as soaked as we were made us feel we weren't completely on our own. We looked up at the stands at the dry fans and thought 'bastards', pulled our collars a little higher to stop the onset of pneumonia and the shivers for at least another hour, and thought to ourselves, well, at least we're the real fans.

Annoyed, frustrated and wet. This was all we knew and felt as the game opened up. Tommy McGuigan got the opening score on two minutes for Tyrone and it took 15 minutes for Dublin to get theirs to make it 0-02 to 0-01. In the meantime Dublin kicked four wides — reminiscent of the Dublin we remembered who would snatch at and waste valuable chances — while Tyrone were being more composed on the ball.

A flash of lightning followed by a clap of thunder reminded us that we were only here by the good grace of the weather gods who decided — only just — that they weren't going to have a monsoon just yet. The pitch was slippy, as was the ball, and the supply into the Dublin corner forwards was wasteful as time after time the ball was overplayed and skidded off over the end line.

A few minutes later, however, and Mossy Quinn and Diarmuid Connolly found themselves two v one against

Justin McMahon; a goal is begging as the players move in on goal, but Quinn's hand pass to Connolly, which would have put him clean through, is too long and Connolly watches agonisingly as the ball flies past him and goes wide. It's a golden chance and yet another one gone abegging. Is this going to be the story of our afternoon, we wonder.

Tyrone's Brian Dooher soon began to take control of things and was popping up everywhere dictating the game as well as grabbing points himself. After 25 minutes Tyrone are already starting to pull away and are 0-05 to 0-02 in front. And then disaster and eight minutes that we could scarcely believe could happen.

Once again the Dublin defence is opened up and Seán Cavanagh bursts through to score a goal and put Tyrone six points in front. But it looks like the Dubs are right back in it when Conal Keaney beats the keeper to a high ball and punches it into the net to bring us back into the match.

The wild celebrations on the Hill are short lived however, as only a minute later Tommy McGuigan gets past Barry Cahill and finds Joe McMahon, who slams the ball to the back of the net. The Hill is in shock and we're back down by six points. We've conceded two goals in five minutes and are being torn asunder every time Tyrone hone in on our defence. Add to that the reckless wides from our forwards and its obvious we're not firing in any part of the pitch.

It's soon half-time and the Dubs are down 1-03 to 2-05. It's only five points — not an impossible lead — but on a day like this it doesn't seem likely that the Dubs can climb back. The Hill is muted, wet and in shock. We're all too depressed by the match and the weather to say much. The rain has stopped — for now — but we're all soaked through and can feel the wet clothes sticking against our bodies. It doesn't help that the match isn't doing much to take our minds off our soaked misery.

But we live in hope. There are 35 minutes left and if the Dubs come charging out of the blocks, get a few early scores and put Tyrone on the back foot, then the game will be there for the taking.

As the second half starts there's still a buzz of anticipation around the ground and on the Hill especially. We know this Dublin team can come out all guns blazing and make a game of this; we know they're better than what we've seen; we still believe.

But only one team comes out blazing for the second half. In the first five minutes Tyrone knock over three points and they're now eight points ahead. The uneasy silence on the Hill grows while every Tyrone point is cheered loudly by their sizeable support in the Lower Hogan and Lower Cusack sides close to the Hill.

'Ah fuck off back to Britland, ya British bastards, and fuck you and your British fuckin establishment,' screams one Dublin voice behind me. The rest of the Hill can't even muster a 'Come on, you Boys in Blue' to drown him out, and you're left wondering once more about the Dubs' mentality on days like this. Every Tyrone score is now greeted with the same riposte from the fan behind us, and it feels like I've stepped back 20 years into the Troubles again when anything Orange or British seemed fair game for many fans on the Hill.

Watching the game was like watching a match in slow motion. Everything seemed inevitable and we could see it coming. Now everything seemed to be going Tyrone's way. We all knew there was only going to be one winner.

It had all come down to this and we were able to take it all in and digest the sad reality of the Dubs' demise while the game unfolded before us. Throughout the whole year from the Blue Stars to the freezing O'Byrne Cup matches, to the National League games home and away around the country, the fracas against Meath while I listened down in Kerry and the early summer promise of hope and potential, the victories in Leinster and the unfolding summer, these had all brought me to this point and it was all about to vanish as quickly as it had come.

This was the end. And what was worse, we knew it 20 minutes before the final whistle. Another defeated season. At least in our defeats to Armagh, Mayo and Kerry in recent years it was close and made you feel proud of a team that gave it their all to the very end. Today they may as well have walked off the pitch and thrown in the towel. It was a humiliating and galling way to end the summer, the season and the year.

I thought of Ciaran Whelan and the decades of sacrifice he had put into Dublin. And for it all to end like this. Was it worth it, I wondered. How can you dedicate yourself so completely to something that delivers nothing but disappointment and heart-break in the end? Would he still have set out ten years ago knowing what he knows now? Would we the fans have still been there in Naomh Mearnog in December or Parnell Park in January if we had known it would end like this?

Yes we would, unfortunately. And one hundred times yes would be Ciaran Whelan's answer. The heart-break and disappointment are what we have to live with as a Dublin fan, for we have no right to expect so much.

It was like watching a train crash unfold before your eyes and with each Tyrone score that went in I could feel my heart sink lower and lower. The final ignominy came on just 50 minutes when Davy Harte, the wing back, went past two Dublin defenders and slotted the ball past Stephen Cluxton to give Tyrone their third goal and put them ten points clear. Not only were we being beaten; we were being humiliated, and that hurt.

The sound of bucket seats being emptied could be heard and we watched as the Dublin fans began streaming out from Croker. Ten minutes later Enda McGinley slotted over another fine point and now Tyrone were 3-13 to 1-06 — 13 points in front.

And then to cap it all the heavens once more decided to open up and began to pour down on us sad souls standing on the Hill. It wasn't enough to be humiliated by Tyrone, but now, just as we were beginning to dry off, we began to get soaked again. As the rain pelted down, we had little stomach to be even raising our hoods in protest. What use now? We were already wet and we were stuffed. The year was over.

I couldn't take it any more. Thirteen points down and even the weather wanted to humiliate us. This was the final straw and I turned to my mates and told them I was off. 'I can't take any more of this,' I said. 'This lot aren't worth getting penumonia for.'

The others said they'd stick it out 'through thick and

thin, you know'. I said good luck to them, but I was too sickened to put myself through any more torture. We shook hands and with a rueful smile I said, 'See you next year.' I headed down the steps and out of the Hill for 2008 and I couldn't even bear to look back one last time.

It wasn't supposed to end like this. Soaked to the bone and walking down Clonliffe Road, hearing the groans from inside the ground, this wasn't supposed to be the ending. It was going to be Dublin against Kerry in the final and Jason Sherlock would score the last minute goal in front of the Hill to win Sam Maguire for us. I would be on the Hill living every moment of it and lapping it up, going delirious and surrounded by 14,000 other ecstatic Dubs. This would be sporting heaven and my book would have its fairytale ending.

But real life doesn't do fairytales. We never got to a semi-final never mind the final. Our last game watching the Dubs from the Hill was a pallid, soaking experience as we watched our beloved Dubs get hammered.

The disappointment was too much to take as I headed away from Croke Park, leaving what was left of my memories inside. I had given my all to the team for the whole year and it wasn't enough. Once again there would be no happy ending and we, the Dubs fans, would carry our hopes into the next season.

It would be another year of winter matches, spring league games and a summer championship and heading into it all, we would keep our dreams alive and think, maybe, just maybe, this is our time.

But why do we keep on deluding ourselves? Why spend so much time and effort following a team that ultimately and nine times out of ten will bring only heartache and disappointment?

Why? Because life is already full of such realities and it's nice for even just a few Sundays in the year to dream big and think maybe there will be a happy ending after all.

# POSTSCRIPT
## THE AFTERMATH

**AUGUST 16 August**

I was fit for nothing for the rest of the day. I sat on the DART heading back home and looked down at my soaked jeans and felt sorry for myself. Other people on the DART looked at me with pity in their eyes; not pity because Dublin lost, mind you, but more the kind of pity that wonders, 'What kind of a retard goes to watch a game in that kind of weather? And you wonder why you're wet? God love you, you must have mental issues.' Or something along those lines. I realised I still had the programme curled up in my hands and it was now a useless relic of the day. The ink had run and the pages were all stuck together; it was destined for the scrapheap — like so much of the season in fact.

And then I heard two people sitting behind me, talking, and they mentioned how they'd heard that Ronnie Drew had passed away. Ronnie Drew, the last of the Dubs — dead. I'd read that he was sick, but to hear such final news that he was now gone shook me out of my self-pity.

Life still goes on for us after this game, but for Ronnie Drew his time was up. It's hard to believe we won't get to hear that gravelly voice any more, or hear him tell stories about Luke Kelly and the good old, wild days of the Dubliners.

There won't be his like again, that's for sure. Dublin has changed too much to ever have characters like that inhabiting the city once more. The folk and ballad revival they helped create will never be seen again and the songs will be sung instead for the tourists in Temple Bar on a Saturday night.

I think part of Dublin's soul died with Ronnie Drew tonight. The wit, the repartee, the stories, the bravado and even the wildness: all are part of an older city of a time gone by. In a way we all try to hang on to a little bit of that on the Hill every summer, but it's hanging on to something that was in the past, a fading memory.

The Dubliners. The very name characterised them. Nothing more to be said after they chose that name, really; and the fact that it was inspired by James Joyce's book made the lineage of the group all the more tied into the city's history.

The Dubs lost more than a game today; they lost a favourite son. And as Don McClean once described the death of Buddy Holly as the 'day the music died', so too part of Dublin's musical heritage died today.

The city will be muted tonight and many Dublin fans in pubs will bow their heads in remembrance — and sink another pint in his memory. They might even sing a verse or two.

I awoke from my thoughts on the DART and realised we had not moved beyond Howth Junction station. The train driver then came on the speaker and told us that due to flooding 'this train will not be going any further. This is the end of the line.'

I headed out into the road, wondering how I was going to make my way home. It was the end of the road for us all this evening.

Many of the Dubs fans headed out after the game — more to drown their sorrows than anything else. But for me, after somehow making my way home from Howth Junction, I lay on the couch and didn't move. Depression, sickness — call it what you will — but I didn't have the heart or the energy to talk or even think about the game. I just felt gutted that it could end like that and in such a morbid way. We'd been knocking on the door each year and seemed to be getting closer and closer. Now this slap in the face was a wake-up call as to where the Dubs' place in the hierarchy of things really stood.

We've taken two steps back today and it will be hard to see how this team can take the next big leap forward. Are we going back to the bad old days of the late 1990s when we didn't win a Leinster title for seven years and lost four provincial finals on the trot before finally breaking our duck in 2002?

This morning I couldn't open a newspaper, knowing what I'd be reading, although I do hear on the radio that Pillar Caffrey has resigned. Fair play to him. At least he didn't drag it out and have it as an ongoing story for the next few weeks. He wasn't good enough; simple as that. He may have brought four Leinster titles to Dublin, but in this era provincial titles aren't good enough — just ask Kerry or Tyrone.

Watching the Dubs you always got the feeling that tactically we weren't at the highest level, that a Mickey Harte or John O'Mahony would be able to get the upper hand. Dublin were too often predictable — shooting hopeful ball into the corners seemed to be our only attacking plan. Watching Tyrone change things around so fluidly yesterday was a reminder that the gulf at the top isn't always about the players.

We have to look outside the county now; it's as simple as that. Already they're saying a Joe Kernan or Jack O'Connor would be possible candidates and that's the right road to be going down. We need someone from a hugely successful county who has that innate winning mentality and who can come to Dublin GAA circles without any baggage or politics around them, someone who doesn't give a damn what the crowd thinks. We need to start learning from the likes of Kerry and Ulster (although I will tear up my Parnell Park pass if we start playing puke football like the Nordies) and innovate tactically instead of trying to copy them.

All of this has got me thinking now and I decide that I can handle reservoirdubs to see what other Dubs fans have been saying. Sure enough, it only takes the first post to sum it up for me:

*Not a defeat, a humiliation.*

*Heartbroken, for the 13th year running. After all the expectation and hope.*

*Don't even know where to start. Don't even know if I want to keep thinking about it.*

Signylin was spot on as well:

*Probably better not to think about it for a while . . . go into the cave.*

Mr Greene's post, while hard-hitting, would also have reflected much of the raw hurt and pain being felt:

*13 years of disappointing, heart wrenching, last minute winning scores, been out classed but at least some sort of fight I have endured, but today has been the first time I have been completely and utterly embarrassed of a Dublin team.*

*Blah, blah, blah — you can dissect it anyway you want, but it all boils down to having no heart and no pride in the shirt you are wearing. After 13 years of failure I'd promised myself years ago never to get my hopes again when it came to winning an All-Ireland. But lo and behold seeing Wexford in a semi-final made me lose the run of myself. This shit won't happen again. The Dublin football team has made me the biggest pessimist on Hill 16.*

*I'm stupid drunk. Heart-breaking Cossie hitting the post in the last minute defeats are one thing but to be pissed on like that by a bunch of Nordys is the last straw, this Dublin team/management has turned me into the biggest disbelieving pessimist there is.*

*Pillar waited way too long to make any subs, by the time he did it was too late. He has to go along with the back room staff, I don't care who they bring in next I've lost all faith . . . away to drink myself into the cesspit that today's performance deserves.*

Interestingly, many of the posts blamed the players and the team as a whole and talk about lack of pride and all that. I'm shocked that not more blame is being put at the management's door. There is little talk about tactics and team selection and the players have become an easy target for the fans' ire.

As for the next manager, some of the Dubs' small town syndrome is still alive and well unfortunately. You get some fans saying they'd burn the Dubs flag if a culchie were ever put in charge, while others think Brian Mullins would be the man. Crazy, crazy stuff some of it, but that's what sport is all about isn't it? Everyone has an opinion, right, wrong or crazy. And obviously the posters that write the things I agree with are the ones that are spot on and very clever indeed . . .

I manage to lift my head far enough up from the couch to watch Waterford beat Tipp in the All-Ireland hurling semi-final. Fair play to Waterford for reaching their first final in 45 years, but my gut has taken some pounding now from the weekend's results. I'm going to bed early and hoping when I wake up tomorrow morning that this has all been some sort of nightmare that has come to an end.

**AUGUST**
**18**
**Monday**

I have enough things to be thinking about to wake me from my self-pitying stupour this week. It just so happens that I have the small matter of my wedding on Thursday to get ready for. Between our house renovations and me fretting about the Dubs game against Tyrone, the wedding plans became just part of the mix. Now, though, it's all guns blazing for Thursday. Suit fits: check; church and reception all ready: check; family sorted: check. Everything in place: fingers crossed, and check.

I'm sure there are a million and one other things that will suddenly need to be done this week, but surprisingly the nerves are holding up. It doesn't help when every other person is asking, 'So are you nervous yet?' Why?

Should I be? We're having a small wedding, thank God, so it will be a relaxed and intimate affair. And now I realise I won't have to be worrying about not being there for the Dubs in the All-Ireland semi-final.

I won't, after all, be watching them from an Irish bar on the beach in Thailand during our honeymoon. I was actually half looking forward to the whole experience; sitting there cheering on the Dubs in my shorts, sandals and T-shirt, drinking beer and watching the match while hearing the waves lapping against the shore. Certainly beats my most recent experience on the Hill. And if you can't be there on the Hill in person, being in Thailand in the summer heat is probably the next best thing . . .

**AUGUST**
**22**
**Friday**

Well, that's it, done and dusted. The ring is on the finger and I feel like a grown-up now. We had one of the best days of our lives yesterday and everything went like a dream. The nerves held up after all and most importantly we made sure we enjoyed ourselves thoroughly right to the end. After all, this day will never come round again. I can't stop fiddling with the ring on my finger — it will take some getting used to. Does this mean I will become like all the other Dublin fans I know of, that started drifting away from the Hill as soon they became husbands and fathers? Will things change forever now?

**AUGUST**
**24**
**Sunday**

I manage to catch the Cork v Kerry football semi-final this afternoon; with ten minutes to go and with Kerry six points up, it was game over. But just as the Cork hurlers have done this year, the footballers dug deep and didn't give up. They got a flukey goal to give them a lifeline, and then the converted penalty in the last minute showed that Kerry are looking weak under pressure.

I still don't give Cork a chance in the replay though. Kerry shouldn't have lost today and will be kicking themselves that they let Cork back into it so softly. Kerry were dominant throughout and will be sure to shake Cork off their coat-tails in the replay. Still, though, Kerry are picking up some poor Dublin habits by not closing the game off completely; that's twice now that they've let Cork off the hook. Maybe The Kingdom aren't as mentally strong as they'd like to make out; maybe this year would have been a good time for Dublin to have been meeting them — maybe, maybe, maybe. The thought that Wexford are in the semis and could be into an All-Ireland final instead of us galls me.

**AUGUST**
**28**
**Thursday**

Laid up with a stomach bug isn't fun at the best of times, but being laid up in a Bangkok hotel is not an experience I'd recommend. It's a strange thing to be washing your teeth with bottled water, but fail to heed the warnings and you can end up like me. Laid up in bed all day means I'm restricted to the best that Thailand TV has to offer.

In many ways it's just like home; the Thais love their soaps and they even have their own Bangkok version of *Fair City*, plus I'm sure I saw a *Glenroe* there while I was flicking the channel. I definitely spotted a Thai 'Biddy' for a second on the screen!

Their obsession with the FA Premier League is also something we have in common with the Thai people and there are match highlights and soccer discussion shows most nights of the week over here. 'Is this what it's going to be like now? Sport, sport, sport?' herself asks in weary tones. 'I'm afraid so, my dear,' I reply with a cheeky grin. It's still just the honeymoon so I'd better not push the boat out too far just yet. Wait till we get back home, though, and have the Premier League, Champions League, Heineken Cup and internationals to look forward to. And then we're into January and the O'Byrne Cup at Parnell Park before the National League kicks in, and then we're into the Championship. I keep all this to myself of course. I moan a little to get some attention and curl up on my side. I realise you can go anywhere in the world, and sport — like the wife — will still be there. That's a good thing I'm sure . . .

**AUGUST 31 Sunday** We've made our way to Ko Samui island in the Gulf of Thailand and it feels like we're in paradise. Beaches, jungles, sunsets, relaxing by the pool and on the balcony: life does not get much better than this. It takes a while to figure out how to chill and relax and not be having to *do* something, but there's a lot to be said for days spent reading, eating, drinking, swimming and doing nothing in particular. Life is good at the moment and I won't let anything spoil it: not even the fact that we can't as much as win at handball any more, and that a Meath team has beaten us in the All-Ireland men's doubles semi-finals; not even the knowledge that Dublin should have been playing in the All-Ireland semi-final against Wexford today where we would have beaten them and then would have been into our first final in 13 years where we would have faced Kerry. Our dreams might actually have come true this year.

But, mine have come true in other ways, and the only dilemma I have at this moment is whether I should get up for a dip in the pool or close my eyes for a nap. Tyrone v Wexford can wait for another day.

**SEPTEMBER 7 Sunday**

*All-Ireland Hurling final, Kilkenny 3-30, Waterford 1-13, Croke Park*

In keeping up with my theme this year of always seeming to be somewhere else when it's the other place you really want to be, I miss the All-Ireland hurling final between Kilkenny and Waterford. Or, perhaps more accurately, what should have been the final with Kilkenny on the pitch while Waterford acted as ballboys. We were in the air flying from Abu Dhabi back to Dublin when hurling perfection was being played out on the Croke Park pitch. As we walked out into arrivals in Dublin Airport, the glum Waterford faces around us told the whole story. No need to ask who won, I thought to myself. But I do make sure to watch the highlights on the *Sunday Game* that night, to see with my own eyes just how good this Kilkenny performance really was.

How bad were Waterford and how good were Kilkenny? That is talk for the pub at the weekend, but seeing how 15 players on a team can play and gel so well together for an entire 70 minutes, and you do come close to sporting perfection. I feel sorry for the Waterford fans, particularly my mate Dermot who is a die-hard and goes to League matches home and away to watch the Deise in action. He's been on a year out, travelling around the world, and before he left he said in near-prophetic terms,

'Knowing my luck, the Dubs and Waterford will get to All-Ireland finals and I'll be somewhere in a South American jungle!'

We all got it wrong about the Dubs; but for Dermot, trying to catch Waterford's progress throughout the summer as he travelled through Chile, Peru and Argentina is a book in itself. Thanks to the internet and radio streaming he was able to listen to their games, and for the final I believe he was somewhere in Buenos Aires, stuck with his ear to a computer in an internet café. He'll probably stay in Argentina and never come back after that result, and I wouldn't blame him. As a Dubs fan you'd feel like emigrating many's the time too, to somewhere you won't be tortured, year in, year out, by the Championship; probably only Antartica at this stage would suffice.

**SEPTEMBER 10 Wednesday**

Just when you think it's safe to go back out in public, there for all to see in today's *Irish Independent* is an exclusive by Martin Breheny who reveals the existence of a 'little Blue Book' which every member of the Dublin GAA team had this season.

It seems to be part sports psychology/part waffle, and in the context of the Dubs getting hammered in the All-Ireland quarter-final, it makes the team — and the management in particular — look like a county peddling as much in voodoo and tarot-card reading as anything else.

According to Breheny, the Blue Book was presented to the Dublin squad the week before the infamous Meath clash in Parnell Park in April. You can only imagine the players' reactions as they were handed this little publication. Now bringing in sports psychology is fair enough, but when you're handed a 52-page publication for your own personal possession which declares on the front cover and on every page, 'Dublin All-Ireland Champions 2008' and that 'It's 31 v 1' or that 'Winning is everything', you start to wonder at the sanity of those involved. Why would you need to be given a book to be told these things in the first place? And why try to turn the Dublin squad into some sort of secret unbreakable fraternity?

For those that didn't know or weren't sure about their purpose this summer, here then was the players' seven-point creed to live by. (Don't try this at home, I might add; it will only end in depressing humiliation and failure at the hands of a more worthy opponent.)

*Accept the Blue Book with pride. It's an honour to become part of a group representing the greatest city in the world.*

*I promise to adhere to all areas of THE BLUE BOOK RULES OF ENGAGEMENT.*

*I promise to utilise THE BLUE BOOK to its fullest in the hope of gaining that extra inch.*

*I will not show or admit the existence of THE BLUE BOOK to any other person except another Blue Book holder.*

*I will accept any disciplinary measures including withdrawal of my BLUE BOOK, should I not apply myself as a BLUE BOOK HOLDER is expected to.*

*I will not divulge the meaning of our BS logo to anybody.*

*Finally, I appreciate that for the duration of this campaign it will be thirty-one versus one. I am quite happy with these odds.*

And my name is John and I'm an alcoholic and where do we all sign up for the Twelve Steps programme? Now there's going the extra inch and then there's taking the piss. The fact that the book was leaked in the aftermath of the campaign shows how not all the players were signed up to the Blue creed. The mumbo jumbo reads like something Glenn Hoddle or Clive Woodward would have invented.

With all the Blue Book's talk about extra inches and doing whatever it takes to win, the Dubs now have egg on their faces after their 12-point defeat to Tyrone. You'd think they'd have been better off concentrating on the simple matter of kicking points, finding a settled spine for the team and following some tactics instead of playing these silly mind games.

Some Dublin fans see this as another opportunity for the media to take a swipe at the Dubs while others don't see anything wrong with the book; after all, they say, what if Dublin had won Sam, wouldn't this have been a work of genius?

To me it just smacks of desperation. If you have to play these types of mind games to try and get the best out of your players, then as a manager you should question your own techniques in the first place. The fact that a player leaked the book indicates that some of the same players questioned those techniques as well.

The Dubs' Blue Book story is all over the media today and the piss-taking has well and truly begun. We're being laughed at and made to look foolish; it feels like this season's ending can't get any worse.

As one fan said today: 'I didn't know so many of the Dublin players could read . . .' Maybe therein lies the rub.

You'd wonder what Brian Cody and those in Kilkenny make of it all.

**SEPTEMBER 11 Thursday**

Reading Mickey Harte's thoughts on the Dubs' Blue Book and on sports psychology in general throws up some interesting perspectives on the whole affair and also shows us just how far behind in the management stakes we have fallen.

When asked about the use of mental preparation in Gaelic football, Harte says it should be about 'normalising the psychology of sport — not making it some high-falutin stuff that comes with degrees or whatever. It comes with degrees of experience . . . You've got to be thinking players nowadays.'

That's the difference. Harte trusts his players enough to allow them to think, to analyse and to use what life has taught them to bring about a balance to their game and their personal lives. One is not exclusive of the other, after all. In contrast, the Dubs think that like making a bold pupil write lines, having 'Dublin, All Ireland Champions 2008' written on every page of a book will suffice.

When you contrast the mentalities and intellectual approaches to the game, you'd wonder how we even won Leinster.

## SEPTEMBER
# 21
**Sunday**

# All-Ireland Football final, Tyrone 1-15, Kerry 0-14, Croke Park

The third Sunday in September is always a hard day to take when the Dubs aren't involved; but having said that, they rarely are, so it's not like we're not used to it. As I was reading online during the week, a Dubs fan pointed out that we've won two All-Irelands in the last 25 years; Kerry have two in the last two years, and Tyrone have won two in just five years. Two All-Irelands in a quarter of a century, one in the 80s, one in the 90s, and now as we approach the end of the 2000s, none to show — not even a damned final.

At least the 90s team were knocking on the door for a while. They had finals in 92 and 94 and were able to give Dubs fans some hope until they finally won Sam in 95. The Dubs in the twenty-first century don't even have false hopes. We have an odd semi-final here and a regular quarter-final there. Don't bother mentioning Leinster titles — as if they're some recompense; they're not. Leinster is fine if you're a county coming back from a half-century's decline — like Wexford — or if you're looking to make the breakthrough like Laois and Westmeath did in the early 2000s.

We haven't sunk so low yet that winning a Leinster title would be a bonus for the county, but then depressing defeats in the All-Ireland series aren't doing our state of mind any good either.

So when Sunday, 21 September, rolled around this year, it was another case of the blues. You breathe deeply, sigh and resign yourself to the way of the world once more. Invariably you're watching a team that has beaten the Dubs to get to the final — Tyrone, Kerry, Mayo, Tyrone, Kerry, Armagh. Spot a pattern here? Maybe that's the hardest pill to swallow, knowing that it might have been us out there walking in the parade and seeing the Hill going wild and filled with blue flags flying proudly in Croker.

I'm sitting in my living room watching the telly and trying to imagine what it would be like. Outside in the city, most of the pubs are filled with punters watching Chelsea v Man Utd; the Dubs turn their noses up at the Gah if it's not their own that's involved. Otherwise it's just bog ball for culchies who get their big day out in the city. All the more reason to turn away, they seem to say; another round of Bulmers is ordered and they shout in more advice at Ashley Cole, Cristiano Ronaldo and Didier Drogba.

Meanwhile, the pageant and one of the finest days on the sporting calendar continues in Croke Park. Soon Kerry and Tyrone start walking around the ground for the traditional pre-match parade. There's nothing to match the uniquely GAA parade — the buzz, the colour, the cheering, the screams even. This is an opportunity for the fans to let their team know how much it means to them before battle commences.

The two sides look determined and intense. Between them they have been in All-Ireland finals for the last seven years. While people speak of Kerry domination and their three in a row, we all seem to have forgotten that this is Tyrone going for their third Sam Maguire in just six years. They are both battle hardened and streetwise as well as being terrific footballers working under shrewd management systems. Is it any wonder then that both of these teams have played us off the park between this and last year?

There was no room for Paul Galvin on the Kerry team for the final either — the Galvin affair was probably the dominant story of the summer and says much about the way GAA coverage is going when it starts to focus on personalities more and more — but still, most pundits were predicting a Kerry win and their first three in a row since the 1980s. Kerry just seem to have this aura of invincibility about them. How much of it is psychological and gets into opponents' heads before they even take to the field?

Not Tyrone, however, and as the game gets going they show how much they are on form. Brian Dooher is having an incredible season as is Seán Cavanagh and Enda McGinley and, a bit like they did to the Dubs, they are carving Kerry open up the middle. The difference though is that Kerry can match Tyrone up front and aren't panicking. Every Tyrone score sees Kerry pick one off themselves, although Donaghy and Walsh aren't getting quite the service they'd like.

It's nip and tuck all the way to half-time and you can't see much daylight between the teams. Kerry are 0-08 to 0-07 up at the break and you're expecting them at any moment to move up another gear and show Tyrone what they're made of. After all, this Kerry team needs to exorcise the ghosts of Tyrone hanging over them and until they beat them in the Championship they can never be considered truly great.

And then it happens. But not what the pundits told us would happen, or what most neutrals expected either. Just 30 seconds into the second half and Tyrone are the ones striding ahead. A scrappy ball breaks through in the full back line and, while the shot from Kevin Hughes is saved, the ball rebounds to Tommy McGuigan who manages to steer it goalwards. It rolls as if in slow motion over the line from about three yards, and there's nothing Kerry's Tom O'Sullivan can do except stick a despairing foot out, realising he's not close enough. The ball is in the back of the net; in such a tight match it could prove to be the crucial score and the difference between the teams.

It's a soft goal to concede and an unusual one for Kerry to let in, but in truth they haven't been at their flying best consistently throughout the season and they look vulnerable. Tyrone are the team with the momentum and despite Kerry pegging them back to two points, The Kingdom fail to score for the last ten minutes and Tyrone pull away winning by four points in the end. Their free-scoring antics near the end was all too reminiscent of their play against Dublin. It's their third All-Ireland in six years and now people are saying Tyrone are the team of the decade. Once again Kerry have failed to beat them in the Championship and their three-in-a-row dream has been shattered. Kerry have been made to look like mere men again and suddenly the green and gold doesn't seem so invincible. Let's hope, from a Dublin point of view, that the damage is lasting.

One interesting point though. This meeting of Kerry and Tyrone was the first All-Ireland football final between two teams to have come through the back door. It all points to how important it seems to be now to get a run of games in the qualifiers instead of winning your province and sitting on your arse for four weeks before playing in the quarter-finals. It's food for thought for all GAA fans, and I wonder if it's a tactic we'll see being employed more thoughtfully come next season — especially in Dublin's case.

As Brian Dooher lifts Sam Maguire in front of the adoring Tyrone crowds who are gathered on the Croke Park pitch, the RTÉ cameras pick out a Garda with his cap askew helping to keep the crowds back from the players on the steps. It's none other than Pillar Caffrey and as he looks up at Dooher he must be thinking, 'if only, if only'. It's the closest any Dub got to the All-Ireland final this year.

**SEPTEMBER**
**24**
**Wednesday**

At least there'll be something to keep us going over the coming months. There's the return of the new and improved 'International Series Lite' in a few weeks' time; it's the biannual Aussie thumping of some Paddies for which sponsors and fans pay good money. But if they take out the violence will we be interested any more? It would be like the WWE without the wrestling.

And then of course there's the small matter of who the next Dublin manager will be. True to form, speculation has it that Dublin will be picking one of their own. The smart money is on Brian Mullins or Mickey Whelan. Whelan you can understand, having brought All-Ireland success to St Vincent's, but his unsuccessful stint in the 1990s as the Dublin manager and the rancour he left behind him are not too long in the past.

Brian Mullins is a name often bandied about in Dublin circles whenever they are looking for a manager. Mullins is to the Dubs what Kevin Keegan is to the Geordies, a legend and a saviour who can come in and take them to the promised land of the 1970s.

But times have changed. And the game has changed with it. Stick and hairdryer approaches have little impact nowadays on modern players; modern sports psychology (and we're not talking 52-page handbooks of quotes and Freemasonry language here) and sports management techniques need to be blended in with tactical nous. Are we going to get that by harking back to the past?

On reservoirdubs.com one fan summed it up right I reckon: 'I was day dreaming, and imagined Kerry winning the all-Ireland by beating Tyrone in a classic, Harte calls it a day and bows out in style, it causes a certain amount of controversy and he is later revealed as the new Dublin manager.'

Harte has confirmed his standing in the game even more now after winning a third All-Ireland and it would be extremely unlikely that he would leave Tyrone. While many Dubs online want to see Mullins the saviour riding over the hill, it's heartening to see that one poll on reservoirdubs has 'some culchie' in the lead on 38% to Deegan's 29% and Mullins's 29% in the survey for the next Dublin manager.

As they've said, the smart money is supposed to be on Mullins and Whelan, and once more Dublin will look to their own and refuse to countenance 'some culchie'. Either way it's all gossip and speculation that is keeping us fans fed on a diet of GAA that we won't let end just yet.

And we're all the more grateful for any of these morsels as we face into the barren months ahead.

## September, October, November, December

So that's it done and dusted. Kilkenny confirm their status as one of the greatest hurling teams of all time while the rest scratch their heads and wonder how in the name of jaysus they're going to beat them next year.

Talk of Kerry's brilliance and sublime domination of Gaelic football has thankfully been put to rest by Tyrone's victory in the All-Ireland football final. Now there's talk of Tyrone's brilliance and sublime domination of Gaelic football. God only knows what they'll be saying about the Dubs if we ever actually do win an All-Ireland again.

It was also the summer of L'Affair Galvin — of temper tantrums, thrown notebooks, disciplinary hearings, suspensions and then back-tracking on it all — all part of a normal GAA summer, of course. There were manager resignations and sackings, and who could forget the Cork players' strike? There was the Parnell Park punch-up, a fourth Leinster title and a humiliation in the quarters. And, of course, there was the poxy rain, rain and more rain.

It was an anticlimactic end to the season for the Dubs. Even Caffrey's resignation brought a mere sigh of little interest before fans moved quickly on to other matters. The most colourful and entertaining part of the whole summer was probably the revelation of the Dubs Blue Book and how this 52-page masterclass in spoofery was supposed to be the extra one per cent in winning an All-Ireland. Problem was, it was more than one per cent we needed to make up a 12-point deficit. At least it gave us some laughs. But everyone else was laughing at us as well.

As these last few words are being written, the news has come through that the new Dublin manager is in fact Pat Gilroy who will have Mickey Whelan as his trainer, and many Dublin fans are still shaking their heads in confusion at the decision. This one came out of the left field and caught everyone on the hop. Gilroy? we're all asking. The Vincent's full forward? The man who hasn't actually managed a team yet? This could either be a stroke of genius or our own version of the Steve Staunton reign. And the Dublin County Board aren't renowned for their strokes of genius. It all gives extra interest now to the 2009 season, but many doubt that Gilroy is the man to end the Dublin All-Ireland famine.

I've packed away the blue jersey and scarf now. They're at the bottom of the drawer hidden underneath the rest of the summer T-shirts that barely saw the light of day these past few months. We're getting quickly to that time of year when the nights are becoming darker earlier and earlier and you can feel the first bite of cold in the mornings.

We don't have Championship Sundays to look forward to and even TG4's *All-Ireland Gold* is getting repetitive. There are only so many times you can watch reruns of the Dubs in the 70s. Two All-Irelands in 25 years has been our lot and we're now going to be 14 seasons and counting since 95.

The end of the summer and the approach of autumn and winter is always tinged with sadness. Nature dies off and hibernation sets in. For the fan it's a double-edged sword, a chance to reflect with sadness at the passing of another empty season and an opportunity to look with a lighter heart to the possibilities for next year. Do we live in false hopes or real expectations? A bit of both maybe, but only by dreaming can we be really free.

We're all still our younger selves as fans, putting our hopes and dreams in a team that gives us mainly heartache, pinning our faith on players who neither know us nor how much we care, standing on the Hill as the crowd sings, chants and cheers as the Dublin team in blue sweep the ball across Croke Park and put it over for another score, celebrating wildly with the thousands of others and getting swept up in the swell of fans, regrouping, and singing from the bottom of our lungs. On the Hill supporting the Dubs we are all little boys again, and for 70 minutes we live our dreams of youth once more.

That is why, as the season ends and I pack away my jersey and scarf, I wonder if maybe now is the time to leave the Hill — and what it means and represents — far behind me for ever. I'm 30 years of age and scrambling around for career dreams that have yet to be realised. Am I now holding on to something with the Dubs that I should have let go by now? I'm one of the last of the friends still clutching my Hill tickets on a Sunday with glee, but maybe I should be growing up with those friends who have moved on.

By staying on the Hill, I wonder, am I delaying the onset of life's seriousness and problems? If I take my seat in the Hogan Stand and join the other fathers and husbands and accept the serious business of sitting and watching the Dubs in passive emotion, am I finally accepting that whatever life held out for me has long since passed me by too?

When the Championship next comes round I will be 31; I'll be settled into married life and have mortgages and bills increasing by the day. I've tried to pursue my dreams of writing and following what my heart tells me, and have come up short so far. Maybe that is why I stick to the Hill.

But closing the drawer on my Dubs jersey and scarf, I feel as if I need to stop clinging on and face up to what life throws my way from now on. As a man I face into an uncertain future, but as a fan I can face into hope and expectations for the coming year. Maybe I'm not quite ready yet to turn my back on the Hill and all that it stands for after all.